Angus in Deir but basically (handwritten annotation)

CW00670877

SUTTON-IN-HOLDERNESS.

South Town to Wacana [Wawna] on Road Wawna — Preston (handwritten annotation)

THE MANOR, THE BEREWIC,

AND

THE VILLAGE COMMUNITY.

BY

THOMAS BLASHILL, F.R.I.B.A.,

THE SUPERINTENDING ARCHITECT OF METROPOLITAN BUILDINGS.

SEAL OF SIR THOMAS DE SUTTON.

HULL: WILLIAM ANDREWS & CO.

AND

A. BROWN & SONS, LTD.

AND AT

5, FARRINGDON AVENUE, LONDON, E.C.

—

1896.

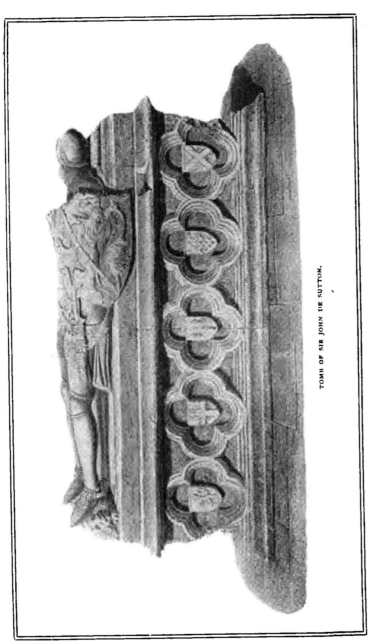

TOMB OF SIR JOHN DE SUTTON.

PREFACE.

THE Domesday record of the Manor and the Berewic which, at the time of the Conquest, were intermixed under the name of SUDTONE, describes a tract of land containing no more than a fifth of the area of mediæval and modern Sutton. It is in the earlier chapters of the *Chronica Monasterii de Melsa*, which deal with the twelfth century, that we first recognise the broad meadows and far-stretching pastures out of the midst of which there rose, on a group of gently swelling hills, the carucates and oxgangs of the more ancient town. But since the days of our great-grandfathers, both the older and the newer lands have been seen in a changed aspect, under the network of hedges, tree-bedecked, which, since 1767, has covered the old meadows and pastures and the open arable fields.

Long ago I formed the idea of making more familiarly known the condition of the parish at two or three of the most notable periods of its history. In 1892, impressed with the accuracy and the interest of the monastic Chronicle, I read before the British Archæological Association a paper on "Sutton-in-Holderness and the Monks of Meaux."* In the Transactions of the East Riding Antiquarian Society,

* Pron. Mewse.

vol. 2, I shewed that the " Hull " of thirteenth century writers was not, as had been supposed, the same as Wyke, now the central portion of Kingston-upon-Hull, but a tract of land by the river-side in the western part of Sutton, and that old references to Dripole usually refer not to any part of the present parish of Drypool, but to the south-western corner of Sutton, now called the Groves. I intended to shew finally, out of the ample materials that exist, how, before the Enclosure, the fragments of the old-fashioned farms lay scattered and intermingled over the Ings and Carrs and tillage fields. The gaps between these portions of the history of the parish were, at first, wide and deep, but as they began to fill with new materials, essential to a correct understanding of the matters in hand, it became necessary to make the whole into one story. Thus, without premeditation, I felt myself responsible for a book.

The work has had to be taken up in the intervals of many absorbing occupations, as its structure and arrangement must, no doubt, indicate. It deals with the great variety of occurrences which, in the course of eight centuries, mark the history of a manor or a parish, and hardly any period has failed to furnish some illustrative examples. Sometimes I have been writing for those to whom ancient documents and family pedigrees and customs, long extinct, would be of especial value ; sometimes for those who would be more interested in the long array of names of fields and roads and boundaries which I have been enabled to trace and identify. As a rule I have dealt only with events long past, and with persons mostly forgotten, but in a few cases I have not refrained from using a modern name, or a recent incident, when these helped to illustrate some old-fashioned habit worthy of remembrance. Whether the matter of the book is, or is not, of general interest, a reference to the table of contents will shew.

I have to acknowledge gratefully the assistance which I have received from the custodians of many public and private documents. I have been allowed to search the manorial records in the possession of the Corporation of Kingston-upon-Hull, and the manorial and family records of the late Colonel W. H. Harrison Broadley, as well as papers of the families of Priestman and Ross, of Sutton. I have received very cordial assistance, in many ways, from Mr. R. Hill Dawe, the Town Clerk of Hull; from Dr. Walter de Grey Birch, LL.D., F.S.A., of the British Museum, who shewed me the newly-acquired charters in the Stowe collection; from Mr. Edward S. Wilson, F.S.A., particularly with respect to Ann Watson's College; from Mr. J. Travis-Cook, F.R.H.S., and Mr. Fred A. Scott, as regards modern dealings with the land. I have also to acknowledge much kindly help in relation to ancient legal documents, and in other ways, from Mr. E. W. Oliver, of London. The Rev. H. A. Holme, the late Vicar of Sutton, and the Rev. G. A. Coleman, the present Vicar, have much facilitated my examination of the parish documents. To the latter is owing the original photographs which so effectively illustrate the church. From Mr. T. Tindall Wildridge I have received great assistance in many details of local history, and I am much indebted to Dr. G. B. Longstaff, of Putney Heath, the Rev. John Ellam, formerly Vicar of Drypool, Mr. J. R. Boyle, F.S.A., Mr. Godfrey R. Park, Mr. J. G. Hall, Mr. W. G. B. Page, and many others, for information and suggestions bearing upon certain sections of my subject. In many ways I have benefited by the judicious advice of Mr. William Andrews, F.R.H.S., of Hull.

Without the assistance and suggestions of Mr. A. Gibbons, F.S.A., of Heworth Green, York, Miss Martin, of 250, Portsdown Road, London, and Miss Parker, of 39, Wellington Square, Oxford, I could not have utilized in any material degree the documents stored in the Registries at York, in the Record Office, London, and in the Bodleian Library at Oxford.

Some new matter which was obtained while the book was going through the press, and some additional references, will be found in the appendix, which should be referred to after reading each of the chapters. There also are noted some errors in the text. I hope there are few that have failed to be noted.

THOMAS BLASHILL.

29, TAVISTOCK SQUARE,
LONDON, W.C.

CONTENTS.

* See Appendix.

ILLUSTRATIONS.

SUTTON-IN-HOLDERNESS.

THE ISLE OF HOLDERNESS.

Land deposited by the sea.—Separated from the Wolds by the great hollow.—
The ancient inhabitants.—The Romans.—The Engles.

THE long line of the Yorkshire Wolds, stretching
from the Humber at Hessle to the cliffs at
Flamborough Head, is the upturned edge, or rim, of
a thick bed of chalk rock that underlies the whole of
Holderness, extending eastward far out below the sea.
For a long period the sea lay deep over this basin of
chalk, dashing against the lower portion of the
wolds at Hessle, and northwards where the shore line
then ran. How came the thick deposits of clay,
gravel, and mud, that throughout Holderness have
been heaped upon the chalk? If we pick up any one of
the pebbles or boulders, that are mixed with the clay of
the low hills, but are most easily obtained from the
cliffs or the shore, it will tell its own portion of this
long and interesting story. Some of these rounded
and water-worn stones were broken from such rocks
as we may still see at Whitby, or in West Yorkshire,
in Durham, or Cumberland, while others came from
Scotland and Norway, or at least from these neighbour-
hoods. Those which travelled the farthest are most
perfectly rounded and smoothed by wear. The clays
which embed them, preserve also the water-worn
remains of very ancient animals washed out of the old
rocks, and mixed with the remains of more recent
animals that lived during the formation of the clays.

1

These clays came from the same general direction as
the rocks and fossils, the carriers of the whole being
water and ice.   The composite mass of clay and gravel
was left in heaps, with intervening hollows, where
afterwards strong excavating currents flowed, and
pools or marrs stagnated.   Some of these became
filled, during long. ages, with thickening beds of peat.

THE ISLE OF HOLDERNESS.

The tall Irish elk stalked over the land, and the fallow
deer, fore-runners of mankind.   Where the carrs now
lie, yew trees grew up, fell, and were buried, to be
replaced by oak, alder, and hazel, that in their turn
met with a like fate.   Then came up Scotch firs that
died where they stood.   In cutting the deep drains in

Ing = meadow near river
Carr = marsh land.
holm = islet in a river or by the sea
CLOUGH - OUTFALL [FROM A DRAIN]

THE ISLE OF HOLDERNESS.   3

the Carrs, the prostrate trees have been unearthed, and
some may still be seen.   Where the tide flowed over
the wide areas that now form our Ings, thick beds of
mud and silt were deposited, and Ings and Carrs
alike were covered with a final layer of clay.

The most ancient inhabitants of the eastern slope of
the Yorkshire Wolds, looking eastward towards the
far-off sea, would have a prospect very different from
that which meets the eyes of their descendants.
Instead of the broad, low-lying plain that now extends
from the Wold foot to the comparatively high ground
of Holderness, they would look down on a wide tidal
inlet or hollow, branching northward from the Humber
past Beverley and Driffield, and curving round towards the sea in the direction of Bridlington Bay.   It
had no depth of water, but its width was three times
that of the Humber at Hull.   At flood-tide, and when
the upland waters were flush, the opposite shore would
seem a great island, with small islets standing out
from its brink, the smallest of them forming green
patches or holms on the face of the shallow water.
But when the tide ebbed out, it would leave an
expanse of grey mud, varied by brackish, stagnant
pools, and by the green holms then inaccessibly
stranded in its midst.   Indeed this must have been
their most usual outlook.   At such times might be
traced a current of fresh upland water scooping out for
itself a track down the middle of the muddy waste,
from pool to pool, past one and another of the solitary
holms in something like the same general course as
that in which the river Hull now winds its way—the
shrunken representative of the immemorial ebb and
flow.

The low margins of the promontory or isle and its
dependant islets, where they bounded the inlet, would
be wide-skirted with salt marshes, the general surface
of the land being seamed with boggy valleys helping
to mark out manors and parishes, and dotted over

with sedgy marrs, of which Hornsea Marr, a veritable lake, is practically the last survivor. The whole district would be populous with sea fowl, whose range was no less over the inlet than over the Humber, and off the North Sea shore.

The most striking feature of the whole district was this inlet or hollow that parted the naze, or ness, or promontory, from the wold country. It must have been a dreary region, for the most part neither navigable water nor firm shore; impassable except by voyaging from holm to holm during the brief periods of the highest spring tides. That it bore the name of the Hul or the Hol, either of which would express the notion of such a hollow, is probable. The first of these forms is found at the earliest date in Holderness, the name of the district cut off by it from the mainland. When we first hear of the river which resulted from the subsequent reclamation, it was called Hul.

To reach the "isle" of Holderness by any land route, it would be necessary to skirt the lower slope of the wolds curving round northward and eastward, as far as Bridlington Bay, then turning to the south along the higher ground by the sea. There stood the great Castle of Skipsea, begun in a remote time, and enlarged, no doubt, by successive owners. After the Norman Conquest, those enormous banks and ditches, and the Castle mound, would be completed for the purpose of controlling the only convenient entrance to the isle.

The condition of this district, in the times of its most ancient inhabitants, may to some extent be con- jectured. The high grounds must have been cultivated in a rude way, and their cattle would graze on the lower slopes. The Castle Hill, which is the most ancient evidence of their occupation now existing in Sutton, was formed down in the submerged Carr, just clear of the high land of Bransholm, from which only it could be attacked. The Romans left but scanty traces of their presence in the isle ; coins have been found at Swine. Five centuries before the Norman Conquest the German invaders called " Engles" or "Angles," included Yorkshire in their conquests and gave their name to England. Those who occupied the East Riding, which extends to the valley of the Derwent, called their country Deira, a name that has been thought to survive partially in the middle syllable of Holderness.

Whatever these pagan Engles may have found here, their little clusters of farmsteads must have occupied all the most eligible sites on the higher grounds of the isle. Each would have its ditch or enclosure forming a "tun," the nucleus of the modern town or village. From it the cornlands, meadows, and pasturage extended down to the rough margins of marsh and marr. Subject to intermixtures with any survivors of earlier races, or with their fellow-countrymen, the Danes, who swarmed here in the eleventh century, these Engles probably form the main stock in our own ancestry.

THE SUDTONE OF DOMESDAY.

Almost an island.—Bransholm and the Castle Hill.—The Domesday Manor and Berewic.—An Agricultural Community.

THE most prominent portion of the land on the west side of Holderness, facing the hollow, then bore the written name of "Wagene," afterwards Waghen, now Wawne. It is said to have been so named from the ancient highway which ran through it. As an ecclesiastical parish it was closely connected with the Cathedral Church of York. It included all the holms scattered over the waste to the southward as far as the Humber, particularly that long tract of land stretching out to the south and east, along which the ancient highway was continued, so as to communicate with south-eastern Holderness. This connecting tract of high land was known as "Sudtone;" it was the South Town of Wagene. In secular matters it was independent, belonging to the manor of Brocstewic, or Burstwick, while Wagene was attached to Aldenberg, now Aldbrough.

The high ground of Sudtone consisted of three very slightly connected parts. Nearest to Wagene was the round hill or holm called Sefholm, the name of which is still preserved in Soffham Farm. Next came the long ridge where Sutton village now stands, and, last, the round hill called Riseholm, but slightly connected with the main land of Holderness to the south-east.

Behind this long stretch of dry land lay, towards the east and north, a wide expanse of shallow waters, where are now the North and East Carrs. There the streams issuing from a great breadth of country beyond Swine met and mingled with the salt water of the higher tides.

Beyond the waters in the North Carr was Bransholm, a cultivated island, which originally belonged
to Swine, but which became attached to the manor
and parish of Sutton. Bransholm is particularly interesting because of the ancient mound with its moat that
stands out into the Carr and is called Castle Hill.
Near to it is a small mound, that probably marks a

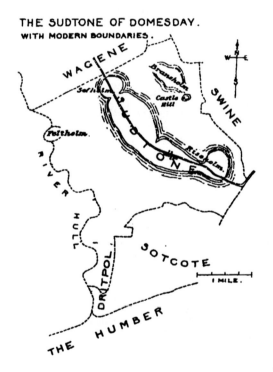

THE SUDTONE OF DOMESDAY.
WITH MODERN BOUNDARIES.

burial place, and there is an embankment leading
towards the Castle Hill from the higher ground. No
doubt these earthworks, like some smaller ones at
Swine, and the great mound and banks at Skipsea,
were begun by a race that has left no precise records,
and, like them, they became in the middle ages useless
for purposes of defence.

About the middle of the eleventh century, in the time of Edward the Confessor, the chief portion of Sudtone was held under Earl Morcare by Grinchil, who is probably the same as Grinchil the owner of Holmpton, near Withernsea.

The first historical record of the condition of the parish is found in the great survey of all his rents in England, ordered by William the Conqueror for financial purposes, and completed in 1086. William had given the lordship of Holderness, which Earl Morcare had held, to a Flemish follower, Drogo de Brevere, who had married the King's relative, and who occupied the Castle of Skipsea, which he, no doubt, strengthened after the method of the time. Several of his manors were, however, intermixed with lands belonging to the See of York and to the College of St. John of Beverley, afterwards called Beverley Minster. The entries in Domesday Book relating to Sutton are in two parts, which are here translated from the contracted Latin. Amongst the manors in Holderness is this entry :—

> "In Sudtone Grinchil had three carucates and two oxgangs of arable land to be taxed. Lanbert, a vassal of Drogo, has now there two ploughs and four villeins, and nine bordars, and sixty acres of meadow, rough pasture two quarentens long and one broad." It is "two miles long and a half mile broad. In King Edward's time worth fifty shillings, now fifty shillings."

The entry relating to Sutton amongst the lands called Berewics, held by the College of St. John (of which the Archbishop was the head), is as follows :—

> "In Sudtone are nine oxgangs of land to be taxed. One free man had there three villeins with one plough and a half."

A carucate was as much arable land as a plough with its team of eight oxen could cultivate during the year, which in Sudtone was a hundred and twenty acres, the usual quantity. An oxgang, or bovate, was the eighth part of a carucate representing the share of one ox, and measuring about fifteen acres. The three carucates and two oxgangs in the manor would contain about three hundred and ninety acres. The nine oxgangs in the berewic would measure about one hundred and thirty-five acres. The ploughland reckoned in Sudtone thus amounts to five hundred and twenty-five acres "to be taxed." Many attempts have been made to account for this peculiar expression, which seems to suggest that there was other plough land that was not taxable. By the old system of cultivation it was not possible to produce a crop off the same land more frequently than two years in three ; or, if the land was poor, one year in two. There is little doubt that in Sudtone the land had always produced a crop two years in three, there would, therefore, always be at least one-third part of it lying fallow. It may be that this was the land not liable to be taxed.

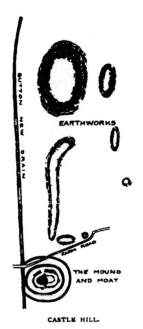

The five hundred and twenty-five acres in Sudtone producing a crop would thus be associated with half as much fallow, making a total area of seven hundred and eighty-seven acres, and this is almost precisely the quantity of tillage that was found to exist in Sutton when the open fields were enclosed, a hundred and twenty-seven years ago.

The sixty acres of meadow in the Manor lay outside the arable fields. The rough pasture would be the worst of the grass land, on which the cattle grazed when they were not turned on to the mown meadows, or on to the bare tillage fields.

This description of the Manor gives no idea of
Sutton as it is known to us.   But it very fairly
describes the ridge on which the village stood, except
that the length of two miles would not include
Sefholm and Riseholm.

It will be observed that the nine oxgangs in the
berewic formed fully a fourth of the whole of the arable
land in Sudtone.   The tillage and meadows belonging to it would generally be intermixed with the lands
held by the vassal of Drogo.   We shall see that the
principal house with the homestead, belonging to the
berewic, and occupied by the free-man, was in the centre
of the village on the east side of the churchyard, where
a terrace has been built in recent years.   It is possible
that Sefholm belonged to the berewic.

Lanbert, vassal of Drogo de Brevere, was the fore-
runner, if not the ancestor, of the Lords of the Manor.
He was responsible to Drogo for taxes, and for services
of various kinds in peace and in war, as Drogo was to
the King.   The " free man " who held the berewic
was the fore-runner of a long line of important men,
who were tenants under the College of St. John.   The
villeins were small farmers or cottagers holding their
portion of the land under the Lord of the Manor,
'assisting in the cultivation of his lands, and giving
him part of the produce of the land which they held.
The bordars were cottagers, no better than serfs or
bondmen, who worked as farm labourers, and were as
much attached to the land as the four-footed farming
stock.

The fact that the Manor was worth as much per
annum in 1086 as in King Edward's time, indicates
that it had escaped the ruin which had fallen on more
prominent places in the north, where manors in
general are said to have been greatly reduced in value,
and many are reported in the Domesday record as
" waste."   Few places in Yorkshire would be less
accessible to the spoiler than Sudtone.   Its remote-

ness and obscurity would be its best protection. It was a hamlet of a few households, settled chiefly on the site of the existing village. Their principal outlook would be across the waters to the nearer holms where Frog Hall, Marfleet, Southcoates, Drypool, and Central Hull now stand. Bransholm, with its castle mound, Swine and Ganstead, would be their nearest objects of interest beyond the tide-covered Carrs. The Wolds of Yorkshire and Lincolnshire would seem to most of them strange countries far away. The ordinary operations of farming, with some help from fishing, would supply nearly all their wants. There were for them neither fairs, markets, nor shops. Until the chapel was built in Sutton, there would be no priest nearer than Wagene, but they would not be without the offices of the church, keeping its fasts, and, let us hope, its feasts. They would have the comforts of social and family life. It is not necessary to suppose that they were unhappy as long as the Danish pirates kept away.

By the end of the eleventh century, old men in Sudtone would notice that the salt grass was encroaching upon the mud flats, that the beds of purple asters were jutting out further into the hollow, and that the flood tides visited their shores more rarely, sooner hurrying away. There would be rumours of hollows like theirs, and of a Holland across the ocean, then being embanked and reclaimed. But for the Conquest they might have waited longer for the enterprise and the organization which turned their surrounding waste into green pastures four times as extensive as their ancient cornland, meadow, and marsh.

MEDIÆVAL SUTTON.

*Flight of Drogo.—Holderness said to be barren.—Embankment and drainage.—
Marrs, sikes, and drains.—New meadows and pastures.—An Oxgang, with its
appurtenances. —The Lords of the Manor.—The Berewic and its owners.*

AFTER the Domesday record of 1086, the Parish
is missed from history during some seventy
years. It then reappears as Sutton, but no modification of name could adequately express the transformation which it had undergone in the interval.

Drogo de Brevere, Lord of Holderness, had
decamped at the beginning of this period, after
murdering his wife, whose ghost was left at Skipsea
to keep fresh the memory of his crime. He was
succeeded in his possessions by Odo, Count of
Champagne, who had married the king's niece, and
who begged for other lands upon the plea that
Holderness was a barren country, that grew nothing
better than oats. Historians treat this as a mere
scheme for obtaining additional manors, by practising
on the ignorance of the king, but it may be doubted
whether Odo himself knew much of the capabilities
of his new possession. Wheat could be grown then,
as now, on the high arable fields, but there would be
no object in growing more than was wanted
for home consumption. The absence of roads, and
the intersecting marshes, would render it difficult to
convey corn from the more fertile districts to Skipsea
Castle.

During the period between 1086 and 1150, the
great hollow had been reclaimed by embankments,
which confined the Humber to something like its
now existing limits, and by drains which carried the
upland waters to the channel of the river.

The practical effect of the embankments and drains, was to change the waste of muddy water into a wide expanse of land, more or less dry, which would in time improve into meadows, called ings, and marshy pastures or carrs. The Manor of Sutton was not at first a very clearly defined area, for on all sides, except the west `where the river ran, it was separated by marshes, or by marrs, from the neighbouring manors. The mud flats would require time to become fairly solid and covered with grass. Meanwhile the labourers who made the embankments would be employed in cutting ditches and grips, which might lead the waters along the lowest places' to suitable cloughs, or outfalls, at the river or Humber bank.

But after all that had been done during the seventy years which are missing from our story, the drainage was very incomplete. A great sheet of water, called Sutton Marr, lay between Sutton and Swine, extending over much of the North Carr. The marr was large enough to be used for the conveyance of farm produce by boat, and for centuries the fishery in its waters was an important right of the lords of the manor.

To the south of the village was another marr, called Stanmer, or Stainmar, which gave its name to certain allotments of meadow in the Ings, and is still commemorated in the So-mer-gangs, or Summergangs, pasture. For a long time the waters in the Ings and the West Carr found their way to the Humber, or the river, by means of certain low marshy channels called "sikes," the names of which should be remembered.

Landsike began near to the place where Sutton House now stands, or at the eastern end of the Tween-dikes Road, running between the Eastfield and the ings in front of Sutton Grange, Tilworth, and Bellfield. It is now partly represented by the old Lammas drain.

Lambhelmsike ran where the Ings Road joins the

Holderness Road, and probably drained off the water from the Stainmar.

Depesike ran from the back of Soffham Farm to a marr, which was afterwards drained by Foredyk.

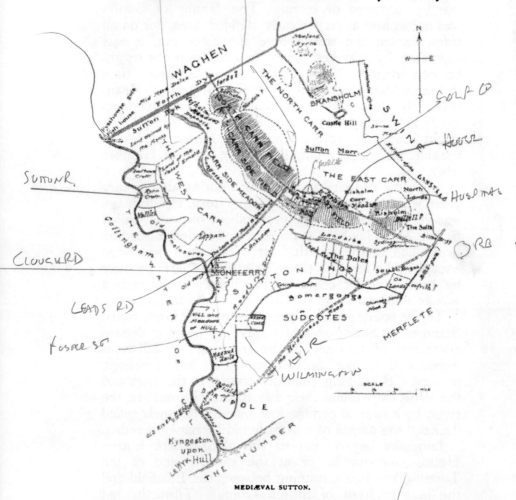

MEDIÆVAL SUTTON.

The fields called Midmeredales, in Wawne, preserve the name of this marr, and of the allotments of meadow near to it.

Langsike ran from near the Soffham end of
Depesike southward till it crossed the Stoneferry
Road,* and joined the ancient dike called Ankedam,
which drained the water from the Ings and West
carr into the river at Stoneferry clough. This dike,
so far as it still exists, is now called Antholme, or
Hantom, but its old course has been in a great
measure superseded by the artificial ditch, or canal, or
"leda," which gives its name to the Leads Road.
But, in spite of Langsike and Ankedam and the leda,
the low land which they drained was so subject to
floods, that the hamlet which grew up at Sutton-ferry
became a township distinct from the township of
Sutton.

There was then a Lord of the Manor, who was the
ancestor of the family which held Sutton until the
time of Richard the Second. His house and its
surrounding land most probably occupied the hilly
ground on the west side of the church. His ancient
ploughland, meadow, and pasture were intermixed
with the lands that were held by the villeins or small
farmers under him. The holding of each of these
might be as little as one oxgang, or fifteen acres,
of arable land, or perhaps less, "with the appurtenances," but two oxgangs, or thirty acres, with the
appurtenances, seems to have been the common
quantity. Before the reclamation of the new meadows
and pastures, these appurtenances consisted of definite
shares in the old meadows and pasturage, and there
would be a small homestead in the village for each
farm. But no man's land lay together, forming a farm,
as is the custom now. The whole area of the tillage
fields was laid out in "lands," or "selions," the breadth
from centre to centre of each selion being twenty-
seven to thirty-three feet, and their length about

---

* The earliest mention of Langsike in the Meaux Chronicle makes it to run from
Foredyk. Depesike seems to have been the northern end deepened so as to drain
into Foredyk.

two hundred and twenty yards—averaging about half-an-acre. Each oxgang consisted of about thirty selions, of which about ten would be in each of the three great fields into which the plough-land was divided, but no two of these would lie near to each other. They would be spread about in some sort of rotation with the selions belonging to other oxgangs, the original arrangement having probably been made by lot.

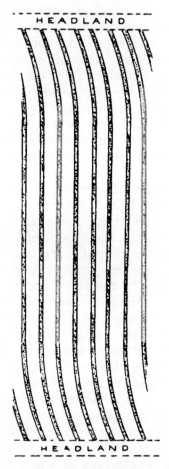

SELIONS WITH GRASS BALKS IN A TILLAGE FIELD

There is some reason to believe that the ancient practice in Sutton was to change the lands of the free tenants or farmers by lot or by rotation year after year. It may be that the meadows only were so changed. As recently as the year 1713 the meadow lands of two proprietors were occupied by each of them in alternate years. The ploughed portions of the selions did not adjoin each other, for between them were strips of grass land, that might be half as wide as the portions that were ploughed. These strips were called at a later time

" mere-furrows," or " balks;" they separated each man's tillage from that of his neighbour.   When the ploughed portions were not growing a crop, the cattle were turned out into the arable fields, and fed on the balks as well as on the stubbles.   When a crop of corn was growing on the ploughed land, the balks would produce a crop of hay.   The cattle were therefore not entirely dependent on the meadows and rough pastures for their food.   In a grass field on Low Bransholm farm, that was once tillage, the lands now measure alternately eighteen feet and nine feet.   This seems to have been laid down to pasture in ancient times before the old grass strips had become reduced in breadth by the plough, as generally happened in the course of time.

To each oxgang in the common fields belonged, as I have said, definite portions in the old common meadows, which were kept clear of cattle from March to Lammas-tide, or the beginning of August, so that the hay could be cut and gathered.   Each oxgang carried also the right to turn out a fixed number of cattle or sheep on the old rough pasture.   The whole arrangement was exceedingly complicated, and liable to engender disputes.   The scattered selions making up an oxgang were wedded to the meadows and rights of pasturage, and could not be separated without disturbing the farming arrangements of the Manor.   In later times we shall see that oxgangs were divided into halves, and thirds, and sixths, but each group of fifteen, or ten, or five selions carried with it the proportion of ancient meadow and pasturage.   So much for the ancient arrangements of the farms before the embankments were made.

But the reclamation of the Ings and Carrs introduced an entirely new element into the farming arrangements. Large portions of the new lands lying near the river were enclosed with ditch and bank, so as to become

the exclusive property of the owners, who would be
the Lord of the Manor, the owner of the berewic, and
any other persons who had taken an important part in
the embankment and drainage. Benedict de Sculcoates seems to have been one of them. These
persons had to keep the bank in repair. In this way
Stoneferry, as distinguished from Sutton, came to
consist largely of enclosed lands, the total quantity
there being about four hundred and forty acres, while
Sutton township only contained about eighty acres.
Large shares of the new meadows that were not
enclosed seem to have gone to the lord of the manor,
and to other persons who may have had special claims.
These meadows are sometimes called in deeds "the
meadows of Sutton." But a very considerable portion
of them, lying chiefly in the ings, were called dailes, or
dayles, each daile being the deal, or dole, that was
dealt out, perhaps by lot.* The Ings Road and the
Sutton portion of the Holderness Road ran across these
dales, and some smaller portions elsewhere seem to
have borne the same name. The "meadows of Sutton
called Sefholm" are now included in Soffham farm,
and the meadow land continued southward from
Sefholm as far as Leads Common, beyond the
Stoneferry Road. The whole was afterwards called
the Carr Side Meadow. There was also a meadow to
the eastward of Sutton called Riseholm Carr.

The new pastures were the West Marsh or West
Carr, that extended from Stoneferry to Waghen, the
East Carr and the Salts, with the North Lands, that
lay in the eastern corner of the parish behind Riseholm. In addition to these, there would be marshes
and new rough pastures on the borders of the marrs.

The result of this great accession of meadow and
pasture was that every owner and occupier of land in

* The improved marsh of the East Kerre of Wawne was divided amongst the
free tenants "so that each one of the said tenants received his share, marked
out in the said marsh according to the quantity of his tenements."—*Meaux
Chronicle.*

Sutton found his farm very largely increased in proportion to his oxgangs of tillage, and it is important to bear in mind that these new grass lands were quite distinct from the old. They were not necessary to the ancient farms, which were complete without them. They would not be very valuable until a great deal of labour had been bestowed on them in ditching and in clearing away weeds. There was no town of Hull, and no market for cattle and other farm produce, until, at a later date, sheep farming became profitable, owing to the foreign demand for wool. Owners of the new meadows and pastures might be glad to sell them, and might even be ready to give them to pious uses, thus alienating them from the ancient oxgangs in respect of which they had been allotted. Indeed these dealings with the new meadows and pastures furnish the most valuable and interesting source of information as to the affairs of the parish during the 12th, 13th, and 14th centuries.

The entries in Domesday, already quoted, shew that the land in Sudtone was held under two distinct tenures—the Manor by Lanbert, under Drogo de Brevere, who held the Isle of Holderness of the king; the Berewic by a free tenant under the College of St. John of Beverley, which held several such berewics of the King. The relation between these two properties, and the genealogy of the families that held them, are matters of considerable interest.

Lanbert, who, like Drogo, is supposed to have been a Fleming, is heard of no more after the Domesday record. He was succeeded by Siward, who appears to have been named after the great Saxon Earl of Northumbria, and is said to have been contemporary with William the Conqueror. After Siward, the family which took the name of Sutton, and may have been descended from him, held the manor for two centuries and a half. The following list of the Lords of the Manor and their family connexions has been compiled on the basis of the pedigree given by Frost, which is, however, very imperfect. Although I have made material amendments, the dates are still somewhat uncertain, until the accession of the first John de Sutton. From the first Sayer de Sutton, the manor descended from father to son, until the succession of Thomas, the last of the Lords of the Manor.

SIWARD DE SUTTON.

SAYER DE SUTTON—the first—living about 1156.

WILLIAM DE SUTTON—mentioned in 1173. He had a brother Richard, whose wife was Basilia, and also a brother Robert. In addition to the lords of the manor, Rainer and Alan de Sutton are mentioned in connection with the parish.

AMANDUS DE SUTTON—mentioned 1186 and 1195.

SAYER DE SUTTON—the second. Mentioned as early as 1211. The King's Bailiff of the Port on the river Hull. His brother William is said to have been priest of the Chapel of Sutton, but a William is mentioned who was a knight, and may have been a brother. Sayer's eldest son, Amandus, entered the Abbey of Meaux, and died before him.

1350. SAYER DE SUTTON—the third, whose wife's name was Johanna. A branch, bearing the names of Ralph and Stephen, and descended from a William de Sutton, existed about this time.

1370. SAYER DE SUTTON—the fourth, whose wife's name was Christiana. His brother William was the priest of the Chapel of Sutton. Administration of his estate was granted to Ernald de Saltmarshe, 9 Kal. Feb., 1289.

1289. JOHN DE SUTTON, SENIOR—married Constantia, daughter of John Sampson, of York. His brother William was priest of the Chapel of Sutton. His brother Nicholas had a son John, a priest, and perhaps a son Nicholas. Another brother Herbert is mentioned by Burton.

1339. JOHN DE SUTTON, JUNIOR—His wife's name was Alicia. He had brothers, William, Edmund, and Thomas, and a son, John, who did not survive him.

1357. THOMAS DE SUTTON—the brother of John. His wife's name was Agnes. He had a son John, who married Elizabeth, but died childless in his father's life-time. The Manor was therefore divided among his three daughters.

Constance became the second wife of Peter de Mauley the sixth. Upon his death she married John Godard, knight. Margery was first married to Peter de Mauley the seventh, and afterwards to William Aldbrough, Baron of Harewood Castle. Agnes married, first, Ralph Bulmer, knight, secondly, Edward Hastings, knight.

In Burke's "Dormant and Extinct Peerages," John de Sutton, senior, is styled "Baron by writ 20th July, 1332," his son John being called 2nd Baron. The Ashmole MS. 834, part iii., p. 30, contains a long and absurd pedigree of the family. According to it, Sayer the first married Idith, sister to his over-lord, William le Gros, Earl of Albemarle. William de Sutton married Mabell, Lady Bardolf. Amandus married the "dowghter of Albayne, Earl of Arondell." Sayer the second married Johanna, the daughter of Lord Ayncourte. Amandus, the novice at Meaux Abbey, whose marriage is doubtful, and who predeceased his father, is said to have married a daughter of Sir William Watton, and to have been the father of Sayer the third, who was really his brother. Sayer the third is made to marry Anne, the daughter of William, Lord Rosse. Sayer the fourth marries Dunstance Delsey; their third son, Sir Richard Sutton, is said to have married the heiress of the Baron of Dudley, and to have been the ancestor of the Suttons, Barons Dudley. No faith can be placed in any of these items; they appear to have been gathered together by an expert genealogist, in order to supply the Dudleys of Queen Elizabeth's day, with a showy list of ancestors.

The free man who held the Berewic under the College of St. John of Beverley, disappeared, as his neighbour Lanbert did, during the period in which the embankments were carried out. It is probable that he or his successor had taken an important part in this work.

I do not think that the relation of a berewic to the manor with which it was associated is anywhere very clearly explained, but there is sufficient evidence to shew how they existed together in Sutton.

The church stands within a considerable area of land anciently enclosed. A large house which stood upon a part of this land, to the eastward of the church, was known from the 15th to the end of the 18th century as the Hastings Manor House, and this land was undoubtedly the site of the chief house and homestead of the owner or occupier of the berewic. It seems probable that, when the original chapel was founded, this land, and perhaps the whole of the land to the east of the chapel, was acquired by the College of St. John of Beverley. Belonging to the homestead were the nine oxgangs of tillage, with their appurtenances, and the meadows and the rights of grazing in the common pastures. Besides this there were, belonging to the berewic, certain shares in the enclosed lands by the river. As the Archbishop claimed to exercise authority over the river, he or the college probably acquired these lands at the time of the embankment. The tillage and meadow, with the pasturage, seem to have been dispersed all over the township, just like the lands of the free tenants and those of the lord himself. Thus the Lords of the Manor were only partial owners of the township or parish, another family of equal rank being in possession of nearly one-fourth of all the land in Sutton, in the end calling their berewic a manor, and claiming all the usual manorial rights. It appears, indeed, that the Lord of Sutton made no important arrangement as to drainage or fishing without the concurrence of the owner of the berewic. Yet there is no trace of any difference between them or their tenants.

It does not appear at what time the berewic came into the family of de Melsa, or Meaux, of Bewick, but early in the 13th century, grants of land in Sutton were being made by members of the family to the

monks at Meaux Abbey. In the reign of Edward the
First, John de Meaux, in reply to a writ of *quo
warranto*, claimed to have the rights of wayf, with the
assize of bread, ale, etc., as holding under the Archbishop of York, who was the head of the College of
St. John. When the berewic came into the family of
Hastings they claimed to hold it of the Archbishop
by the service of a pepper-corn, an easy tenure, which
may account for the freedom with which portions of
the land were granted away. The property descended,
with only one break, from father to son for eleven
generations, according to the following list.

> KETELLUS DE MEAUX—of Brie, in Champagne, a companion of
> the Conqueror.
> GAMELLUS.
> JOHN.—In King Stephen's time. He exchanged Meaux for
> Bewick, with William le Gros.
> THOMAS.—A priest. The eldest son.
> ROBERT.—The brother of Thomas. About 1164.
> JOHN.—In the reign of Richard I.
> GALFRIDUS, OR GEOFFREY.—In the reign of Henry III.
> JOHN.
> GODFRIDUS.
> 1311. JOHN.
> 1321. JOHN.
> 1353. JOHN.—In 1372, he died childless, leaving a sister,
> Alice, married to Ralph de Hastings. His monument, with
> effigy, is in the church at Aldbrough.

Thus, by a coincidence, both these ancient families,
in which the manor and the berewic had descended
for many generations, became extinct in the male line
a few years before the beginning of the fifteenth
century. The berewic descended in the family of
Hastings, as will be detailed in the chapter upon the
history of the parish during that century.

THE EARLY LORDS OF THE MANOR.

The Monks of Meaux and their chronicle.—They acquire lands in Sutton.—Their legacy from Amandus de Sutton.

OUR knowledge of the earlier Lords of the Manor is derived principally from records kept by a community of monks, who, about the middle of the 12th century, became their neighbours and tenants.

In the year 1128, there was introduced into England, a reformed branch of the Benedictine Order, that had been founded at Cîteaux in Burgundy, from whence these monks were called Cistercians. They were soon settled at Fountains, Rievaulx, Kirkstall, and other places, where the remains of their magnificent abbeys still exist. A few years later, William le Gros, Earl of Albemarle, was Lord of Holderness, and owner of the old castle of Skipsea, which had been dismantled. The drainage of the great hollow had, by this time, changed the current of the traffic to such places as Stoneferry and Wawne-ferry, where new routes were established from Holderness towards the Wolds. In his search for a new place of residence, William had fixed on an excellent site at Meaux in the parish of Wawne, which he took steps to obtain by an exchange with the owner, John de Meaux. He had, however, made a vow to go to the Holy Land, but, being too stout of body for such an enterprise, he arranged with Adam, a Cistercian monk, to found an abbey in Holderness instead. Although the Earl had not yet obtained possession, Adam chose the site at Meaux, and would take no denial, so the new monastery was there founded in 1150.

It is from the chronicle of the abbey, compiled by

Thomas de Burton, Abbot of Meaux, that the list of Lords of the Manor of Sutton, and particulars of the possessions of the abbey, are chiefly derived.*

Amongst its earliest endowments, were lands at Waghen, adjoining the Manor of Sutton, which would be divided from Waghen by some marshy boundary or sike, in the place where Foredike was afterwards cut. From the corner of these lands by the river bank, where the monks had established a fishery, they would see at a distance of less than half a mile the extreme point of the enclosed land that stretched northward from Stoneferry. It consisted in part of one of those holms that may have stood out above the surface of the muddy hollow, except in times of extraordinary flood. This was called Feltholm, part of which, at least, had belonged to the demesne lands of Siward de Sutton ; the whole being now comprised in the ancient enclosed lands of Frog Hall. Between this old enclosure and their fishery in Waghen lay the northern part of the open pasture of the West Marsh. It would only be natural for the monks to conceive a wish to acquire this property, and their proceedings in respect of lands and pasturage in and near to what is now called the West Carr form an interesting portion of their own story.

Very soon after they came to Meaux, two houses with lands in Sutton, probably small cottage farms, had been given to the monks. These they exchanged with the first Sayer de Sutton, the Lord of the Manor, for the farm called Herneycroft, which had belonged to Herney de Hull, together with pasturage for forty cows with their young calves, in the West Marsh. It is easy to see how Sayer might undervalue land in such a remote place, and pasturage in that ill-drained marsh, while he would be glad to get into his own

* "Chronica Monasterii de Melsa," edited by Edward A. Bond, and published under the direction of the Master of the Rolls. The statements relating to the abbey for which I quote no other authority, will be found under the corresponding dates in that work.

hands any small properties near to the centre of his
Manor.

Between 1160 and 1186, Rainer de Sutton granted
to the monks, at a rent of fourteen shillings a year,
five acres of meadow in Feltholm, and the whole
meadow which he held at the north part of the croft,
which had belonged to Herney de Hull, who was, I
doubt not, so called because he dwelt by the river.

Amandus, the son of William de Sutton, gave them
the half of an exit called " Le Outgange," that they
might have free ingress and egress for their animals.
An ordinary outgang was a place where the cattle
of a village assembled, when they were to be driven
out together to graze in common.   This outgang
seems to have run between the old enclosed lands and
the southern part of the West Carr or Marsh, where a
very muddy road still exists.   It was a grassy drive,
and was to be shared with one Ernald, who held, under
Amandus, the southern part of the West Carr.   But if
it should improve into a meadow, the monks were to
have half the produce, whether it was mown for hay
or grazed by cattle.

Amandus gave them besides, twelve acres of meadow
which Siward had held, and by other gifts and
exchanges, they, in the result, possessed two estates,
separated only by a narrow strip containing five acres
of grass land that ran to the river.   This strip, now
called Crab Close, has always been distinct from the
adjoining lands ; it must have formed an access to the
river from the lands of Ernald.   One of these estates,
obtained by the monks, was afterwards called Hyrn
Croft, and measured thirty-six acres ; the other they
called South-hows-croft, it being the enclosed land
that lay nearest to their Waghen property.   It had
been held by Huck, and measured thirty-six acres, all
but a half pole or perch.   Thus they had obtained, on
very easy terms, seventy-two acres of enclosed land,
some of which was tillage, also pasture for forty cows

with their young calves. They would have to perform services, or make payments, in respect of their lands to the lord of the Manor, like all other tenants, unless they managed to get these dues remitted, but in any case they were the possessors of a valuable farm.

No doubt they were sorely in need of all they could acquire, for, in addition to their own very moderate wants, they had undertaken the costly work of building a great monastery, and of distributing alms to the poor who presented themselves at their gate. If we find them rather exacting or encroaching, we should remember these things, and bear in mind, also, how unscrupulous were the practices of the times. It is, however, pretty clear that they had deliberately planned the acquisition of the whole of the northern portion of the West Carr.

In the latter part of the twelfth century, the Archbishop's berewic, in Sutton, was held by the family of de Melsa or Meaux, who had exchanged their lands at Meaux for Bewick, where they now lived. From Thomas the Clerk, brother to Robert de Meaux, "a man of great authority, and large means," who lived in the time of Henry the Second, they received as much pasture in the West Carr as appertained to the third part of three oxgangs of his tillage—and the whole meadow, which is called Le Gayre, in the western part of Sutton. This would, I think, be part of the meadow called Sefholm. Robert gave them, for the health of his soul, and the souls of his ancestors, all his land on the south side of Gyselfleth, six perches wide, and extending from the river to the "fossatum marisci." This appears to be their earliest acquisition of land between the river and Summergangs dike, where they formed their estate of Magnusdaile. At a later time, they got from his son, John de Meaux, in an exchange, all his pasture in the West Carr belonging to ten oxgangs and a half of tillage; and by gift, six acres of land in the New Ings, by the river. Then Ralph, son of Rayner de Sutton, and Robert, his brother, who held tillage near Foredike, gave them their shares in the pasturage of the West Carr. It is to be observed that these gifts, and many more that will be mentioned, were new meadows, and new rights of pasturage, resulting from the embankment. They were quite distinct from the ancient appurtenances of the oxgangs. Such of these acquisitions as were made in the time of Amandus de Sutton were stepping-stones towards more important operations to follow.

Early in the thirteenth century, during the reign of King John, Amandus, finding himself drawing near his end, gave to the monks, by charter, and also by his will, "whatever he had," in the West Marsh in length between Forthdyke and the land of Ernald, the "man" or vassal of Amandus. Its breadth on one side, was from the river along Forthdyke as far as Landsyk, which is between Sefholm and the said marsh, and on the other side "it runs by the common exit, which lies between Hernyscroft and the land of Ernald, leading straight from the river as far as the aforesaid Landsyk." The Chronicle says that this transaction had the assent and goodwill of Sayer, the son and heir of Amandus, but, though he may have felt unable to make any open opposition at such a time, we may doubt his cordial acquiescence in a death-bed gift which would so materially diminish his inheritance. We shall see how this able and vigorous personage handled the matter, when he came into his estate.

SAYER THE SECOND—THE KING'S BAILIFF.

The forfeiture of his control over the river.—Drainage of the marshes.—Dripole in Sutton.—The monks and the West Carr.—Drainage of the West Carr.—Mills, canals, and fishery.—The legacy of young Amandus.—Death of a bondman.—Sale of bondmen.—Large grants to the monks.

SAYER, the son of Amandus de Sutton, appears to have succeeded his father about the year 1210, in the reign of King John. He was a knight in 1218. He is said (Frost, p. 119) to have claimed "by inheritance, through a long line of ancestry," the fisheries on both sides of the river. About the year 1126, in the eleventh year of Henry the Third, he was, as the Bailiff of the King, in charge of the Port that had been established on the river. For many years during which he held this position, he seems to have been engaged in disputes with the Archbishop of York, Walter de Gray, who, as Lord of Beverley, questioned his authority over the river. He was scarcely ever free from disputes with the Monks of Meaux about their title to lands in Sutton. During his time, Godfrey the second, and his son, John de Meaux, held the Berewic in Sutton, that lay intermixed with the lands of his Manor; and William de St. Luce, as the husband of the heiress of Benedict de Sculcoates, also held lands in Sutton.

His connection with the river, as the Bailiff of the King, whose dues he would collect, had a tragical ending. His men having discovered that a vessel, said to be laden with wine, carried also rich jewels, he ordered them to bring the treasure to his house, even if it cost the lives of the crew. In the contest the crew were killed, and it was only by resigning to the Archbishop his authority over the river, and thus making him his friend, that he escaped a worse punishment for this crime.

In addition to his Manor of Sutton, Sayer had a large interest in the lands of Southcoates, as tenant of the berewic, under the College of St. John of Beverley, and in Drypool also. His lands extended northward, into that part of Swine which lies between Bransholm and Fairholm, but, notwithstanding the embankments and drainage of the low ground, the greater part of his inheritance must have been no better than marsh or marr. By his efforts to drain and improve the low-lying lands of Sutton and Southcoates, he is best known in local history.

In his time, the river Hull turned westward at Sculcoates, and, after a winding course, discharged into the Humber. Drypool probably took its name from a creek that jutted out from the Humber, where the old harbour now runs. Sayer de Sutton seems to have chosen this creek as the outlet for the ditch, or sewer, that he made through the marshes, which ditch was used as a boundary between Sutton and Southcoates, the outlet being called Sayer Creek. The ditch was evidently so designed as to run along the boundaries of two or three pieces of old enclosed land of his own, that were used as sheepfolds, and it cut off from the ancient Dripole a large portion, which was thenceforward included in the Parish of Sutton.

The Marr, called Stanmer or Stainmar, that lay to the south of Sutton Ings, would be drained by Sayer's new ditch. I am not disposed to speculate as to how, or by whom, the old creek was extended northward into which Sayer's dike was discharged, so as to join the river at Sculcoates. It is likely, that, at least in times of flood, some of the water had always passed along that route, but, in any case, its formation into a navigable channel would readily be contrived, and easily executed, by the parties who were interested in forming a new and more direct outlet for the river.

The territory of Dripole extended along the east side of the new channel of the river, over the district now called the Groves, as far, at least, as the land occupied by the Flax and Cotton Mills. I cannot say how Sayer became possessed of the portion of Dripole. It may be that he acquired it from the College of St. John of Beverley, or it may have been one of the fruits of his drainage operations. It is frequently referred to as consisting of three oxgangs of land and is called a manor, distinct from the Manor of Sutton.

The disputes between Sayer and the monks of Meaux, together with his plans for draining and improving the lands in which they and he were interested, occupy a large space in the Chronicle of the Abbey. We have seen that in the north-western corner of the great pasture of the West Marsh or West Carr, the monks had acquired, from the first Sayer de Sutton, pasturage for forty cows, and rights of pasturage from Thomas and John de Meaux, and other persons. To these acquisitions had been added the vague gift or bequest from Amandus de Sutton, of " whatever he had " in that portion of the West Carr. It is not clear whether Sayer altogether repudiated his father's gift, to which he had seemed to assent at the time, or whether he only disputed the right of the monks to turn out more than the precise number of cows that Amandus had kept in the pasture. The monks, however, claimed the whole interest which Amandus had possessed in that pasture, hoping to become in time, through gifts or purchases, the sole owners of the grazing rights, so that they could enclose and improve the pasture for their own advantage.

It seems probable that the monks attempted prematurely to enclose the land, or to do some other thing contrary to the custom of the Manor, for even Sayer could hardly have ventured to act towards them as he did without some kind of justification. They say that he turned them out of the West Marsh "by the violent hands of armed men," pillaged their sheepfolds, seized twenty-two quarters of their corn, extorted from them one hundred shillings, and, besides taking other things, assisted the Prioress of Swine to abstract the body of their brother, Amandus the butler (of Benningholm) who had bequeathed it, together with an oxgang of land and ten acres of meadow, to Meaux Abbey.

The monks appealed, not to the law, as they might have been expected to do if they were altogether blameless, but to the Pope, who, on October 12th, 1218, directed the Abbot of Jervaulx (a Cistercian monastery) the Abbot of Easby, and the Dean of Richmond to settle the difference. It was Pope Honorius III., or his officials, who, although intensely interested in the promotion of a new Crusade, found time to intervene in this quarrel. After many sittings, to which Sayer and his adherents were summoned, all parties agreed to a compromise, (see Lansdowne MS., 424. fol. 111ᵇ-112ᵇ.) by which the monks yielded to him the matters in dispute. In exchange, they got pasturage in the West Marsh for forty more cows, besides their original pasturage obtained from the first Sayer de Sutton. But, as this additional pasturage for forty cows must have included all the grazing rights that they had acquired from other persons, they could hardly have gained by the compromise. It seems, however, that the referees, who, as clergy, would not be unfavourable to the monks, thought the above was all to which they were entitled under the circumstances, and the monks complain that they could get from Sayer no confirmation of his father's charter.

About this time their cow-houses in Hyrncroft and Southowscroft, became dilapidated, and they turned them into sheepcots, on account of the rising demand for wool. The proportion of sheep admitted to pasturage in Sutton, was five for each cow or ox, so the monks who, like all the Cistercians, became great wool growers, would be able to depasture in the West Marsh, in lieu of eighty horned cattle, a flock of four hundred sheep.

Sayer, having succeeded in limiting the grazing rights of the monks, set about improving his lands in and near to the West Carr by drainage works, carried out in conjunction with Peter de Waghen, the monks of Meaux, and the free tenants of Sutton and Waghen. Then the drain called Forthdyk, Fordyk, or Foredike, which now divides Sutton from Wawne, was cut of a breadth of sixteen feet and a depth of six feet, draining the water from parts of the low lands of Sutton, Waghen, Bransholm, and Swine into the river at the Fishhouse of the monks. It was a clever and complicated piece of engineering. Mills were set up by the monks on the river bank, which were worked by the water that ran into the river at low-tide, and also by the water that ran back into Forthdyk at high-tide. The new drain was to be used as a canal. Two bridges were to be made over Forthdik, one near to the river bank for the use of the monks in driving their cattle between the West Marsh and their land at the fishery, still called the Fishhouse Vaccary; the other at Forth-cross for waggons and passengers. This last was at the spot where Foredike bridge now carries the Wawne Road. These bridges were to be so con-structed that boats without "rostra," or high prows, could be hauled under them. By this dike, farm produce was carried by water from the low country of Bransholm, Wawne, and Swine, where roads are still very deficient. And in order that a waterway for this important traffic might always be available, whether the stream of Forthdyk was running outwards or inwards through the Abbey Mills, or whether it was dammed up, the monks granted to Sayer and his free

3

tenants leave to make a second ditch or drain of the
width of ten feet along the West Marsh, parallel with
Forthdyk. This ditch was called "Sutton-dyk;" it
began at a distance of twenty perches, or about one
hundred and twenty yards, from Forth-cross, and was
provided with sluices at each end. At the fishery
near the Abbey Mills a mill pool was formed, which
would also be a fish pond, and the right of drawing
nets for fish in Forthdyk was given by the monks
to John de Meaux and to William de St. Luce, who
evidently had considerable interests in the neighbouring
meadows. If Sefholm was part of the Meaux berewic,
that will help to account for the deficiency in the
Domesday measurement of the length of Sudtone.

Besides these various uses, a road was to be maintained on the narrow strip of bank between Foredike
and Sutton dike, leading from the Waghen Road to
the Abbey Mills and to the river. There was then,
no doubt, an important traffic in connexion with the
mills, the canals, and the road. At the present time
the most solitary corner of the parish is where the
remains of Old Forthdyk and Sutton dyke, with
the bank between them, extend beyond Soffham
Farm nearly to the river. In my earliest years at
Soffham it was a place in which one might get lost
in a tangle of wild roses, and where the only sign
of life was the broad sail of some vessel gliding
noiselessly beyond the trees. It has been called at
various times the Raw, Fishhouse Rawe, the
Helpster bank, and Roe bank, which name it still
retains.

The relations of Sayer with the monks did not
improve with time. A fresh quarrel which arose
between them forms an important chapter in his family
history, and also furnishes us with many interesting
particulars of lands within the Manor.

Sayer's eldest son was called Amandus, after his
grandfather, and about the year 1245 was already a

knight.   He was about to be married to a daughter of
Hugh Paynell, and, in view of this match, Sayer
arranged to give him twenty-five pounds worth of land
to enable him to make a settlement upon his wife.
Of this, the half, reckoned at seven and a half oxgangs,
or about a hundred and twelve acres of tillage, with a
house, and with meadows and pasturage, and other
appendages, in Sutton, was actually granted by
charter.   All this was given out of Sayer's own
demesne lands, and would form a very substantial
farm, much beyond the holding of an ordinary free
tenant, and would indeed be next in importance to the
lands of the berewic.   Although Sayer parted with this
large property in this way, it would be in the full
expectation that, when Amandus succeeded him, he
would bring these lands back into the estate.   Sayer
could never have dreamed that they would be permanently severed from his property, yet this was made
possible by that endowment.   It appears probable that
the match never came about, for Amandus entered the
monastery of Meaux as a novice, dying there soon
afterwards.

It was at that period common for men who were
stricken with death to enter a monastery, to assume
the habit of the order, and to be buried in the sacred
precincts.   A rich man would make a large endowment in return for such a privilege.   If Amandus
found himself likely to die, he might naturally adopt this
course, and he would certainly make some gifts to the
monks for receiving him among them.   He did indeed
make certain gifts, which were distinct from the lands
that he had from his father, having been obtained from
Peter, the son of Thomas de Sutton.   They consisted
of a sheepcot, with pasturage for six score
sheep, and also an acre and a half of meadow
adjoining "le Mikeldayl" on the south side, and
abutting upon "le Led," which was the leda or
canal that gave its name to the Leads or Stoneferry

Road.* This was subject to a rent of a pair of white gloves worth a halfpenny, payable to Peter annually at Easter, but afterwards remitted by him. These would not seem inadequate contributions from a young man, and were probably all the land that he was then free to give.

But when Amandus was dead, the monks produced a deed of gift by which he conveyed to their monastery the whole of the estate which his father had given him as a dower for his intended wife. The list of these lands supplies us with much interesting information as to names and places in Sutton, in the middle of the thirteenth century.

The charter granted by Sayer to Amandus, in view of his marriage, is copied in the Dodsworth MS. 53, fol. 2. It is witnessed by P. de Falkenberg, of Rise, William de Sutton, and John de Bilton, knights, Master John de Swine, who was, probably, one of the Canons attached to the Priory, Benedict and Peter, the Chaplains, with others. The charter given by Amandus to the abbey is entered in the Lansdowne MS. 424, fol. 3. The following list of the lands is founded on Sayer's charter; with the addition of some of the names in the charter of Amandus, which differ from or explain those in the charter of his father. The positions of some of the lands can be identified. Although the names are simply entered in a list in the order here given, they appear to form three groups, corresponding with the three arable fields. Each group begins with the names of the sections of the field in which the tillage lay. The lands were conveyed with their "appurtenances, and easements in meadows, in ways, in waters (that is fishing and hauling), in paths, in pastures, in turbaries, and all other easements within the town and without." The appurtenances would include the ancient meadow land

---

* This seems a more probable position than any site near Magnusdaile, which was in Dripole. There was, however, a ditch there, but it does not appear to have been called a "Lede."

and pasturage that was always attached to the tillage.
The newly-enclosed meadows are specially mentioned
under the names of the particular dayles in which they
lay ; with them would go the new pasturage.   The
term "culture" is applied to tillage and meadow alike.
The first item in Sayer's list refers to the house to
which the lands belonged, and where Amandus may
have intended to live.   Sayer specifies : " My Capital
messuage of Sutton, enclosed with a ditch under my
garden wall, and with the same ditch and one acre of
land."   Amandus adds that this land is " adjacent."

The cultures are :—

Grenedic.
Watelandes.
Sefures.   *At Sefholm ?*
Litelstayndale.   *In the Ings by Summergangs.*
Gatesflat.
Le Dayl, alias Hou.   *In the Ings near to Hougcote.*
Le Dayl Allede.   *By the Leda or Canal.*
Le Dayl at Fulsic, towards the South.
Bildesdayl.   *In the Carr side meadow.*

Scotlandes.
Blakemildes, towards the West.
Stokethaye.
Cartegatedayle.
Staynmardayle.   *In the Ings.*
Le Daile ad Fontem.
Le Dayle ad North Lagghes.
Le Dayle super Halle, towards the South.

Yarleshon (or Jerlshon).   *Tillage in the East field between the
    Bilton Road and the East Carr.*
Le Dayl which belonged to Robert Bodi.
A moiety of Sideng (or Sidehenges).   *The Side Ings is a piece of
    ancient enclosure near the Salts, probably the site of a Sheep-
    fold belonging to Sayer.   It now forms the lower part of
    Bellfield.*
Two butts towards the East Carr.   *Pieces of meadow at the
    lower end of the Selions, in or near to Jerlshon.*
Ninety acres of meadow in the marsh of Sutton, towards the
    West, between Ford dike and Ankedam.   *That is in the
    Carr side meadow.*

To this list Amandus adds the toft called in the Chronicle an oxshed,

"which I began to rebuild outside of the town of Sutton, on the west part of the town of Sutton as included in a wall, and it is to be remembered that all the above is computed at seven and a half oxgangs."

We can easily imagine the feelings of Sayer de Sutton, when he learnt the contents of the charter of Amandus granting all this property to the Abbey. But at the head of the witnesses stood the name of William de Forz, or Fortibus, Earl of Albemarle, and Lord of Holderness, under whom he held his Manor, and he would feel it advisable to restrain himself for the time. He, indeed, went so far as to withhold his consent, but, with the aid of the Earl, the monks kept possession, until by an act of violence of their own they placed themselves at his mercy, and had to yield a portion of the gift.

The Chronicle says :—

" At the false advice of a certain perverse Councillor of ours, Hugh de Pontebelli, we disseised the aforesaid Sayer of his own meadow by force of arms, and in some strife which arose over the affair, one of his officers, who was a serf or bondman, was killed."

Sayer, therefore, laid a serious charge against them before the King's Justices at York, and the wife and brother of the bondman were able to bring an action for manslaughter against the abbot, the monks, the lay brethren, and their servants. Then, in fear of an irrecoverable loss, they, acting on the advice of friends, paid to Sayer sixty marks, and gave up half of all the properties in dispute, and also the fishery in the Marr, and the chief residence, and the oxshed or toft, with its enclosed land, and all the other appurtenances belonging to that which they gave up. Thereupon Sayer confirmed to them the other half of the property left by Amandus, and let them have the right of haulage by boat in the Marr, and got the action for manslaughter withdrawn.

But, two years afterwards, Sayer ejected them from certain meadows which appertained to the half of the lands that they had been allowed to keep. These were the grass butts that ran down from the ends of six of their selions of tillage on the south side of the Eastfield to Landsyk, the six pieces being reckoned at less than seven acres. The monks issued a writ against him, but, before the case came on for trial, they came to an arrangement by which he gave them the meadows in dispute for the support of the alms at the gate of their monastery.

This is the last of their recorded struggles with Sayer. Although they had not been so successful as they wished, they had made very considerable inroads upon his property, and, in addition to their acquisitions of his own demesne lands, they were rapidly acquiring new meadows and pasture rights belonging to the tenants on his Manor.

The following details refer chiefly to pasturage in the Salts and to lands in Magnusdayle, which lay in that narrow part of the parish between Southcoates and the river just to the north of the field, anciently called Drypole field, and afterwards called the Clough-field. But they include also gifts of tillage, with its appurtenances of meadows and pasturage, both ancient and reclaimed. These details will show how actively the monks were proceeding to make good their footing in the parish, and particularly how, without forgetting the West Carr, they were striving for the exclusive possession of these two properties—Magnus-dayle and the Salts.

Peter, the son of Thomas de Sutton, gave them, in addition to his other gifts, two acres and a quarter of tillage and meadow in divers places, and all the grazing rights that he had in the northern part of the West Marsh. Godfrey de Meaux, who then held the Arch-bishop's Berewic, gave them, in exchange for two selions of their own in some other part of Sutton, two

selions of arable land in Magnusdayle, saving a
sufficient and reasonable way for those passing along
the bank of Hull, which bank they were to keep in
repair.   Andrew de Branchester, clerk, gave them,
with his body for burial, all the pasture in the "West
Kerre" next Foredike, that appertained to one oxgang
of tillage, also a toft in Sutton, they being bound to
pay to Ralph, son of Stephen de Sutton, one penny
yearly.   Richard, son of Roger, son of Ralph the
elder, of Sutton, gave them thirteen acres of land for
which they·were to pay to Ralph, son of Stephen, a
rent of twelve pence.   This Ralph, son of Stephen,
gave them a toft, five perches and a half of land,
and pasture for one ox, in all the ox pastures, and
remitted to them a rent of twenty pence, which they
had to pay him.   Also for supporting the gate-alms he
remitted to them a rent of eighteen pence, that the
porter of the monastery used to pay him.

Amandus, the son of Alan de Sutton, gave them
meadow, about thirty-nine yards in breadth, in "le
Gayre" before mentioned.   Henry de Hull gave them
all the land called Bludetres, and a yearly rent of
four pence out of the tenement of Simon Wolf.
Avicia, Simon's wife, sold to them, for five marks,
five acres of tillage, with all the meadow appertaining
thereto.   Stephen, the son of Ralph, son of Rayner
de Sutton, confirmed these grants, and added one or
two strips of meadow to them.

Their acquisitions from the family of William de
Watton are carefully given in detail.   William
possessed two oxgangs, or thirty acres, of arable
land, with its appurtenances of meadow and pasturage,
which would make up a full-sized farm.   He gave to
the monks his rights of pasturage, which were in the
West Carr, next Foredike, and, dying, left a son and
heir, Amandus, who also died, and the two oxgangs
were divided between his three sisters.   Of these,
Beatrice married Robert, son of Alan de Sutton;

Matilda married William, the son of William de Ruda, or Routh; and Margaret married Robert, the son of Peter de Otringham.

Nearly all these lands appear to have come into the possession of the monks either directly from the ladies and their husbands, or from the persons to whom they had sold certain portions. They included the thirty acres of tillage, and all the meadows and rights of pasturage in Magnusdayle and Salts, and in the Oxfryth, which was either the enclosure called the Oxlands, or the ox pasture called the Northlands, close to the Salts. Of these grants, one section was for broadening the courtyard of their Grange or Farmstead. Other portions were for keeping up the distribution of alms at their gate. But, though parts of these properties appear to have been gifts, the bulk of them were purchases made by the payment of money by the monks to certain Jews of York and Lincoln, for debts due to them from the owners of the lands. For these payments, the monks held the receipts of the Jews.

The Chronicle says that Sayer de Sutton confirmed all these grants to them, and gave them three acres in Magnusdayle for their gate alms, and four acres near to the same in exchange for eight acres in other places. But the most important thing was, that as lord of the Manor, he allowed them to enclose their acquisitions in Magnusdayle with ditch and bank, and to make all manner of improvements for their own advantage. Thus was formed a little estate of some thirty-two acres of enclosed land, which, with some difficulty, they managed to keep until the dissolution of their monastery.

Besides these gifts, the chronicler recites in the time of Sayer, Junior, how Sayer the Elder had given to the convent twenty acres of land and all the exit called "Arnald Outgange," for the support of the woollen-house for clothing the monks. The Cistercians wore a long tunic of unbleached wool, their lay brethren, who managed their farms, wearing a similar garment. No picture of Sutton during the Middle Ages would be complete without the figures of these white monks, their heads covered each with a large cowl, going to and fro amongst the free tenants and bondmen.

In reference to the condition of the serfs or bondmen in Sutton, in the time of Sayer, the charter No. 194 in the Lansdowne collection, is of great interest. It is a grant by Stephen, son of Ralph de Sutton, for the health of his soul, and the souls of all his ancestors, to God, and to the Altar of St. John of Beverley, of his bondmen, John, Henry, and Roger, sons of Richard, son of Robert of Hul, with all their children then born, or in future to be born. The witnesses appear to be chiefly members of the College of St. John. They include W. Scot, who became Archdeacon of Worcester, with S. de Evesham, and W. de Wisbeche, both of whom became Archdeacons of the East Riding. None of these persons could have seen any impropriety in such a transaction, and the serfs themselves would be clear gainers by being transferred to the service of a religious corporation.

In 1247, Walter de Gray, Archbishop of York, released to Sayer his right to the advowson of the chapel of Sutton, which had before been made, to some extent, separate from Waghen. After the separation, the parish would have its own priest, subject to compensation to the Rector of Waghen in respect of dues, mention of which will be found in great detail in the chapter upon the fifteenth century. Henceforth, the priest seems, as a rule, to have been a son or brother of the lord of the Manor. No part of the church now visible can have existed at this date.

Sayer de Sutton, the King's bailiff of the port of Hull, was, no doubt, the most interesting of all the lords of the Manor. Our knowledge of him comes chiefly from the records left by his enemies. By their accounts, his faults were those of a strong and active character, but they were displayed under considerable provocation. One would like to hear his side of the questions in dispute. If the violence of some of his proceedings should need excuse, his efforts for the improvement of the whole district under his control, and particularly the wide areas of meadow and pasture ground reclaimed from marr and marsh, will plead for him, at least with those who enjoy the fruits of his labour.

William, the brother of Sayer, is entered in Frost's pedigree as "persona de Sutton," there is, perhaps, some confusion arising from the succession of two or three parsons of Sutton called William, who were brothers of the lords of the Manor. William de Sutton, knight, was one of the witnesses of Sayer's grant to Amandus. He also appears in the Meaux Chronicle as having granted a mill, etc., at Hessle, to the monks. Dodsworth gives (71, fol. 27) a charter from Osmund de Stuteville, rector of Cottingham, of similar property which he had "of the gift and sale of Saer de Hesel, son of William de Sutton, knight." Sayer de Sutton is one of the witnesses.

In the pedigree of the family of St. Quintin, given by Poulson (vol. 1, p. 266), William St. Quintin is said to have married Beatrix, daughter of Sayer de Sutton. The families were neighbours for several generations, branches of the St. Quintins being landowners at Brandsburton and Ganstead. This is one of the old Yorkshire families still existing.

In the time of Sayer and his successor, several of his relations held lands in his Manor, descendants, as it seems, of Rayner de Sutton and of William, the ancestor of Sayer. There were successive generations of Stephens and Ralphs, with Peter and Thomas and Alan de Sutton, besides others who bore the name, but who may not have been relations. Their names appear through their grants of land, which may indicate that they were breaking their connection with the place.

Sayer's name appears amongst the witnesses of grants to the Hospital of St. Sepulchre at Hedon, and of a charter of William de Fortibus, the second. See B.M. Add., 24, fol. 188, and 24, fol. 190 ; also Harl., ch. 50 D. 39.

The site of Sayer's house, to which he ordered the contraband jewels to be brought, is a matter of considerable interest. He could not have lived at the Castle Hill, where the ancient owners of Bransholm had lived in the time when they needed a defensible position in the margin of the tide-covered Carr. He might have fixed his residence at Stoneferry, where he could control the river, and the road which then formed the most southern access to Holderness. But, upon the whole, it is most likely that he and the other lords of the Manor lived in the town or hamlet from which they took their names. The only part of the town that bears evidence of having been occupied by the Lords of the Manor, is the western part, and particularly the hilly ground to the west of the church.

Sayer the Second died about the middle of the thirteenth century, in the reign of Henry III.

SAYER DE SUTTON THE THIRD.

IF the Chronicle of Meaux Abbey gives events at this period in their proper order, "Sayer, the son of Sayer, the son of Amandus," was lord of Sutton before the great and fatal floods near the Humber and the river, by which the monks lost buildings, men, and cattle, in Sutton and elsewhere. The editor of the Chronicle adopts the date of 1253 for these floods, which seem to have simply poured over the tops of the banks, into every part of the reclaimed district. Sayer probably succeeded his father about the year 1250, he was certainly contemporary with William de Fortibus the Third, his over-lord, who died in 1260. It was, I think, in the earlier portion of his time that Sayer granted to Martin de Otringham, burgess of Hedon (Dods. MS. 53, fol. 2^b) five acres in the meadows of Sutton, under Dodersykes, abutting upon "le Led," or "le Lede," for a length of fifteen perches, or ninety yards. With this, he granted pasturage for a hundred sheep in the West Carr. By another charter, he granted to the same Martin pasturage for four hundred sheep in Somergangs, with the sheepfold called Hougcote enclosed with ditches, also a piece of meadow named Catstertdayle in the Ings, and pasture for his lambs in the meadows for eight days, when they were separated from the ewes. After hay-time, the sheep were to pasture throughout the meadows. This grant was subject to a payment of six shillings at Whitsuntide and Martinmas. William, the son of Robert de Sutton, was one of the

witnesses to this charter.   Hougcote, and a daile
called Hou, were probably near to the south end of the
Ings road.   In the eighteenth century, the Casterd
gate of Sutton led out towards the Ings ; Catstertdayle
would be near to the Sutton end of the Ings road.

A few years afterwards, probably in 1264, there was
a huge commotion in the parish.   The young Prince
Edward, afterwards Edward the First, being on his
way to Scotland, had summoned the knights and
freemen of Holderness to meet him in arms at York,
but the sub-prior of Meaux had been deputed to make
excuse.   The last William de Fortibus, lord of
Holderness, having died, his heiress, Aveline, was
placed under the wardship of Prince Edward, and it
was perhaps on this account that he asserted his
authority over the feudal tenants.   Upon his return
from Scotland, he repeated the summons with no
better success.   Soon afterwards, a strong force under
seven barons, sent by the King to bring the men of
Holderness to reason, was posted at Cottingham, and
the Sheriff of Holderness led the rebels to the grange
of the monks, on the site of Frog Hall, an excellent
position for defence, where they watched for two nights
to prevent the passage of the river.   But when the
monks saw that they had to feed a crowding, hungry
host, they made haste to bring about a peace.   This
local rebellion, nowhere else recorded, fits in fairly well
with the history of the struggles then going on between
the King and the barons under the Earl of Leicester.
We are not told how Sayer and the men of Sutton
acted in what might so easily have led to a small battle
in the West Carr.

Sayer seems to have spent his time chiefly in his
own neighbourhood, occupying himself in the affairs
of his manors.   His name appears in charters, either
as grantor, or as witness, more frequently than that of
any other member of his family.   The Priory of Swine,
which was conspicuous across the East Carr, would be

the place to which he and his household would resort
for such of the offices of religion as could there be performed with a grandeur of ceremonial not possible in
the little chapel of Sutton.   There they would meet
the lords of all the neighbouring manors with their
families, and in the Priory Church many of their
business transactions were consecrated.   The charters
by which property was conveyed from different persons
to the prioress and nuns of Swine, add very materially
to the information given by the Meaux Chronicle as
to the land in Sutton, and its owners, at this period.

I have generally credited Sayer the Third with the
charters here given, which bear the name of Sayer, the
son of Sayer, because these all appear to have been
granted by the same person.   But his son and
successor was also named Sayer, and the documents
do not always clearly distinguish between them, the
son sometimes styling himself as the father had been
styled, "Sayer the son of Sayer."   In the Meaux
Chronicle, Vol. 2, p. 169, Sayer the Third is called
Sayer Senior, and the son Sayer Junior.

Swine Priory was founded by Robert de Verli in
or before the reign of King Stephen, for fourteen or
fifteen nuns of the Cistercian Order.   It is said to
have at one time consisted of brethren and sisters,
living together under a prioress, but in the charters
the prioress and nuns only are mentioned.   There
were, however, two canons at least to assist in the
offices of religion, who did not refrain from meddling
in secular affairs.   The nuns had also several lay
brethren to take the outdoor management of their
property.

The Parish Church of Swine, the chancel of which,
with its aisles, only remains, is commonly spoken of as
the church of the Priory, but this must be a mistake.
The Meaux Chronicle mentions that, in a dispute with
the monks about tithes, the nuns being contumacious,
the ecclesiastical court closed first the parish church,

and afterwards the conventual church with the adjacent church of the lay-brethren. These two churches would disappear soon after the priory was dissolved.

The Swine Charters, from which I shall quote, are partly in the Lansdowne and Lord Frederick Campbell collections, but chiefly in the Stowe collection in the British Museum—small parchments beautifully written, and as legible as when they were taken from the priory at the dissolution in 1540. They were evidently written on the spot, being executed at times of festival when all the great people in the neighbourhood were there assembled. From the lists of witnesses we learn the names of several of the ordinary associates of the lords of Sutton, and the humbler frequenters of the monastery in the thirteenth century. The lords of manors are named first in these documents; then come names of lesser note, including officers of the convent and servants, the writer of the charter being sometimes specially named.

Geoffrey de Watton gave two of these charters. By the first (Stowe 493) he grants to the nuns a piece of arable land at Jerleshon, three perches—that is eighteen yards—in breadth (which would be two selions), and extending from the Bilton Road down to the meadow of Risholm Carr; a piece of meadow land thirty yards in breadth in the daile called Brun, a similar piece at Stainmar, and another at Kalvegaire. These and other grants of meadow in the dailes are usually described as extending from the Landsic of Sutton to the pasture of Sothekotes or of Dripole, which is Summergangs. The common pasturage belonging to the above lands is included in the gift, making altogether a little group of about an acre of tillage with its appurtenances. For this and a similar quantity of land in Dripole he reserves a rent of six pence, in two payments, at midsummer and on the thirtieth of November. His second charter, No. 494, is a more solemn document. It is a grant by Geoffrey of lands to the Church of St. Mary, at Swine, and the nuns therein serving God, for his soul and the souls of his father, mother, and wife, and the souls of all his ancestors, in free and perpetual alms, with his body for burial at the priory. Besides an acre of tillage in the east part of the town of Sutton, extending from the great street of the town to the East Carr, which might be in Jerleshou, he grants three pieces of meadow, similar to those before mentioned which he formerly held " de domino Willelmo de Sutthona ; " not, I think, the former lord of the manor, but his grandson, William, the brother of Sayer the Second. The meadows are situate in East Stain-mar-daile, in Horse-daile, " extending from Landsike to the dyke of Cothecroft," and in West Stain-mar-daile. There is no mention of pasturage in Geoffrey de Watton's second charter. The rent reserved for these lands, with others in Dripole, is sixpence, in two payments— at Michaelmas and Easter. An endorsement states that these two charters refer to the same lands, but though one of them does explain the other, the descriptions do not quite tally. The witnesses to one or both are the knights Adam de Merflet, Simon, his brother, William de St. Quintin, and John de Belton ; also Simon de Preston, William de Muberai, John Lubens, of Dripole, Robert and William, sons of Alan, Robert the Clerk, who probably prepared both the charters, Hugh, son of Agnes of Swine, Richard, son of Thomas de Newton, and Peter de Rue.

Stephen, son of Peter, "filius domini Willelmi" de Sutton (who may have been the former lord of the manor) makes a free grant (Stowe 492) to the priory of five acres of meadow in Howed-dailes, which had belonged to Ralph, son of Reiner de Sutton, stretching from the arable land of Sutton (the East-field) to the pasture of Sothecotes. The witnesses are Hugh de Verli, Sayer de Sutton, Simon de Seifling, Alan de Danethorp, and Henry Coleman. After the death of

4

Stephen, Wimark, his widow (Stowe 491), gives up her claim to dower, and Ralph, his son (Stowe 490), confirms Stephen's gift. The witnesses to one or both these charters are William the Constable, William de St. Quintin, Henry Coleman, and Richard, his brother, Richard Marschall, Alexander de Wyton, Robert, son of Alan, Simon, son of Hugh of Swine, Hugh, son of Agnes, and Robert de Stanernia, whose name appears at the end of other charters. He may be identical with Robert, the clerk.

Ralph, son and heir of Stephen, son of Ralph de Sutton, granted (Stowe 489) seventeen acres and a half of meadow, of which five lay nearest the Horse-daile towards the east, four lay nearest the Stain-mar towards the east, three and a half lay next to the daile of Sayer de Sutton in Calvgaire towards the east, and five lay next the daile of Sayer towards the east, in the daile called Brune. He granted, also, one selion of arable land, eighteen yards wide, lying between the daile of Sayer and the daile which Richard, the son of the priest, held of Sayer ;* also pasture for two oxen or cows in the oxpasture, for thirty wethers in the West Carr, and anywhere in the common pastures except the Salts, and for ten oxen or cows everywhere in the common pastures, with the digging of four cart-loads of turf yearly. This grant is subject to a rent of two shillings in silver, in four payments—at Easter, Mid-summer, Michaelmas, and St. Andrew's Day. The witnesses are Sayer de Sutton and John de Bilton, knights, Robert de Hilton, Herbert de St. Quintin, Andrew de Sutton, clerk, William, son of Robert, and Richard, son of Hamo, both of Sutton, Simon, son of Hugh, of Swine, Richard Marescall, of Swine, Robert, the cook of Swine, and Robert, the clerk, who is described as " Notary of this document."

---

* Although the marriage of priests was discountenanced by the Popes, the practice was not long discontinued. Their children had succeeded to their property, and in many cases even to their benefices.

The names of two of these witnesses—John de Bilton and Andrew the clerk—are appended to a grant by William, son of Robert, son of Alan de Sutton (Dods. MS. 53, fol. 1ᵇ), to the Abbey of Meaux, for their alms, of two acres and a half of meadow in Staynmar, in "the South Enges" named in these documents. The frequent occurrence of the name of one amongst the witnesses with the addition "clerico" makes it probable that, besides the officer of the priory who wrote the documents, there was a person present who would take care that the grantor did not put his seal to parchments which he could not understand.

By a very interesting series of charters, Sayer, the son of Sayer, grants lands and rights of way to, and exchanges lands with, the Priory of Swine, the effect being to increase Sayer's property in the Dailes, and to give the nuns an estate in Sutton near to their property in Southcoats ; their new acquisitions being in the district now called Wilmington. These lands extended to the river or to the lands by the river that had been anciently enclosed.

Where the railway from Hull to Hornsea crosses the Sutton Drain, it enters some ancient enclosed lands that belonged to the lords of Sutton. The ditch which separates Sutton from Drypool was evidently so cut as to go round the southern side of these lands, which are now laid out in three fields, one of them being still called "Hedon Close." By the charter L.F.C., viii. 7, Sayer grants the site of that sheepfold, with its appurtenances, which is situate in the land which lies next to the land called "Hedoncroft in Sutton,* just as it is bounded by the dykes," the witnesses being Robert de Lisset, Henry de Stuteville, Roger de Dol, and others before mentioned, including the Swine folk, who were always at hand for such a

---

* The grant dated 1217 by Sayer the Second to Thornton Abbey mentions land of Hedun de Hedun and a sheepfold close to the " Led."

purpose. To this charter is still appended a seal bearing a crescent and star, surrounded by the legend, " S. Saeri fil Saeri de Sutt." This small lump of green wax has suffered little during the six centuries and a quarter that must have passed since it was impressed by the hand of Sayer himself.

SEAL OF SAYER THE THIRD.

By the Stowe charter, 487, "Sayer, the son of Sayer," grants twenty-one acres of land in the meadow of Sutton, whereof eighteen and a half lie next to Hedon-crofts on the northern side near to the sheep-fold of the nuns, between the lands of the chapel of Sutton on the southern side and the land of Andrew the clerk on the northern side, and extending from the common pasture of the Sumer-gang as far as the arable land by the river, also a similar slip of two and a half acres lying between Sayer's own land and the land of Amandus de Fittling. Sayer receives in exchange sixteen acres of meadow, less by "three falls and a half," lying in three dayles, viz., in Brune, in Stannmardayles, and in Fritholm-daile, with the release to him of five acres of his own meadow in Soddecotes, which the nuns had held in lieu of the tithes of his hay there. The Stowe Charter 498 is a copy of this document, in which the grantor is styled " Sayer tercius." Sayer warrants the lands granted by him against all claim of his over-lord the Earl of Albemarle. This charter must therefore have been made before the death, in 1260, of the last William de Fortibus. Among the witnesses are Godfrey de

Meaux, Walter de Faukonberg of Rise, and John Surdeval.

By the Stowe charter, 484, Sayer grants thirty acres of land and appurtenances, "measured by the perch of eighteen feet" (which measurement I have followed throughout), between the closes formerly belonging to Amandus de Watton and to Simon Scot at Hull, extending from the meadows of Sutton to the river, with common of pasture for their cattle, after the hay and corn harvest until the middle of March.   Simon Scot lived, I presume, by the river Hull :—there was as yet no town of that name.

The Stowe charter, 485, appears to relate to the same land.   The witnesses include Stephen Palmer, Richard de Buton or Ruton, and Laurence his brother, Robert de Bern and Thomas de Flinton, with the other usual witnesses great and small.

The following charter, Stowe 486, bearing a bad impression of Sayer's seal, is very interesting in relation to the roads in Sutton at this period.   By it, "Sayerus de Suttona miles, filius Sayeri de Suttona militis," after greeting in the Lord all who may see the document, granted to the nuns freeways for carts and wains, men and horses, and for driving the rest of their animals from the bridge of Bilton through the midst of the meadow of Sutton—that is, the Dayles—as far as Sumergang-dike, and through the pasture of Sumergang as far as Dripole and Sotecotes, and to their sheepfolds.   This is the track which, in the time of John de Sutton, the grandson of Sayer, was made into the road to Hedon for the convenience of the new town of Kingston-upon-Hull, and is now called the Holderness Road.   We must bear in mind that there was as yet no public way in the parish except the ancient road coming from Wawne and going towards Preston, and probably the road to the river at Stone-ferry, though there must have been many rights of way-by which the free tenants got access to their lands, which lay scattered all over the parish. Amongst these was a bridle path and footway that led out of the back street of the village nearly along the line of the present footway to Hull; but at Thisleton, where that footway now turns by the side of the Sutton Drain, it went straight on across the meadows, by way of Wilmington, towards the river bank. These lands were called by Sutton folk "the meadows of Hul," and those further south "the meadows of Dripole," where the unsavoury modern suburb called the Groves has since been built. Sayer now grants to the nuns that, with their men riding or going, they may use the path that reaches from Sutton as far as Dripole through the meadows of Sutton, and of Hul, and of Dripole, as the men of Sutton and Dripole now use it. Besides these ways, he grants them a path for their milkmaids from the land of Sutton beyond Catesterte as far as the sheepfold of Martin de Otringham. Moreover, he grants a path from the Marr of Swine through the middle of the East Carr as far as the way nearest to the close of Thomas de Flinton, and on the east thereof, with liberty to carry their corn and hay from their lands, and the tithes which they may collect anywhere over his manor. This gave the nuns rights of way from Swine, through the parish of Sutton, to their new properties at Wilmington, and to their pasturage and sheepfolds in Southcoats.

At the end of the charter, Sayer says with solemn emphasis :—

"I have granted and sworn, by touching the holy vessels, for myself and my heirs, that we will never impound the cattle of the nuns for trespass, but only for farm rent."

If their cattle should trespass on his corn or meadow, they should be sent back at once upon surety being given, and the damage made good upon the oath of the keeper of the cattle, or on the view of good and lawful men, chosen for that purpose.

These things were granted for the health of the souls of himself and his ancestors, mutual faith to be faithfully kept, but should he fail in this, he would forfeit to the King sixty shillings, and the Sheriff of York, or the bailiff of Holderness, might distrain upon anything of his, movable or immovable, for the penalty and the damage, as sworn by those in charge of the cattle.

All this shews the strictness with which rent would ordinarily be exacted, even from the nuns, the severity with which trespass would ordinarily be treated, and the tightness of the bonds wherewith the lord of a manor had to be bound. Witnessing his oath and deed, standing before the altar at Swine, were John de Bilton, Symon de Preston, John de Surdeval, William de Brustwicke, Roger Dole, William de Wydthon, Robert de Berthe, with others. This weight of testimony neither he nor his heirs could very well gainsay.

With the monks of Meaux, Sayer seems to have been on tolerably friendly terms. The portion of the West Carr where they had their pasturage, had by this time proved insufficient to feed the stock allotted to it, particularly when sheep were substituted for the fourscore cows, named in their original grants, the proportion being, as we shall see, five sheep for one cow, the young calves and lambs being of course included. Therefore, by arrangement, the monks released to Sayer their grazing rights there, and he granted to them in return the whole of his pasturage in demesne in this same northern part of West Carr, which lay between the river and the marshy streams called Langsyk and Depesyk, which divided the West Carr from the meadows of Sutton, called Sefholm. It extended southward from Forthdyk, as far as a line drawn from the corner of Southowscroft almost in the direction of Swine Church, now, no doubt, represented by the road from the homestead of Soffham to Frog Hall. Along this line, posts were to be set up, until the ditch, which Sayer authorised them to make, should be dug. Neither he nor his heirs were to have any rights within this enclosure, and the monks might impound any cattle that trespassed therein from the southern part of the West Carr, and improve it as they would. The contemplated improvement would consist in cutting ditches and grips to carry off the water from the more moist portions of the marsh. We shall see, however, that owing to some grazing rights of other persons in the same portion of land, which rights the monks could not acquire, the ditch was never made, and this caused trouble at a later time.

The successive transactions by which they acquired the grazing rights in the pasture then, and still, called the Salts, are of great interest as illustrating the customary mode of dealing with such property. Poulson's slight allusion to this pasturage is made void of meaning through his reading of "in salinis de Suttona," as "in Sutton Willows," instead of "in the Salts of Sutton."

From the Almonry near the gate of the monastery of Meaux, relief was doled out practically to all who presented themselves, upon whatever excuse, the poor traveller on honest business, the outcast labourer, not so happy as to be even in bondage, or the vagabond who was the precursor of the casual tramp. This business was under the monk who held the important office of porter, and who had the distribution of considerable gifts that had been settled on the monastery for the gate-alms. Sayer gave for this object two selions of arable land at Bylhylle, with a piece of meadow that probably ran down from the ends of the selions to the edge of the carr or marsh. They received also a good deal of the pasturage which they held in the Salts for the same object.

Besides the land in Bylhylle, Sayer gave for the gate-alms as much pasturage in the Salts as belonged to nine oxgangs of his tillage, also the remaining part of a piece of meadow of which his father had given the other part. The sheep which they would be thus entitled to turn into the Salts might be turned, after hay-time and corn harvest, into the common meadows and arable fields until the middle of March. The Chronicle says that he also granted them free passage with their carts and wains anywhere in Sutton, so that they might cut their corn, mow their hay, dig turves, and carry away all their things at their pleasure. But his son disputed this grant, as will be seen.

Among the gifts of Peter, the son of Matilda de Routh, for their gate-alms was an acre and a half of meadow in Newenge (the New Ings) of Stoneferry. John de Brystalle (in Brandesburton) gave them, for gate-alms, two acres of arable and meadow land. Benedict, the son of Peter, gave half an acre of tillage and a piece of meadow, three perches, or fifty-four feet, in breadth, with a rent of a halfpenny payable in respect of half an acre of tillage. John Poke also gave, for their gate-alms, one toft and three perches of meadow, and Ralph, son of Stephen de Sutton, confirmed the gift. The Lansdowne MS. 424, f. 118^b., describes these lands. This gift included one selion of land, extending from the Wawne Road to Sutton Marr, and lying between the land of Peter the Provost and that of Robert le Gray.* The meadow was at Bildesdayll, and extended from "where the plough turns" at the bottom of the tillage in the Carr Side meadow, between lands of Robert le Gray and Wm. de Stuteville. Walter de Wyk gave them a toft, with a

---

* This Peter may have been a Reeve only. Robert le Gray, *miles*, was the grandson of Robert de Gray, of Rotherfield, who married Beatrice, the heiress of William de Seynt Luce. He held the lands of the family that took its name from Sculcoates, which lands were afterwards granted by Michael de la Pole to the Carthusian priory there.

building upon it, in Drypool. But William de Dryffeld, the ninth abbot—a man of such remarkable sanctity that miracles were attributed to him (though he was the worst manager they ever had)—let to William de Thorne, knight (Lansd. MS. 424, f. 113), three perches of land with seven "rodefallis" in Sutton. It lay between the toft of Alice, sister of Sayer, and the croft of Ralph, son of Stephen, and extended from William de Thorne's own croft as far as Croftdyk, next to the Marr; for this he was to pay his homage and two shillings annually. But as to this and some other properties, the Chronicler, writing a century later, sadly records that it is quite impossible to say anything about either the land or the rent!

We hear little of the interference of the lords of Holderness in the affairs of their vassals, the lords of Sutton; but we must not forget that the lords of Sutton were answerable for rents and services to their over-lords, just as the free tenants and cottagers were to them. William de Fortibus the Third, having died in 1260, his only child, Aveline, succeeded to his possessions, subject to the right to dower of her mother, the Countess Isabella. Aveline married, in 1269, Edmund Plantagenet, called "Crouchback," the brother of the King, and in 1273 died childless. Among the more splendid of the tombs in Westminster Abbey, the effigy of the young heiress Aveline, lies under its gorgeous canopy, statuettes of relatives, as mourners, surrounding the base. Isabella de Fortibus, herself a great heiress, survived her daughter for many years, and, through her bailiff, Robert de Hildyard, was active in the affairs of the parish. The castle of the lords of Holderness was then at Burstwick, from which place the affairs of the Seigneury would be chiefly managed.

By a charter (Dods. MS. 94, f. 90ᵇ.) Sayer grants to the lady Countess de Fortibus and her heirs for ever, a hundred and twenty acres of meadow in the meadows of Sutton, with pasturage for a thousand sheep in Sottecotes, Drypool, and Sutton. The patches of meadow lay scattered in the fourteen places following :—

	A.	R.	P.
Forde, *near Foredike* - - - - -	6	0	0
"Eight oxgangs" in Forde - - - -	5	2	10
Hou, *in the Ings* - - - - - -	3	0	27
Blakmildes - - - - - - -	3	1	0
Gayres, *near Foredike?* - - - - -	11	0	0
Arnald croft - - - - - -	18	0	0
"Eight roods" - - - - - -	4	2	24
Bretes - - - - - - -	15	1	10
The Culture of Robert son of Rayner - -	14	2	20
Gesekeld - - - - - - -	4	2	0
Bildesdeyle, *in Carr side meadow* - - -	3	2	0
Ledeholme - - - - - -	13	1	0
Dedersigdeyle - - - - - -	8	0	0
Norhundeldeyle, *Nordale or Noddle?* -	9	0	29
	120	0	0

This very considerable alienation of property was made subject to an annual payment to Sayer at Easter of a pair of gloves or a penny. When next heard of, in 1296, the lands were in the possession of Robert de Hildyard.

Towards the close of his life, Sayer granted two charters, which are recorded in the register of the Archbishop of York (B.M. Lansd., 402), and are of considerable interest. By the first of these he gave, for the health of his soul, and the souls of his ancestors, all his rights of setting up weirs in the water of Hull between Beverley and the Humber, so that he would make no obstacle to the free passage of ships to and from Beverley. The witnesses were John de Oketon, John de Meaux, John de Reygote, Symon le Constable, John de Frysmareys, and Geoffrey Aguylum, Knights, with John Hesel and Nigel de Waudebi. The date is no doubt 1269, for there is a similar grant of that date (Dods. 28, f. 20), by Johanna de Estutevill, who thereby relinquished her right as owner of the Cottingham side of the river. This grant also is witnessed by John de Oketun as well as by Sayer the Third.

I have noticed the ancient connexion of Bransholm with Swine, where the Archbishop was the over-lord. By another charter Sayer the Third granted to Arch-bishop Walter Giffard all his pasture called Braunseholme, in length between the Marr of "Schwine" and Thirty acre-dike, and in breadth from the Leda or canal of Swine, as far as the boundary between Sutton and Braunseholme.*

This grant included the pasture of Sutton (the North Carr), for cattle going out and returning as far as the arable land of Sutton, and free chase "as well by boat in the water as by land," with all appurtenances, from the quinzaine of the Blessed Virgin Mary (or within the fortnight following Lady Day), 1270. For the first two years the rent was to be a peppercorn at Michaelmas, and afterwards for the term of ten years, twenty pounds by the year. Sayer warranted to the Archbishop all the fruits and profits for the ten years, so that if he should suffer loss through time of war or otherwise, he might hold the pasture for the full term of ten years, at the rent of a peppercorn, until his loss should be fully satisfied. In those last years of Henry III. such a stipulation was not unnecessary.

By the following January, and probably earlier, Sayer the Third had died, as is shewn by an arrange-ment as to dower made with his widow Johanna, by his son, Sayer the Fourth, who about the same time

---

* The scribe who copied this charter has written "Chrecti Akerdyk" and "Ledeswine." I do not doubt that he misread two letters of the word which in the original was "Thretti." The Thirty Acres is a very old name for land just outside Sutton in the direction of Fairholm, that belonged to Sayer the Second. The ditch enclosing it on the north, and extending within six feet of the Leda of Swine, is described in the Meaux Chronicle after the account of the making of Foredike. This Leda was the boundary of Swine afterwards called Bransholmdike.

having "inspected and understood" this grant, confirmed it to the Archbishop.

Upon the death, in 1260, of William de Fortibus, it had been found (Dods. 98, f. 119) that Sayer the Third held two carucates and one oxgang of tillage in Sutton, four carucates in Ganstead, one carucate in Coniston, half a carucate in Rotheringham, and three oxgangs in Drypool, with all the meadows and pasturage that then belonged to this land. As he had neither the rank nor the responsibilities of the great nobles of the time, we may hope that, notwithstanding the considerable amount of property which he granted away, he would be able to keep up his position fairly well among the lords of the neighbouring manors.

———

Note.—The charter, dated 1217 (Add. MS. 26786, f. 60) by which Sayer the Second granted for fifty marks, for the term of twelve years and three months, meadows and pasturage to the Abbey of Thornton in Lincolnshire, should have been quoted in the preceding chapter. The pasturage is for six hundred and sixteen sheep (at six score to the hundred), and twenty cattle, in the fields and marshes of Sutton, Hull, Sotecotes, and Dripol, with free entrance and exit between Hull and Wilflete, that is between the river Hull and the ancient outfall into the Humber at Marfleet. The meadows of sixty acres included the whole except sixty acres of Ledeholmdale, of Dodersicdale, and of the meadow which abuts upon the "Led" in which "Hedun de Hedun" had four acres, also the site of a sheepcot of an acre in the meadow on Led.

Ledeholm and Dodersike are so mentioned in different documents as to leave it doubtful whether they were near Summergangs-dike, or near the Leads or Stoneferry Roads, but as the Leads common lay

close to that road, and the leda or canal which superseded the ancient Ankedam is there, this is the more
probable position. A conveyance, dated 1723,
. mentions Dother Sykes as being near the Casterd
Gate, which was probably near the Tween-dikes
road.

Jerlshon or Yarlshon, near Risholm Carr should be
written Jarlshou or Yarlshou. If it means the Earl's
landing-place, it may point back to a time when the
high land of Sutton was accessible from the eastward
chiefly by boat.

SAYER DE SUTTON THE FOURTH.

Sayer's grant of dower to his father's widow.—Fishery in Sutton Marr—New apportionment of the pasturage.—An oxgang with its appurtenances.—A cottager's rights to meadow and grazing.—The monks as sheep farmers.—List of their Sutton possessions.—The export of wool.—Projected foundation of Kingston-upon-Hull.

SAYER, the son of Sayer, the son of Sayer, or Sayer Junior, or Sayer, the son of Sayer, as he is styled in different documents, succeeded his father in the year 1270.

In January, 1270-1, his father's widow, Joan, found it necessary to get a regular assignment of her dowry out of the family estate, and, in the octave of St Hilary, she, by the writ of dower called "unde nihil habet," impleaded, in the court of Westminster, Walter Giffard, Archbishop of York, Isabella de Fortibus, Richard de Thornton, tenth Abbot of Meaux, Matilda, Prioress of Swine, with others who were probably trustees for Sayer. Thereupon "Sayerus de Sutton, filius et heres domini Sayeri de Sutton," in order to avoid costs, and labours, and grievances, by a charter (Dods. 94, f. 90) assigned certain lands and privileges to his mother for her dower. They comprised the entire manor of Sottecottes, and all his holding in Drypool, with all their liberties, gates, customs, and "all that entire close in Sutton called Cotecroft,* as it is enclosed with ditches," and eighty acres of meadow, with all their appurtenances in the towns of Sutton and Hull, with which she was formerly dowered by the bailiffs of the Countess of Albemarle; also a fishery in Sutton Marr. She was to be at liberty to fish there every day in the year at her pleasure, using one boat with baskets,

* Cotecroft is probably the Oxlands adjoining Marfleet.

and all nets, except the seine-net, and whenever Sayer should use the seine-net, she was to have a third part of the fish taken, or the produce of every third draught of the net. She was also to have a piece of land lying outside his garden towards the west upon which to dry her nets,—this, I suppose, would be behind the existing Church School. She was also to have a third part of the liberty of the turbary of Sutton, to dig, stack, and carry away as many turves as often as she pleased, without waste. Finally, there was to her granted William the Reeve (prepositus) of Hull, with his holding, his family, and his chattels; and she was to do the "service" due to the chief lord of the manor of Suttecotes as Sayer, her husband, had done. A century afterwards, this "service" consisted of the payment of eight shillings annually to the provost of the College of St. John of Beverley. There can be no doubt that "Hull" here, as in other documents of this early date, means the land by the river at Wilmington, William being the bondman in charge of the meadows, who, according to custom, would be taken over with the land.

This charter was given in the Chapel of Sutton, on Thursday next after the feast of St. Matthew, in the year 1271, before Simon le Constable, John de Bilton, the bailiff of the Provost of Beverley, Robert de Hildierd, who was the bailiff of the Countess Isabella, and many others.

In the Meaux Chronicle, vol. 2, p. 149, Sayer, the son of Sayer, is said to have given up to the monks all the claim which he made to their wood-lands near the abbey, confirming to them all the lands and tenements, homages and services which they held of his fee in Sutton. The monks averred, however, that he endeavoured as much as he could to impede their free carriage of corn and hay, which had been granted by his father, and that he revoked this as far as he could by making exception of it in his charter. A copy of the charter, given in Dodsworth MS., 94, f. 91, enables us to check the chronicle.

Styling himself at full length, " Sayer, the son of Sayer, the son of Sayer, the elder of Sutton," he grants and quit-claims to the monks all his rights in the woods of Meaux and the properties in Sutton which they held from his ancestors, " except the carriage of corn and hay, for which they say they have a writing from Sayer, my father." It does not appear that the monks were able to produce any such writing, as they might have done had it existed, for this charter of Sayer the Fourth was given at their abbey. It is dated on the morrow of St. Thomas' in the year 1279, and among the witnesses is Sayer's brother, William, "the parson of Sutton." But however strict the Lord of the Manor might be with them, the monks, on their part, kept up their ancient policy of holding tenaciously to everything which they thought their own. Thus, according to their account, they managed, after all, to continue to exercise the privilege of carriage with their carts and wains.

They had, however, by this time touched the highest point of their prosperity. Henceforth nothing of material value was given to them in Sutton, unless for some substantial consideration. They had indeed to struggle, often with very poor success, to keep what they had got. Writing at a later time, when misfortunes had fallen on them, their chronicler seems to dwell with pleasure on the details of their former large possessions. These details are of the more importance to us, as shewing pretty clearly the composition of the farms held by the free tenants in Sutton, of whose holdings we have very little information from any other source.

In the time of Richard, the tenth Abbot of Meaux— 1269-70—there was a new admeasurement of the pastures of Sutton, and the number of animals that

5

could then be depastured by the owners of each oxgang of tillage is clearly set out. The live stock that could be turned out by each cottager is also recorded. Some twenty years later a statement is given of the proportion of meadow land that belonged to each oxgang, and, by combining these two accounts, we can estimate the proportions of tillage, meadow, and pasture in the farms of the parish, in the latter part of the thirteenth century.

Every oxgang of tillage contained about fifteen acres, in about thirty selions scattered over the three great arable fields. Under the three-course system wheat was grown in one year in one of the fields, to be followed by oats and barley or beans, after which there would be a year of fallow, when the land would be ploughed and prepared for wheat. During the year of fallow, and whenever the land was clear of crop, the cattle of the several owners ran freely over the whole of the tillage, grazing on the grass balks, and picking what they could off the stubbles.

Twenty acres of meadow in the Ings and Sefholm and Riseholm Carr belonged to each oxgang. After the hay was carried, the cattle of the tenants ran over the whole meadow.

For each oxgang, the farmer could turn upon the arable land, the meadows, and pastures twenty head of cattle or horses, with their progeny, four of these being depastured in the ox-pasture called the Northlands behind Riseholm, and sixteen in the East Carr, West Carr, and North Carr. So long as the farmer kept up the supply of plough oxen, he might substitute five sheep for each ox, besides these, he might have four pigs, which, with their litters, would run chiefly on the stubbles, and ten geese, which might be accompanied by their broods until Martinmas. For fuel, sixteen cartloads of turves might be cut in certain of the rough pastures or wastes. Forty sheep with their young lambs, for each oxgang could be turned by the monks

GARTH = GARDEN

into the pasture of Salts, and sixty elsewhere; but this did not apply to the farmers, whose rights with regard to such pasture as the Salts and the West Carr varied considerably.

One or two tofts, or small enclosures, for convenience of cultivation usually existed on each oxgang, where the land lay very far from the village. Sometimes there is special mention of an oxgang without a toft. Enclosures, called sheepcots, existed on some of the larger allotments of meadow. At a later time they were called pighills.

Two oxgangs are generally considered to have constituted an ordinary farm. I think that in Sutton, where the meadows and pastures are so abundant, one oxgang was a more usual quantity, and a half oxgang was, in later times, an ordinary sized farm. Each farm had its homestead in the village, where a few buildings of wood, or of wattle and clay covered with thatch, would abut upon the street, a garth or garden being at the rear.

For each oxgang, the tenant had to send one ox to the common plough. He would also perform the customary services to the lord, by giving a fixed amount of labour per annum upon his lands, delivering to him at stated times the stipulated numbers of poultry and eggs, with other farm produce, and some moderate payment in cash. There were, besides, "boon" days of labour, and other services, rendered at first voluntarily, but which grew into customs. The tendency, however, was now towards fixed rents, which would, in time, be redeemed, and then the free tenant would be on the high-road to becoming a freeholder.

A cottager had his small cottage, or toftstead, with garden and croft. His rights of pasturage at this time, were for four large cattle, thirty sheep, two pigs, and five geese, with the young of each kind, and he would perform his services to the lord in labour, poultry, eggs, and small coin. The officers of the lord of the

manor superintended these complicated arrangements, and the tenants would appoint one of their
number as the Reeve to look after their interests.

The condition of the free tenants and the cottagers
would depend largely upon the amount of the "services"
to which they were liable, but there is no doubt that,
while these were subject to little alteration, the land
was materially improving, so that, unless in very bad
seasons, in the frequent times of plague, or when the
lord of Sutton had to engage in the wars of the period,
the free tenants, and even the cottagers, were fairly
comfortable according to the very low standard of that
age.*

By this time a town was beginning to grow up at
the mouth of the river Hull, partly owing to the
decay of the older ports on the Humber, partly also
through the increasing prosperity of the neighbourhood. The rising town would cause a demand for
corn and cattle and for labour, and whosoever was
poor or discontented or ambitious, might there find an
opening and a career.

As regards the monks, their most prosperous period
in Sutton was during the time of Sayer the Fourth.
They had reduced their tillage somewhat by exchanges,
but they still held six oxgangs and three quarters, or
about a hundred acres. To these, which they
distinguish as their own oxgangs, belonged eighty-one
acres of meadow, but they had seventy-two acres more
which had appertained to the oxgangs of other persons
whose grants have been enumerated. They had
their enclosed lands of Magnusdaile, containing some
thirty acres, also Herncroft and Southowscroft, which
were chiefly meadow, and contained seventy-one acres

---

* Comparisons are sometimes drawn between the condition of the cottager or
labourer of the present day, and that of the cottager of the thirteenth century, when
it is supposed that every man had his piece of land or small farm. But such
cottagers were few. Below them came the labourers without land, who were then
practically slaves on the lord's estate. There is some chance for the landless man
now.

and a half. Thus their meadows measured about 255 acres in all.

By the account of their pasturage we are let into the secret of their farm management, which must have been successful, and could not fail to be copied by their observant, not to say jealous, neighbours in Sutton. Two head of cattle per oxgang were sufficient for keeping up the supply necessary for their cultivation. As the pasturage of each oxgang would keep twenty cattle, they had grazing rights for an overplus of eighteen cattle per oxgang, which they replaced by ninety sheep. They treated the grazing rights in the newer pastures which they had acquired from other persons in the same way. The details of their calculations are intricate, but they need not be unravelled here, for the sum of the account is that, for a long time, they had eight sheepfolds in Sutton, in which were tended upwards of two thousand sheep. The reason of all this contriving is evident.

The Cistercian monks had always been great sheep farmers. Their general system was to obtain the gift of some marshy valley, which to the owner was almost useless for grazing. There they would build one of their monasteries as they built Fountains, Rievaulx, Kirkstall, and Tintern, which are now the ornaments of such sites, and the monuments of their taste and skill. They would drain the marshes to fit them for sheep pastures, and of the wool they would make merchandise. The associated merchants of Florence and Lucca, bearing such names as Friscobaldi, Bardi, Riccardi, and Spini—some of whom traded under the special protection of the Pope, found the money for the costly wars and expeditions of Edward the First. They reimbursed themselves by taking the King's wool, and collecting the duties levied on exports ; the mouth of the Hull being one of the chief ports from which wool was shipped. Without this market for wool, it is difficult to see how the vast area of moist

grass-land in the valley of the Hull could have been profitably used. The value of the sheep and oxen as food must have been a minor consideration, for we can scarcely imagine a population in or near to the broad valley of the Hull that could consume the produce of its pastures.

In the latter part of the reign of Henry the Third, the export of wool was prohibited, but the need of a market was so great that the lords of the manors are said to have connived with the King's officers and the merchants of Florence to smuggle their wool away to Flanders, where the manufactures created a great demand. Let us hope the Sayers were no worse than their neighbours. In 1274 the prohibition was removed, and the whole district would profit by the open market, while a varied commerce would spring up at the river's mouth. Among the thousands of stones of wool, and the thousands of sheep-skins, which were being shipped annually from Holderness and the parts adjacent, would be found every sack of wool and every "woolfel" that the monks of Meaux could spare. If they had managed their affairs with ordinary prudence, they must have prospered exceedingly, but it is evident they were getting poorer year by year. This appears clearly enough from an account of their affairs in Sutton.

At the best, those affairs seem to have been liable to complication. The Lansdowne MS. 424, f. 111^b, gives a letter from Isabella de Fortibus to her bailiff, Robert de Hildierd, directing him not to molest Meaux Abbey as to the pastures of Billeshull * and Saltes. This is dated in 1276, but at a later date they found that they could not depend on her friendship.

It will be remembered that their acquisitions of pasturage in the Salts, were chiefly or wholly for the purpose of keeping up the alms daily given away at the gate of the monastery. The management of the

* Near the boundary of Bilton, probably close to Risholm Hill.

pasturage was therefore in the hands of the monk who held the important office of porter. It happened that in the time of Abbot Richard of Barton, 1280 to 1286, through losses, they were short of the full number of sheep that they were entitled to turn into the Salts. The porter-monk therefore took in strangers' sheep for payment. This was a high misdemeanor in a tenant on a manor, and he would expect at least to be heavily fined if his action were found out. In an agreement respecting lands in Benningholm, that were common between the monks and the nuns of Swine, the penalty for this offence was fixed at half a mark.

But when Sayer found out what the porter had done, he took a more serious view of the matter, impounding the strange sheep, exacting the whole of the money payable for their grazing, and, with the assistance of Isabella, Countess of Albemarle, deprived them of the rights of pasturage in the Salts that they had bought of Sayer his father. But, after all, they still had left the grazing belonging to the six and three-quarters oxgangs of their own tillage, and to fourteen and three-quarters oxgangs of the tillage of other persons from whom they had obtained grants; so that they could still turn into the Salts three hundred and sixty-eight sheep and four large animals.

To the latter part of the time of Sayer the Fourth belongs a transaction that ought not to be omitted from the story of Sutton. The monks, partly through bad management, but very largely, no doubt, owing to the cost of erecting their splendid monastery at Meaux, were reduced to extremity for want of cash. They had been compelled to anticipate their annual revenues by granting long leases of their lands for inadequate sums paid down, and they had on similar conditions bound themselves to deliver annually for many years to come, specified quantities of wool.

At this time the monks had long possessed the Vill of Wyk and the grange of Myton, where now stands

the more important part of the town of Hull, but in
1286 Roger de Driffield, though a reforming abbot,
was compelled to grant to William de Hamelton, a
Canon of York, and Adam his brother, a twenty years
lease of these lands, for eight hundred marks in cash
paid down.   A year afterwards the abbot seems to
have found that the King wanted these properties in
order to establish the improved port of Kingston-upon-
Hull.   The abbot tried to get them back from the
Hameltons, who may have had the same information,
for after long delay, they forced him to submit to
extortionate terms, so that the monks estimated their
loss on the whole transaction at the ruinous sum of a
thousand pounds.

It is, I think, most probable that a charter copied by
Dodsworth (153, f. 52^b) was granted by Sayer the
Fourth.   By it, " Sayer, the son of Sayer," gives to
Robert de Hildyerd common in Sutton and Hull as
much as belongs to an oxgang of tillage.   But
whether he or his father was the grantor, it shews that
the " Hull" therein mentioned was in the same manor
with Sutton, and not upon the site of Kingston-upon-
Hull.

The last of the Sayers was lord of Sutton until
about the middle of the reign of Edward the First.
The register of Archbishop Romain gives 1289 as the
year in which administration of his property was
granted to Ernald de Saltmarsh.   Inquisitions as
to Sayer's possessions made in 1289 and 1292,
have been understood as indicating that his father
died in the former year, and he in the latter, but
the second inquisition may have had reference
to the succession at the coming of age of his
son.   By this inquisition (Dods., 123, f. 27^b) it was
found that he died possessed of a capital messuage in
Sutton, a fishery, twenty oxgangs and a fourth of
tillage, and a wind-mill.   He had also rents coming
from Sutton, Coniston, Ganstead, " Hull," and else-

where, amounting to forty-nine shillings. His wife
Christiana was entitled to one-third of these properties
as her dower. These were no doubt his demesne
lands, which he held in hand at the date of his death.
Beside these, he had tillage and meadow in Bransholm, held of the heirs of William de Hilton, and at a
place called Ernistholm there was a piece of land,
half of which was held under the seigneur of Holderness and the rest under the heirs of Hilton. His
mother, or step-mother, Joan, the widow of Sayer
the Third, to whom he had made a grant of
dower, was still living (Dods., 117, f. 22), and had
married for her second husband John de Hildierd,
probably surviving him also. Her executors, un-
named (Dods., 94, f. 91ᵇ), acknowledged the receipt of
six pounds paid by Robert de Hildierd, in respect of
corn in Riston field in which she had an interest.
This document is dated at Sutton, on the morrow of
the feast of Sts. Philip and James, in the year 1296.

SIR JOHN DE SUTTON, SENIOR.

JOHN, the son of Sayer, came of age in the octave of Trinity, 1291. He had a brother Nicholas, who was a knight, a brother William, who was rector of Sutton, and a sister Joan. William probably succeeded, as rector, Matthew de Grymeston, Archdeacon of Cleveland, who died in 1289. He must have been very young when he was appointed to the benefice, but the old chapel of Sutton was not much favoured with the personal services of its rectors, young or old.

So far we have heard but little of the doings of the Lords of the Manor beyond their own immediate neighbourhood. Roads were few and very bad, and neither business nor pleasure furnished inducements to travel. They would mix with their neighbours in South Holderness, and would go to Swine, perhaps also to Meaux, at times of festival. At Burstwick they might have to see the Lord of Holderness or his bailiff, but Skipsea was still a place of some resort for manorial business. A journey beyond the grey wolds to York might be undertaken upon some great occasion. They must have gone with their over-lord to the wars, where they would mingle with the crowd of undistinguished knights.

But towards the end of the thirteenth century, a season of greater general activity set in. The Lords of the Holderness manors now held them direct under the King, subject to the right to dower of the

widowed Countess Isabella de Fortibus, and the lords
of Sutton were therefore called upon to take responsibilities which had before been taken by their over-lord.
Other causes may have been operating for some time
past to bring them into contact with a wider world.

It is usual to give to persons who in the Latin
charters are called either "dominus" or "miles," the
prefix which in modern times has distinguished the
name of a knight. The frequent result is that the
knight and the priest, whose university degree entitled
him to be called "dominus," are given the prefix
"sir," which was used of neither of them in their own
day. Sir John de Sutton may, however, be so called,
because that style was coming into use at about his
time, and he has been generally so distinguished.
I have already noted his claim to the rank of a baron
by writ of summons.

John, being still under age when his father died,
was the ward of the Countess Isabella. At that time
William de Hamelton, who soon afterwards became
the Dean of York, was making the most of his
speculation in the town of Wyk and grange of Myton,
which he and his brother Adam had leased from the
monks. He now bought from Isabella the right to
choose a wife for her young ward, paying therefor
the very substantial sum of one hundred and twenty
marks. Upon the face of it this also looks like a
speculation, and it was part of the bargain that if John
should marry against the will of William de Hamelton,
or should die before marriage, William should have a
similar right with respect to the next heir. But there
seems good reason to suppose that the marriage which
was arranged came about through acquaintance
between the families in the ordinary way. John
would be brought up in intimate friendship with the
family of Ernald de Saltmarshe, who administered to
his father's will. The tomb of Sybilla de Metham,
the niece of William de Hamelton, is in the Salt-

marshe Chapel at Howden, where the arms of
Hamelton are conspicuous by the side of those of
Saltmarshe. William de Hamelton probably conducted the negotiation simply with a view to make
John de Sutton free to marry as the family and he
himself desired. However that may be, all went well,
and about Midsummer, 1294, John de Sutton was
married to Constance, the daughter of John Sampson,
of York.* His marriage settlement, in Latin (Brit.
Mus., L.F.C. iii., 5), a piece of parchment measuring
seven inches by three inches and three-quarters,
almost perfect, and still bearing the seal impressed by
his own hand, may be read as follows :—

> " Know all men as well present as future that Whereas I John
> son and heir of Saer de [Sutton in Holder]ness, on Friday
> after the feast of Saint Bartholomew the Apostle in the twenty
> second year of the reign of King Edward [I] have espoused
> Custantia daughter of John Sampson at the door of the Church
> of St. Martin in Coningstret as my wife, I have endowed her
> with my manors of Sutton and Braunsholm, and have assigned
> the same to her in dower, to have and to hold in the name of
> dower during the whole term of her life. Wherefore I will and
> grant that, whenever human fate overtakes me and she survives,
> she the aforesaid Custantia shall have and hold my manors of
> Sutton and Braunsholm with all manner of their appurtenances,
> things, and easements, as freely, quietly, and wholly as I held
> them on the day of the making of these presents without
> contradiction or hindrance of my heirs or any other persons
> whomsoever. In witness whereof I have set my seal to this
> present writing and I have obtained the Seal of the Officialty of
> York to be appended to the same together with my seal—these
> being the Witnesses. William, the Rector of the Church of
> Sutton, Maurice Sampson, Nicholas de Seleby, Robert Seg-
> gevans, John Huthriz, Richard Wiles, Alan Baudewin, and
> others."

The seal of John de Sutton, a lion dormant, or
curled up in sleep, is in very fair condition. It seems
that the lion rampant had not yet been adopted as the
cognisance of the family.

* In 1298 John Sampson was one of the members for the county in the
Parliament which met at York.

Early in the time of John, the meadow in the Ings and the pasturage in the West Carr, which the last Sayer had granted to Martin de Otringham, together with a considerable extent of meadows and pasturage in Southcoats and elsewhere, came into the hands of the monks of Meaux. Serious responsibilities were, however, attached to the gift, and the story illustrates the habits of the time.

Richard de Otringham, the grandson of Martin, had inherited the property. Being a priest, the rector of Shelford, near Cambridge, it was natural for him to think of founding a small religious house in Ottringham, the home of his family ; and the priory of Bridlington, which held the church of Ottringham, was selected to carry out his views. This house of

"SIGILL IOH'IS DE SVTTVN."

Augustinian canons might indeed be expected to faithfully execute such a trust. But the law was jealous of these endowments, and the Statute of Mortmain forbad them unless with the consent of the King. Edward the First, being then in negotiation with the monks for their town of Wyk and grange of Myton, in the hope of making better terms for himself, insisted that the endowment should be made to the Abbey of Meaux. Several charters (Lansd. 424, f. 38) show that this matter was in hand for some five years, but on the 8th March, 1293, the King gave licence to the Abbey to hold the property, and in June following John de Sutton, by charter, authorised Richard de Otringham to assign it to the Abbey. He begins with the statement that :—

"By the Common Counsel of the realm of England it has been provided and enacted that it shall not be lawful for men in a religious community, nor for others, to enter the fee of any man so that it may come to a 'dead hand,' without the special licence of the King and of the chief lord of whom that property is immediately held."

Nevertheless, he grants his charter, which was witnessed by William, the rector of Sutton, amongst others. And so the chantry was founded, the founder conveying to the Abbey with the lands his bondmen with their families and chattels. Thereupon seven monks were sent from Meaux and furnished with carefully-considered instructions as to their manner of life. Their services, the psalms and anthems they were to use, their special devotions to the Blessed virgin, "our hope and consolation after God," their reading, labour, and diversion were strictly enjoined. They were to study theology, not to wander about in pairs, nor keep idle company, nor to quarrel, nor enter a tavern, or visit public shows. All this indicates that there were then in the country side these snares for the feet of the unwary, and also that the strict seclusion of the Cistercian rules must have been a good deal relaxed to admit of these monks falling into them. But with all this care scandals arose, so that, after four-and-twenty years, it became necessary to remove, with the consent of the founder, the little establishment to a place outside the gate of Meaux Abbey, where they could be better supervised. Thus, although one chaplain was left at Ottringham, the original intention of Richard de Otringham, who must have pictured to himself a perpetual continuance of Church service on the land of his inheritance, came to naught.

But the monks did not continue to enjoy this benefaction without dispute. The chronicle records that John de Sutton unjustly took away from them thirteen acres and one-third of the meadow, but at

length he restored it, confirming their title to the
whole. The part taken was in the midst of their
thirty-five acres in Cartgatedaile. In the charter by
which he restores the land so taken (Dods. 53, f. 1^b) he
says it was between the meadow of the convent on
either side.

Long before the time of John de Sutton, the free
tenants, looking from the backs of their homesteads
over the green Ings must have noticed the gradual
increase in the groups of houses on the holm where
central Hull now stands. The traffic in wool had
grown from smuggling to legitimate export, vessels
belonging to Beverley would be seen in growing
numbers passing up and down the river, a veritable
port had come into existence at the harbour
mouth. Edward I. sanctioned and promoted this
commerce, and some ten years after John became
lord of Sutton, the port was established as a town
under the new name of Kyngeston-upon-Hull.

But as yet, no one who did not possess some right
of way could reach the place with horses or carts, and
in the year 1302 a commission was issued to enquire
as to the best mode of remedying this defect.
Thereupon the roads to Anlaby and Beverley, and
that leading towards Hedon, were laid out as King's
highways. The last, which is the Holderness Road,
was to begin at midstream of the river Hull, to go
through the middle of the town of Drypool to the
pasture called "Suttecotes Som'gang," thence in a
direct line to the cross standing in Somergangs, thence
to the west end of the town of "Sutcotes," and thence
to the ditch dividing Sutton and Summergangs where
a bridge was to be made near a place called
"Lambhelmsike" on the west, where the Holderness
Road is now joined by the Ings Road. From that
place the road was to be continued of a breadth of
forty feet to the bridge of Bilton, where it would join
the ancient road through Sutton towards Hedon, and

so communicate with such roads as then existed in South Holderness.

This must have been on the general lines of the right of way granted by Sayer the Third to the nuns of Swine for access to their sheepcots in Southcoates. It appears from an inquisition—quoted by Frost (p. 64) —that four acres, three roods and a half of meadow in Sutton, in the dayles, and four acres of pasture in Summergangs were taken for the making of this road. But no compensation could be obtained by John de Sutton for this land, nor yet for the injury to his ferry across the river at Drypool.

The making of the Anlaby and Holderness Roads would divert the traffic between South Holderness and the wolds from the older road by way of Stoneferry, and would greatly promote the prosperity of the town of Kingston-upon-Hull for the improvement of which, "and for no other purpose," the roads are said to have been made.

Early in the fourteenth century, the mills belonging to the monks at the outlet of Forthdyk, had become defective, and a dispute arose as to the repairs of the parallel ditches with their floodgates. Then the monks and their tenants in Waghen agreed with John de Sutton, Godfrey de Meaux, and their tenants in Sutton, by which the monastery was to renew and keep in repair the floodgates and repair the channel of Forthdyk. They were also to find timber for the renewal and repairs of the floodgates on Sutton dyk, the work being done by the lords and tenants of Sutton, for whose convenience that cut had been made. All this is recorded in the Chronicle, and set out in the Stowe Charter, 495, a little dilapidated piece of parchment executed at Sutton in 1304.

Edward II. coming to the throne in 1307, incurred the dislike of his people, by his attachment to Piers Gaveston, to whom he granted the Seigniory of Holderness. John de Sutton and many of his neighbours were amongst those who, although he was their overlord, took part against the favourite. In 1312 Gaveston was captured and beheaded, and John de Sutton, and Nicholas his brother, soon after that event found themselves in the King's prison at York. In the Pipe Roll of the sixth year of Edward there is an entry of a fine of a hundred marks for the redemption of their bodies. On the 16th October, 1313 (7th Edward II.), John's name appears in a long list of those who, with their leader, Thomas, Earl of Lancaster, received pardon for the part they had taken in bringing about the death of Gaveston.

From a charter of John (Dods. 94, fol. 92), it appears that Sir Robert de Hyldeyard had given him a bond for the payment of one hundred marks, but John released him on condition that one hundred and twenty acres of meadow in Sutton and the Sheepcots held by Hyldeyard, should be transferred to John for six years. This appears to be the property granted by Sayer the Third to Isabella de Fortibus. The family of Hyldeyard was closely connected with the property held by Isabella, who had died soon after John came into his manor.

From an entry in the register of Archbishop Greenfield (2nd part, 130), quoted by Dodsworth (28f. 59), we learn that John's sister Joan was a nun at Swine, or at least an inmate of the priory. In the year 1314 " Domina Johanna de Sutton," who had been indisposed, had leave to go to the house of her brother John, and stay with him for two or three days. The Prioresses of Swine were the daughters of persons of position in the neighbourhood, and the nuns would be of like origin. The ancestors of Joan, for at least four generations, had been on friendly terms with the community, her old home could be seen from the Priory, and one must feel glad to know

6

that she could be permitted to visit it at such a time.[*]

John was from time to time called upon with other lords of manors to furnish troops for the royal armies engaged in the wars with Scotland and France. During these wars levies were more than once ordered of all the men between twenty and sixty, and all such as had lands or goods of value, had to come armed either as light horsemen, or in heavy armour and mounted on strong horses, as was necessary for those who had to bear the main shock of the battle. Holderness would furnish a due proportion, and the lord of the manor of Sutton would appear in the field with his neighbours clad in armour, closely resembling that which covers the recumbent effigy in the chancel of Sutton Church. When in 1314, Edward II. returned from his ill-fated expedition against Robert the Bruce, he ordered Robert le Constable, John de Sutton, and Robert de Roos to raise within the Seigniory horsemen and foot soldiers to reinforce him. John was summoned to Parliament on several occasions, first as John de Sutton, and later as John de Sutton, senior. In a writ dated the 12th Edward the Third, the year before John's death, for levying supplies for the war in France, he is named as "Johes de Sutton, Senior, Miles." In 1310, and again in 1336, he acted as a commissioner for the drainage and embankment of the Humber in Holderness.

Once at least, but probably more often, Sutton was

---

[*] So little is known of the wives and daughters of this family that every document relating to them has a special interest. Dodsworth (106, f. 21) copies a Fine by which Thomas Oudely de Reyle (Audley de Rayleigh), in the county of Essex, and Joan, his wife, daughter of John de Sutton-in-Holderness, conveyed to Robert Dumfravyle and William Ryther, Knights, and John Holme, Robert Haytfeld, Thomas Wilton and Richard Haytfeld, Esquires, five messages, three tofts, one oxgang, and nine acres of tillage and seventeen acres of meadow, with the appurtenances in Sutton, Stanfery, and Drypole. This distant connexion may have arisen through the tenure of the lordship of Holderness by Margaret de Clare, who had inherited manors in Essex, and was the wife, first of Piers Gaveston, and afterwards of Hugh, Lord Audley.

honoured by the presence of royalty, Burstwick being
visited on several occasions by Edward I. and Edward
II. In October, 1322, Edward II., returning from an
expedition to the north, turned aside for a very brief
visit to Holderness. On the fifteenth of the month
he was at Bridlington, and on the seventeenth his
Privy seal was affixed to a document (relating to the
wardship of one of his castles) at Sutton. He was
at York on the day following.

In the year 1339, after he had held the Manor for
the long period of fifty years, " human fate " overtook
Sir John de Sutton ; his widow, Constance, being left
in the enjoyment of her dower.

In the quire of Sutton Church, which was built in
the time of his son, there lies on an altar tomb the
effigy of a knight, carefully wrought so as to show the
minutest details of the armour worn in the fourteenth
century. The late Sir Samuel Rush Meyrick, the
great authority on ancient armour, gave an opinion as
to the date of this effigy, which is printed in Frost's
" Notices." He says :—

> " The costume of the effigy proves it to be that of Sir John de
> Sutton, who died in the 12th of Edward III., rather than that
> of his son, who died in the 30th of Edward III., as in the
> latter case it would have been in the short hauberk, covered by
> the jupon, instead of the long one and the cyclas. The last
> mentioned garment, indeed, rather marks the period of the
> preceding Monarch, as it succeeded the surcoat of his reign,
> and went out of fashion early in that of Edward III. On the
> head of the figure is the basinet, to which is attached the
> camail for the protection of the throat ; the arms and legs are
> in plate armour, and the feet in sollerets, that have a scale-like
> appearance."

Admitting the force of this inference from the style
of the armour, it must still seem somewhat strange that
such a monument to Sir John de Sutton, senior, should
here be found. The chapel of Sutton was in his time
dilapidated, and there was nothing to render it eligible
as a place of sepulture. At this period men of con-

siderable position were anxious to be buried in the
church of some religious community, where masses for
their souls would be daily said, and where all the
services of the church would be heard in due season.
The priory of Swine, in which his sister lived, was
such a place. There is now in the parish church of
Swine a monument with a pair of effigies that have
doubtless been removed from the destroyed priory
church to their present position in a recess in the south
wall.   Burnsall, who would have heard the tradition,
says this is the monument of Sir John de Sutton, and
although this may be doubtful, the probability is that
he would be buried there, and would have a monument.
As to the tomb at Sutton, I shall show by independent
evidence that it very probably belongs to the younger
John de Sutton.

SIR JOHN DE SUTTON, JUNIOR.

A Hildyard heiress.—Thomas Sampson, Rector.—Renewed disputes over the West
Carr.—Dispute over an old tunic.—Knighthood of the Black Prince.—The
College of St. James founded, and Sutton Church built.—Its dedication.—
The Black Death.—Thomas Sampson's will.—Death of Sir John de Sutton.—
His son no more heard of.—The tomb in the church.—His wife's dower.

JOHN, the son of John de Sutton, succeeded his
father in 1339, the twelfth year of Edward III.
Frost states that he was then twenty years old,
but there is a document (Dods. 60, f. 80ᵇ) which
makes him thirty, a more likely age. His position
was one of some prominence. He was summoned to
parliament, as his father had been, and was
commissioned to raise troops for the king. His family
connections would draw him towards York, but he
acted with his neighbours as a commissioner for
keeping up the embankments and drainage of
Holderness, and he seems to have attended closely to
the affairs of his manor. He had brothers, Edmund
and Thomas, and perhaps William also.

As to the last named, there is a charter in French
(Dods. 94, f. 96ᵇ) which shews that William de
Sutton, "Chivaler," married Emme, the widow of
Thomas Hildyard of Riston, and thus became step-
father of the heiress, Katherine Hildyard, whose
marriage, with that of her sister, was the subject of a
dispute recorded in the chronicle of Meaux Abbey.*
Katherine's husband, Piers Nuttell, at Candlemastide,
1340, being at Sutton, entered into an arrangement
with William and Emme for the repayment by him of
a hundred pounds, which was probably some portion
of Katherine's fortune, in case there should be no

* No brother of John de Sutton, Junior, could have been more than twenty-nine
years old, but this William could not have been John's uncle William, who was
a priest.

children of the marriage. The Nuttells had children, and Katherine, who had inherited lands in Sutton, Stoneferry, and other places, parted by a charter (Dods. 139, f. 45ᵇ·) with her life interest to William de Melton, the parson of Brandesburton, and others. Part of this property (which seems the same as the grant of Sayer the Third to Isabella de Fortibus) can probably be identified. There are two fields to the north of the Warld's Ends house still called High and Low Nuttles, on which the marks of enclosures or foundations may indicate an ancient farmstead by the river. It seems probable also that the field called "Countess Croft," adjoining Summergangs, now, like Nuttles, belonging to Watson's Charity, was a sheepfold of the Countess Isabella.

In the year 1340, the Rectory of Sutton became vacant by the death of John's uncle, William de Sutton, who had held it for fifty years. John's mother, Constance, who was then enjoying the manor of Sutton as her dower, presented her brother, Thomas Sampson, some time the Rector of Acaster Malbis, near York, and afterwards Archdeacon of Cleveland. He was also a Canon of York, having been appointed to the prebend of Huish Episcopi in 1332. The living was too valuable to be bestowed on a simple parish priest, and Thomas Sampson held it as such benefices were usually held by persons of his dignity—the duties being left to chaplains while he lived at York.

Frost says that John de Sutton, Junior, had a grant of the manor of Barton-on-Humber in 1327. At that date he was under age, and the statement may refer to his father, but I see no foundation for it. The manor of Barrow, or some share in it, did belong to his brother who succeeded him, and may have belonged to himself. There was in his family a similar ownership of the manor of Atwick.

The enthusiasm for the endowment of monasteries

was now on the wane, we are therefore without those
interesting particulars as to gifts of meadows and
pasturage which the records of Meaux and Swine
have before supplied.   On the other hand, disputes
were now arising as to the right of the monasteries to
the lands they had acquired, and John de Sutton,
Junior, did not lose much time in raising such a
dispute with the monks of Meaux.   Through this
difference we learn something more about the
pasturage in the West Carr.

It will be remembered that the monks had not been
able to enclose their portion of the West Carr, because
of rights of pasturage appertaining to seven oxgangs
of tillage, and fifteen tofts which belonged to other
persons.   For that reason they had set up boundary
posts along the line where the road now runs between
Soffham and Frog Hall.   In the course of eighty years,
however, these posts had decayed away, so that all
evidence of the boundary line was lost, and John, "in
spite of the charters of his ancestors," claimed common
of pasture in this part of the West Carr.   But after
long negotiations, during which the decayed feet of the
posts were dug up, the parties were brought to one
mind, and made a new agreement.   By it, John de
Sutton, his heirs and their bondmen, were henceforth
to have common for their wethers and sheep over
the land which the monks called their own, that is over
the low grounds of Soffham and Frog Hall.   The
monks were to have common for five hundred wethers
or sheep in the residue of the West Carr, which extended
to Stoneferry, besides the pasturage for a hundred
sheep to which they were entitled by the terms of
Richard de Otringham's endowment.   Steps were
then taken to renew the old boundary marks by putting
down very large stones instead of posts, "from the
corner of Southowscroft in a line almost direct towards
Swine Church."   Although this arrangement seems to
have been satisfactory at the time, they complain that,

not only John de Sutton, his heirs and their bondmen, but also the rest of the commoners pastured their stock in the portion belonging to the abbey, which the monks say was contrary to right, particularly as the monks had to keep up the river bank, northward of Frog Hall. This is the last that we hear of these disputes about the legacy which old Amandus de Sutton left to them more than two hundred years before.

One of the petty troubles of the monks, recorded in their chronicle, and in the Lansdowne MS., 424, f. 113[b.] is of some interest. In 1344, John de Falconberge, of Rise, raised questions as to the value of the clothing for a poor man, which, about a century before, had been agreed to be given annually in acknowledgment of a gift from his ancestor of so much of the pasturage in the Salts as belonged to an oxgang and a half of tillage. He questioned also the place and time where and when the clothing ought to be delivered. In the end he laid it down that the monks should provide one old tunic, worth eighteen-pence, or should pay over that sum yearly at the gate of the abbey between St. Andrew's Day (30th November) and Christmas, to the poor man appointed by him to receive it. He promised that neither he nor his heirs would seize the sheep or cattle of the abbey, except when the tunic or its value should be in arrear. But in some way the heirs converted this eighteenpence into rent—which looks as if they ignored the charitable nature of the gift, and made the monks their tenants with a view to an increased claim on the pasturage at some future time.

Frost says that John de Sutton, Junior, was knighted by Edward the Third at the siege of Calais which took place in 1346, but he was a knight some years before that time. On Wednesday next before the feast of St. Lawrence, 1342, William de Hornse and Robert de Waghen, chaplain, granted to John de Sutton, " Miles," the lands and tenements in Sutton which they had received from him with remainders successively in case of failure of issue to Edmund de Sutton and to Thomas de Sutton, his brothers, and to his own right heirs.   The deed was executed at Sutton, and was witnessed by John de Monceaux, Nicholas de Sutton, Robert de Withornwyc, John de Bilton, Peter de Gousill of Merfleet, and others.   Nicholas may have been John's uncle.   Thomas was his successor as Lord of the Manor.   Of the existence of his brother Edmund, this is the only evidence I have seen.

The name of John de Sutton appears in connection with preparations for the expedition of Edward the Third to France, in 1346.   Thus, although there were then one or two other knights of the same name, it seems possible that his azure shield with the golden lion and the red and silver bend, which cognisance he was the first of his family to bear, may have been seen at Cressy, and at the siege of Calais, which ended that memorable campaign.

In 1346, Edward the Third had a grant of forty shillings from every knight's fee consisting of forty-eight carucates of land, in order to create his eldest son, the Black Prince, a knight.   John de Sutton, Junior, was rated at nine shillings and two pence in respect of eleven carucates in his manors of Sutton and Ganstead. He paid also two shillings and threepence half-penny in respect of two carucates and six oxgangs of land in Coniston, which adjoins Ganstead, formerly held by John de Blascelles.*

In the time of John de Sutton, Junior, the affairs of the chapel in relation to the parishioners of Sutton, and to the mother church of Waghen, were brought

---

* Hugh Blassel had held this land, 15th Edward III., see (Dods. 98, f. 120.) In 1138, Richard I. confirmed to Thornton Abbey a gift, by William le Gros, of land, which in the 20th Richard II. was referred to as "totum feodum Pagani Blassell."   The surname derived from it has ever since been found sparingly in different forms throughout South Holderness, to which it has been practically confined.

under review. It was high time. No doubt the
amount of the tithes must have been increasing during
many years. The living had been usually given to a
near relation of the Lord of the Manor. John's uncle,
Thomas Sampson, who had been rector of Sutton since
1340, and other rectors before him, so far as was
known, had deputed chaplains to officiate in their
stead. Walter Wylkynson and Thomas Hoton were
such chaplains : their position would be something like
that of a curate-in-charge. They ministered in all
parochial matters, except at burials, and on the feasts
of Pentecost, St. Peter and St. Paul, and All Saints,
on which days the parishioners repaired to Wawne to
hear mass. There they made their oblations to the
vicar, who buried their dead and received the fees, a
very important matter, as we shall see. But baptisms
had been administered time out of mind in the font at
Sutton.

Sutton Chapel was ruinous and dilapidated. The
rector, Thomas Sampson, Archdeacon and Canon,
was aged. He had been elected Dean of York, but
the Pope set him aside in favour of a foreign Cardinal.
Sutton was his especial charge, and he might desire
to leave its spiritual affairs in a more satisfactory
condition. It was a time when small colleges of
priests were being established in many places, and,
with such an income as belonged to Sutton, an
establishment of this kind would be naturally suggested.
So in 1346 John de Sutton granted the advowson
of the chapel to Thomas Sampson and five chaplains
to celebrate offices there for the good estate of Edward
the Third, and Philippa his consort, and of John
himself, and Alice, his consort, while living, for their
souls when dead, and for the souls of Sir John's father
and mother, their ancestors and heirs, and all the
faithful departed. Upon this, the Archbishop William
de la Zouch, on June 13th, 1346, issued his mandate
to the Dean of Holderness to enquire into the

relations between the chapel of Sutton, and the mother church of Wawne, and as to the power of John de Sutton to make such a grant. The enquiry was held on the 27th December, 1346, in the old chapel of Sutton, by the Dean of Holderness, with the rectors, vicars, or parochial chaplains of Routh, Catwick, Sproatley, Swine, Frodingham, Atwick, Aldboro', and Nunkeeling, and seven laymen of Holderness, including Nicholas de Sutton. These found on their oaths that John de Sutton was the true patron of the chapel, and that Thomas Sampson, William de Sutton, and their predecessors had been duly presented, and had deputed certain chaplains who had ministered in the chapels. The king's licence having been obtained, the Archbishop, on the 17th November, 1347, made his decree for the constitution and government of the new foundation.

The college was to consist of a Custos or warden with five chaplains. There was to be a rectory house or mansion with a convenient hall, chambers, kitchen, stable, and granges, to be enclosed with a ditch at the expense of the founder, and there the warden and chaplains were continually to reside. In case of any vacancy in the office of warden, John de Sutton, his wife or his heirs, were to present a successor within fifteen days. If John should die childless, the chaplains must present within eight days. If a chaplaincy should become vacant, John, his wife or his heirs, should present within eight days, and if he should die without children, the warden and chaplains should present within eight days. The tithes, great and small, must be paid to the warden and chaplains under pain of the greater excommunication. As to the mother church of Wawne, the warden and chaplains must not deprive it of its rights, but must pay a mark yearly to the Chancellor of York, in the name of the church of Wawne, as well as the fees on the deaths of all

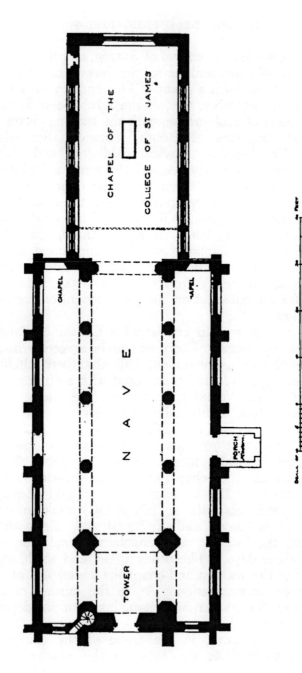

CHAPEL OF THE
COLLEGE OF ST JAMES

CHAPEL

NAVE

CHAPEL

TOWER

PORCH

PLAN OF THK CHURCH.

persons dying in Sutton, and the oblations of all
parishioners on the feasts of Pentecost, St. Peter and
Paul, and All Saints.   Besides all this, twenty shillings
per annum had to be paid to the Archbishop, and
thirteen shillings and fourpence to the Dean and
Chapter of York.

Thomas Sampson being the first warden, the five
chaplains were William de Denford, Symon de
Mirflet, John de Guthmundham, Robert de
Cottingham, and Thomas de Shirburne.

In addition to the new rectory house which was "large
and spacious," the re-building of the dilapidated church
was undertaken, and completed without delay.   John
de Sutton was at the expense of building the nave, and
Thomas Sampson, or his college, built the quire.
This was a very heavy undertaking, and, although
bricks, the manufacture of which had recently been
introduced, were very largely used, particularly in the
nave, very large quantities of stone would have to be
brought up the river to Stoneferry.   It is not likely
that the Leads road could then have borne this heavy
traffic, but the new Antholme dike must have been
intended to be navigable, and would probably
be used.   However that may be, the church was
ready for consecration within two years.   It consisted of a nave of moderate size, having massive
piers of brick, and a very large quire chiefly for
the accommodation of the college of priests.   Very
handsome oak screens divided the portion set apart for
the college from the part used by the parishioners, and
it is probable that the east end of each side aisle was
enclosed in the same way.   Altars were placed in these
positions, as is shewn by the piscina, or drain, still
left in each aisle, for pouring away the water used in
washing the sacramental cups.   The south aisle probably contained the Lady chapel.

The screen which ran across the quire was placed a
few feet to the eastward of the quire arch, so as to

SUTTON CHURCH ABOUT 1830.

From Poulson's History of Holderness.

form a very shallow parochial chancel, having a two-light window on each side, very distinct from the three-light windows of the rest of the quire.   With the altar at the east end there would be four or five altars in the church, a number sufficient for the ordinary services, as well as for those in honour of the Blessed Virgin Mary, and for the masses especially provided by John de Sutton.

The style is tolerably consistent with that of the middle of the 14th century.   In the east end of each aisle was placed a window of flowing, almost flamboyant, tracery, the like of which is best seen in the nave aisles at Patrington.   The other windows are less characteristic.   The door in the tower is a good specimen of perpendicular work, and, like the rest of the tower, looks later than the date at which the nave was built.   The style of the chancel is very heavy, quite different from the nave ; crosses and inscriptions were painted on the walls.   The windows contained stained glass, remains of which, bearing the arms of the Suttons, existed in the seventeenth century.

The work was so far complete as to be ready for the dedication of chapel and graveyard at the end of the summer of 1349, but Thomas Sampson did not live to take part in the ceremony.   His will was proved on the fourth of July in that year, and William de Denford, one of his chaplains, succeeded him as warden of the college.   Thomas Sampson was buried in York Minster.   In his will he describes himself as of York, and makes no allusion to his clerical duties or ecclesiastical dignities.

Fifty-three years afterwards, at an enquiry recorded in a volume belonging to York Minster, the story of the dedication was told by a group of elderly men, who, as children, had witnessed the ceremony.   John Dowson, one of a family which was then of some prominence, believed the day was in the summer, but old books preserved in the college gave the date as the

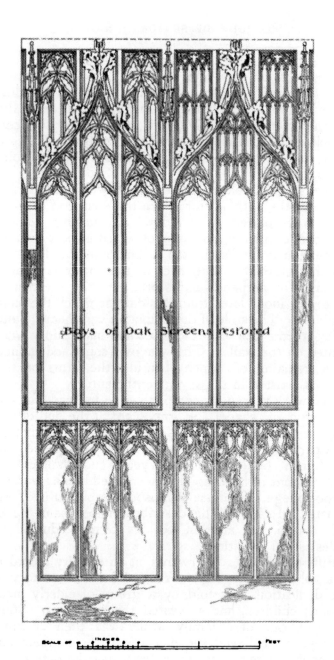

Bays of Oak Screens restored

SCALE OF ‖INCHES‖ FEET

12th of September, 1349, between the Nativity of the
Blessed Virgin Mary and the feast of the Exaltation
of the Holy Cross.   This day was always observed as
the anniversary.   There was "a great multitude" of
the parishioners present, amongst them were Peter and
John Dowson, William Spencer and his son Peter,
Nicholas Baker, Thomas de - Burton, Symon Tailiour,
Peter Carter, John Adamman, Henry Hobson's father
and his grandmother, dame Alice Gaunsted, John
Fyssher, and Robert Stevenson.   Of girls, there were
Katherine Dawson, Alice, afterwards the wife of
Peter Sayer, and others who talked about the event as
long as they lived.

We might have expected to hear of a brave
show of knights and dames, and of the more
striking details of a splendid ceremonial, but
the old men spoke chiefly of their fathers and of
their young companions.   Two or three of them
remembered an Augustinian Friar, whose name they
had forgotten, Suffragan of the Archbishop, who
sprinkled holy water while performing the dedication.
Nothing is said as to the presence of John de
Sutton or any members of his family at this
dedication ceremony.   John would, however,
doubtless be present, for only three days before, on
the feast of the Nativity of the Blessed Virgin, he had
sealed at Sutton a grant of an oxgang of land which
he had inherited from Nicholas de Sutton, to William,
son of Henry le Clerc of Sutton.   There was a
remainder to John's own son, "John of York," and to
another John, the brother of Nicholas de Sutton.
These brothers seem to have been the sons of John's
deceased uncle Nicholas.

It must have been a time for humiliation rather than
for rejoicing.   During that summer and autumn a
dark cloud hung over the whole country, bereavement
and the dread of death being upon every household.
They were in the midst of the greatest of the

7

pestilences of the middle ages, that which is now called
the Black Death.   It was no ordinary plague, but,
coming from the east, it swept over Europe, unchecked
by the science of the learned or by the fasts and
offerings of the faithful.   From one-third to two-thirds
of the population of every country died.   Half the
priests in Yorkshire were carried off.   Harvests rotted
upon the ground, whole parishes lay waste for years,
and cattle wandered without owners through the corn
in the great open fields.

Only four or five miles away, the monks of Meaux,
who believed as firmly in signs and portents as did
their more ignorant neighbours, remembered that on
the Friday before Passion Sunday, while at vespers,
they had been violently thrown from their stalls by an
earthquake ; surely this was sent as a warning !   In
the month of August alone their Abbot, Hugh de
Leven, with twenty-two monks and six lay brethren,
died, the Abbot and five monks dying in one day.
Out of fifty monks and lay brethren only ten survived.
The Abbey, already impoverished, was almost ruined
through the deaths of those who had the best knowledge of its lands and affairs.   Ready money had to be
raised on the most exorbitant terms.   For a present
payment of eighty pounds, they leased their grange in
Sutton, called Gannok, to Sir William de Swine for
his life, but, luckily for them, he was murdered soon
afterwards, so the grange remained in their hands for
the time.

We have seen that baptisms had from time
immemorial been performed in the font of the old
chapel.   Immediately after the consecration, burials
also began to take place in the new chapel, and its
grave-yard, subject, no doubt, to the payment of fees
to the Vicar of Wawne.

The will of the Warden, Thomas Sampson (Dods.
99, f. 1) gives some interesting particulars of the
Sutton family, and of the articles possessed by a

person in his condition at this period. He leaves to his brother William all the houses and tenements which had belonged to his father in Coning Street, York, and had been given to him by John de Sutton, his kinsman. son of Nicholas de Sutton. This John was probably the same as his executor, John de Sutton, then the rector of Acaster Malbis, the living which Thomas Sampson had held some time before. In a codicil he leaves to John and Thomas de Sutton, Knights, his nephews. one cup each.   After other bequests, including the clasp or brooch which he had of Constance, his sister, he gives all his armour to certain sons of his brothers.   To William de Malebys, with whom he and ,the Sutton family must have been intimately acquainted, he leaves two cups, six other pieces, six platters, as many saucers, and two of his best silver basins, with two ewers. These, with the furniture of his hall, are to be kept as heirlooms for the sons of William de Malebys, whom Thomas Sampson calls his kinsmen.

In 1350, licence was given by Edward the Third to " John de Sutton de Holderness " amongst many others, to pass, by way of Dover, to the continent with eight horses on the way to Rome.   He is not styled chivaler, as some others are, nor is he called a priest.   It is doubtful whether the Lord of the Manor or his son, " John of York," was travelling with such a retinue as this indicates.   The latter may have just reached manhood.

In 1353 (Dods. 84, f. 110) John de Sutton, Junior, was fined twenty pounds for having crenellated, or in some way fortified, his castle of Bransholm.   I have failed to find any explanation of this reference to the fortification of the old mound down in the Carr.

On May 5, 1357, John died.   At the enquiry of 1402, before referred to, Peter Dowson said that on the feast of St. John ante portam Latinam (May 6) he saw him buried in the quire.   John Dowson said that he was in Sutton church one day, fifty years back, and "saw

the body of Sir John de Sutton publicly buried in the
quire, where he still lies as by his tomb now appears."
The Dowsons were people of good position, who
had lived in Sutton all their lives.   Peter is styled
"literatus," John was for twenty years procurator for
the vicar of Waghen to receive his burial fees.   They
were not likely to be mistaken on such a question as
the provision of a monument for the lord of the manor.
We have no evidence of any tomb except that which
now remains, and which, until it was removed some
five-and-twenty years ago, stood in the centre of the
quire, the place usually chosen for the tomb of the
founder of a church.

The frontispiece, which is copied from the engraving
in Frost's *Notices*, shews the cyclas, a long loose
garment, the front of the skirt of which was cut away.
The folds of the back part of the skirt extend down-
wards by the side of the thigh.   The sword has been
handsomely decorated.   Upon the shield, and also
upon the front of the cyclas are the arms.   "Azure, a
lion rampant, or, over all a bend gobony argent and
gules."   The hands are executed in a separate piece of
stone, neatly inserted, which may indicate an ancient
reparation.   It conceals nothing.   The armour is that
which John .de Sutton, Junior, must have worn as a
young man.   The effigy would not be a portrait, but
would more probably be bought from a sculptor, whose
work may not have been in the newest fashion.   It
will be observed that the lion which appears on the
seal of John de Sutton, Senior, is dormant, in no way
resembling that on this tomb.   The seal of Thomas
de Sutton, the brother and successor of John,
corresponds with this shield.

We need not suppose that the lord of Sutton
appeared very frequently amongst his tenants and
neighbours in the guise in which he is here represented.
Every detail of his armour was intended for defence or
offence, when the knight was mounted on a strong

war horse, and actually engaged in battle. So laden, he could only mount with difficulty. If he should be unhorsed, or if his horse should fall, he would have to rely on his attendants to help him against any foot soldiers by whom he might be attacked.

Though we may disregard the pedigree which I have quoted from the Ashmole MS., the shields that surround the tomb in Sutton, indicate that the family connections were sufficiently distinguished.*

In the Book of Provosts of St. John of Beverley, there is an entry to the effect that John died seized of a manor and two carucates of land in Sutcoates, in which Thomas, his brother, succeeded him.

The heir, called "John of York," to distinguish him amongst the three or four persons who then bore that name, did not live to inherit the manor, nor is he heard of after the sealing of the deed in which his name appears. It may be that the Black Death is accountable for the disappearance of some of those whose names are missing after that period.

Alice, the widow of John de Sutton, Junior, survived him seven years. Poulson, quoting Ridley, says she held at the date of her death, "one messuage, 59 acres of tillage, 105 acres meadow, and 222 acres of pasture with their appurtenances in Swine, in which the castle of Bransholm is situated, of Matilda, who was the wife of Robert Hilton, by military service." Other references to the tenure of Bransholm under the Hiltons indicate that the ancient connexion with Swine had never been severed, although Bransholm was included in the parish of Sutton.

* Poulson says, "On the south side are five shields of arms within quatrefoils; 1st, Barry, 3 chaplets; 2nd, Lion rampant; 3rd, Arms of Saltmarsh; 4th, a fess vairy between 3 fleur de lis; 5th, Three roses. At the end are two shields: 1st, Lozengy, Fauconberg; 2nd, a Maunch, Hastings. At the west end two shields: 1st, a lion rampant; 2nd, 3 water bougets. On the north are five more shields: 1st, a lion rampant; 2nd, a plain cross; 3rd, 3 Lucies haurient; 4th, Billety a fess dancette; 5th, a Saltire."—History of Holderness.

SIR THOMAS DE SUTTON.

Bondmen transformed into labourers.—Enlargement of the Northlands.—Impover-
ishment of the monks.—Dispute about Magnusdaile.—Fresh mortgages.—
Disputes with tile makers from Beverley.—The Children's Pestilence.—New
Statutes for the College.—Marriage and death of the heir to the Manor.—
Succession of daughters of Sir Thomas de Sutton.—Alice de Meaux inherits
the Berewic.

THE last of the lords of Sutton succeeded his
brother in 1357, at a time of great disturbance
in the relations between the lords of manors and their
tenants and bondmen. The lord was now more
anxious to receive rent than labour, his own demesne
or home farm being often let for a money-rent or cultivated by hired free-labourers instead of serfs. We saw
how, in the preceding century, serfs belonging to Sutton
could be sold with their families and all that they had.
But we also saw that when one of them had been killed
by the servants of the monks of Meaux, his family
were able to obtain a measure of redress. Their
position was by this time so far improving that in their
struggles against oppression they could command public
sympathy and help. The bondman was, in fact, by rapid
strides, reaching a position of practical freedom. He
might be permitted by his lord to hold land, employ
labourers, and move about the country as he thought
fit, though in law he was still in bondage. We have
no record of this further progress in Sutton, but one
of the most valuable evidences of it is found in the
dealings of Meaux Abbey with their bondmen at
Wawne. That which happened in the mother parish
might very well have happened here if the monks had
owned the bondmen of the manor of Sutton.

There was then at Wawne a large family of serfs of
the Abbey, whose history had been somewhat

obscured by their former residence upon the Abbey's manor of Dimlington-by-the-Sea, where they must have enjoyed a great amount of freedom, paying for it by the usual services to the Abbey. But when they had been for some time settled at Wawne, it suited the convenience of the monks to treat them as, by strict law, bondmen might be treated. They therefore broke into rebellion, asserting not indeed that they were free, but that they were the bondmen of the king, belonging to his manor of Easington, in which parish Dimlington is included, and in that way they got the king's officers to take their part. For a long time they struggled with the abbot on fairly equal terms. They accused him of having taken away their hired ploughmen, and when he rode to Hedon to answer this charge they caused his horses to be impounded at Burstwick, so that he had to hire others to carry him home. In successive actions at law the decisions of the courts seem to have been influenced by sympathy for the bondmen when they were not swayed by the bribes of the abbot, and, although finally the bondmen were handed over to him with their families and farm stock, it was with a recommendation to treat them well, and not to punish their rebellion.

But whether bond or free, the condition of the man without land, dependent on others for employment and bread, must have been wretched at the best. The statute of labourers passed after the Black Death, compelled every such man to serve the first master who claimed him at the old starvation rate of wages. The labourer was forbidden to quit his parish under pain of imprisonment or branding on the forehead. The towns were now forbidden to harbour fugitive labourers, so that for a time this avenue for escape was closed to them.

As to the lands of Sutton, the ox-pasture, called the Northlands, lying next to the Salts, had, at this period, proved insufficient to support the allotted number of cattle, and it appears that, perhaps because of the increasing population of the adjacent town, oxen were now becoming of more importance than sheep, so the lord of the manor, with John de Meaux, the Abbot of Meaux, and the free tenants in Sutton, agreed verbally to throw into the Northlands a piece from the Salts, and to make new boundaries "to endure for ever." Thus the extra stock of sheep belonging to the abbey (besides that which appertained to their six and three quarter oxgangs), was reduced from three hundred and sixty-eight to three hundred and one.   By this arrangement they gave up grazing rights for sixty-seven sheep, in order to get the right to turn out only six large cattle more than they had before.

They were about this time in great straits, having reduced their stock of sheep generally, and their crops, so that they were no longer able to keep up the annual deliveries of wool and wheat and barley, on the promise of which they had been raising large sums of ready money.   They had to assign to Thomas and Richard de Holme, of Beverley, their grange of Sutton, with all its appurtenances, for forty years to come, and although they got it back after four years, the whole transaction was ruinously costly to them, as they shew by a full relation of the miserable details.   I assume that this was their grange, called Gannok, and that it was another name for Southowscott, upon which they had before raised money when in need, and which would have to serve their turn again.

It will be remembered that in the time of Sayer, the king's bailiff, the Abbey of Meaux had been permitted to get together the estate called Magnusdayle by the river bank, in that narrow portion of the Groves which has been occupied by flax and cotton mills in our time. This the monks were permitted to enclose with ditches, but with their usual carelessness, they had neglected to keep the ditches cleansed, so that they became filled up nearly level with the land, and Thomas de Sutton, with the free tenants, claimed the right to turn their cattle into Magnusdayle after the hay had been carted away. Thereupon the monks began to clean out the ditches, but the lord and his tenants made forcible resistance. After long wrangling, there was a meeting of all the parties upon the ground, the abbot and his chief officers probably going by the river, and carrying with them their precious charters, the lord and his tenants going along the existing footpath through the Ings. There they compared the charters, examined the vestiges of the ditches, and enquired of the old people as to the ancient use of them. As Sir Thomas de Sutton in the end favoured the cause of the monks, the free tenants withdrew their claims, and the monks were permitted to repair the ditches, so that the enclosed land was worth a mark per annum more than it had fetched before.

Among other ill-advised means of raising money adopted by the monks, was the leasing of their grange of Saltagh, near Patrington, in consequence of which they had to drive their flock of sheep to Sutton. Four hundred of these died from the change, probably because of the moist pasturage into which they were turned.

Once more their grange, called Gannok with Hirncote, which together would be the whole of the old enclosed land of Frog Hall, and several other properties had to be leased, this time to Peter Dowson, of Sutton, for the term of his life, he paying down in advance two hundred marks. The term was afterwards extended to the lives of his wife, his two sons, and three daughters, on payment of three hundred marks more. We have seen that Peter was present with his two sons at the consecration of Sutton chapel. As these sons were living in 1402 aged sixty and sixty-eight, it is probable that this lease also was, in the long run, a bad bargain for the monks.[*]

[*] Gannok is a name for an enclosure or intake like Southowscott.

About the same time a new trouble arose in and near to the West Carr. Certain tile makers of Beverley began coming often, and secretly, down the river in boats, taking away soil between the bank and the channel of the stream. The monks seized the oars and tools, and, finding this ineffectual, they captured one of the laden boats at Wawne. Thereupon Robert de Manfield, Provost of Beverley, who was then in high favour with Alexander, Archbishop of York, and who had other reasons for quarreling with the monks, raised the town against them, reviving the old claims of the Archbishop to the level space that lay between the low bank and the channel, which was accustomed to be inundated by the high tides. Their antagonists used all means, "even threats and blasphemy," to make the monks repair the broken boat. They thrust one of the monks into prison at Beverley, and threatened to do as much for the Abbot himself, his monks and servants, one after another, if they could get hold of them. Eventually, according to the chronicle, shame seized the oppressors, not un-mixed with fear, for the King was coming to Beverley, so they found an excuse for releasing the monk. They were afterwards fain to come before the Abbot at Wawne, when they admitted their fault, begged for absolution, and experienced the mercy of the Abbot's court.

By the river beyond Frog Hall we may still see the low bank with the grassy space, covered by the highest tides, between it and the channel of the river, and may freely sympathise with the monks, who, in this instance, were standing up for their rights, and for the security of the river bank.

Twice in the time of Thomas de Sutton the plague revisited this country, first in 1361, when it was called the children's pestilence, and again in 1369. No special mention of these visitations is made in the documents that I have seen, but the mortality, especially amongst children, must usually have been enormous.

On May 6th, 1380, the statutes of the College of St. James, though only thirty-three years old, were reformed by Alexander, Archbishop of York. It may be that the duties of the chaplains had been badly performed, or it may be that an increase in the ordinary income of the College was the chief cause of the increase, at this time, in its duties, and in the number of its members. By the new ordination there was to be, as before, a master and five chaplains, to whom were now added two clerks, one of whom was to be paid by the master, the other, "the bearer of the water," was to have his allowance of victuals from the College, and also anything he might receive from the charity of the parishioners and the chaplains. As before, one of the chaplains was to be the parochial curate. They were to eat together in one house in common, and to lodge in one house, or two and two together, and each was to say his own mass. The chaplains and clerks, on all Sundays and festivals, were to say matins, parochial mass, and vespers, and on Friday and Saturday, our Lady's mass with music. On week days, the masses, matins, and other canonical " hours " were to be said by the chaplains, and on every day "Placebo et Dirige" * in common, two and two together. On every day one of them was to say the stipulated mass for the souls of John de Sutton, Junior, the founder, and Alice, his wife, of John de Sutton, Senior, and Constance, his wife, and of Thomas Sampson, also for the souls of Thomas de Sutton, and Agnes, his wife, when they should have departed this life.

The book of the provosts of Beverley records that in respect of his land at Sudcoates, Thomas de Sutton paid to the provost of Beverley, eight shillings for his homage. Upon one occasion he was fined a mark for non-appearance, but upon its being proved in court

* From the Office for the Dead.

that he had made his homage, the distress was withdrawn.

His wife's name was' Agnes. There is a record in the Provost's book, of homage done for lands and tenements of the wife at Gembling. This ought to give some clue to her family.

The date of the death of Sir Thomas de Sutton is uncertain. On the 2nd August, 1389, his widow presented to one of the chaplaincies in the College of St. James. In the evidence taken as to burials at Sutton, nothing was said of his burial in the quire, but that would be a matter of course. The Lansdowne MS. 894, f. 115, mentions a gravestone there with the inscription, "Orate pro anima D'ni Thomæ de Sutton." This simple request for a prayer for his soul was likely to form the border to a brass or incised slab.

Frost says that he left no son, and that his property was divided between his three daughters. I am able to give a document that reveals a fact new to the family history, and shews by how narrow a chance this family, which had existed for at least two centuries and a half, failed to be continued in the male line. It is a conveyance by Sir Thomas de Sutton to the master and chaplains of the College of St. James of his reversionary interest in his manor and lands at Barrow, which, had been settled upon a son of his named John, who had died childless. The following is a translation :—

"To all the faithful of Christ unto whom the present writing shall have come Thomas de Sutton knight [sendeth] greeting in the Lord.

Know all of you by these presents that the said Thomas hath granted and by this his present writing confirmed to *dominus* William de Barneby chaplain of the Chantry of Sutton, William de Wandesforde and Robert de Garton chaplains the reversion of his Manor of Barowe and of all other his lands and tenements and rents in the same town of Barowe and Brunhum with the appurtenances in the County of Lincoln which Sir Thomas de Trivet and Elizabeth his wife hold for the

term of the life of the said Elizabeth of the gift and grant of
Thomas Warde Chaplain Robert Sampson and William Spencier
made to the said Elizabeth and John de Sutton formerly the
husband of the said Elizabeth the son of the said Thomas de
Sutton and the heirs lawfully begotten of the bodies of them
John the son of Thomas, and Elizabeth, so that if the aforesaid
John and Elizabeth shall have deceased without heirs lawfully
begotten of their bodies, that in that case the aforesaid Manor
lands and tenements and rents with the appurtenances may
remain to the said Thomas de Sutton, his heirs and assigns
for ever, which John indeed formerly the husband of the said
Elizabeth deceased without heirs issuing of his body and the
said Elizabeth took for husband the said Sir Thomas de
Trivet. To have and to hold the aforesaid Manor lands
tenements and rents with the appurtenances after the death of
the aforesaid Elizabeth to the aforesaid William de Barneby
William de Wandesforde and Robert de Garton chaplains and
their heirs or their assigns for ever of the chief lords of that fee
by the services therefor due and of right accustomed. And the
aforesaid Thomas de Sutton and his heirs will warrant acquit
and defend for ever against all people all the aforesaid Manor,
lands, and tenements with their appurtenances, as is above
mentioned, to the aforesaid William de Barneby, William de
Wandesford, and Robert Garton chaplains and their heirs or
their assigns.

These being witnesses: the lords John Constable, Robert
de Hylton, Walter Faucunberge Knights, Robert Lorimer,
Thomas de Beverle, Thomas Humbercoltes and others.

Dated at Suttecotes on Saturday next before the feast of
Saint George the Martyr in the fourth year of the reign of King
Richard the second after the conquest [A.D. 1381]."

The seal bears the family arms as borne by the
effigy of Sir John de Sutton. It is a handsome seal,
in such preservation that its original design can be
almost completely made out. It will be observed that
the charter is dated at Southcoats, where his brother
had given the foundation charter of the college of St.
James. They may have had some residence on that
manor.

The three daughters of Thomas de Sutton had been
married, not to any of the lords of neighbouring
manors, but to persons in prominent positions in
Yorkshire, living at a distance from Sutton.

Constance, who appears to have been the eldest, became the second wife of Peter de Mauley, of Mulgrave Castle, near Whitby, who was the first Baron de Mauley. Upon his death, left a widow without children, she married Sir John Goddard, who, in 1389, was Sheriff of Yorkshire. They had a son who inherited her share of the manor, which, after passing by marriage into the family of Stapylton, was sold in 1554.

Margery, the second daughter, was first married to Peter de Mauley, the son of her sister's husband, who died before his father. Their son and heir, Peter, died childless, and the barony fell into abeyance, the property being divided between his two sisters, Constance and Elizabeth. The share of Constance, which was a sixth of the whole, descended to her children by Sir John Bygod, her second husband. Elizabeth married George Salvayn, of North Duffield, and from them is descended the present Baron de Mauley, who is the co-heir of the ancient lords of the manor of Sutton. This share, after becoming somewhat diminished, descended in their family until 1536, and is now the property of the Corporation of Hull.

Agnes, the third of these co-heiresses, named after her mother, married first, Sir Ralph Bulmer, and their descendants inherited her property. She married secondly, Sir Edward Hastings, whose name has led to some confusion between the share of the manor belonging to his wife, and the lands of the berewic, which by this time had passed by marriage into another branch of the family of Hastings.

Male heirs, however, continued to be scarce among the descendants of Sir Thomas de Sutton, and some of the shares in the manor became divided and sub-divided among females, so that we hear of portions so small as "the third part of half a sixth." Sometimes the share of one of these owners is called "the manor," as if it were the whole, and the old manor of Sutton, with Bransholm, to which parts of Southcoats were joined, came to be described as the manors of Sutton, Stoneferry, Sutcoats, and Dripole. It would be neither easy nor profitable to trace the smaller of these sub-divisions, but important portions of them can still be identified.

TOMB OF SIR JOHN DE MEAUX.

In 1377, by the death of the last Sir John de Meaux, the succession in the male line of the owners of the berewic came to an end. Poulson's engraving of his tomb in the church of Aldbrough, in which parish his manor of Bewick was situate, may be compared with that of the tomb of Sir John de Sutton. He wears the jupon over the short hauberk, which costume had come into general use several years before the date of his death. His breast displays the griffins of his coat of arms. His sister Alice, who was married to Sir Ralph de Hastings, inherited his possessions.

THE FIFTEENTH CENTURY.

AFTER the death of Sir Thomas de Sutton the most prominent persons connected with the parish were the owners of the Berewic henceforth known as the manor of Hastings. They succeeded to the property in the following order :—

Sir Ralph de Hastings. Married Alice, the sister and heiress of the last Sir John de Meaux.

Sir Ralph de Hastings, his son. Beheaded in 1405, and his estates forfeited, for rebellion against Henry IV. Left no children.

Sir Richard de Hastings, his brother. Had grant of the forfeited estates. Died in 1447, leaving no children.

Sir Leonard de Hastings, his brother. Died in 1456.

Sir William de Hastings, his son. The friend and a chief supporter of Edward, Duke of York, afterwards Edward IV. Created Baron Hastings and a Knight of the Garter. Beheaded in 1483 by order of Richard III.

Edward, Lord Hastings, his son. Baron Hungerford in right of his wife. Died in 1507.

George, Lord Hastings, son of Edward. Created Earl of Huntingdon. Died in 1544.

Francis, Earl of Huntingdon, K.G., son of the above. Died in 1561.

Henry, Earl of Huntingdon, son of Earl Francis. Sold the manor of Hastings in 1565 to Thomas Dalton, a merchant of Hull.

The Domesday berewic of nine oxgangs had received its due proportion of the meadows and pastures gained by the embankments as well as enclosed lands by the river. But material portions of the property had been granted away. Poulson quotes (vol. ii., p. 327) the grant by Wm. Gower and Wm. Gibson, Clerks, John Hastings de Brunby, and Robert Thornton, Esq., to Sir Ralph de Hastings, of 1 messuage, 16 cottages, and 6 oxgangs of tillage, 29½ acres of meadow, and 30s. rental in Sutton. This appears to be the property of Alice his wife, and it was held of the Archbishop of York, as of his manor of Beverley, by the service of a peppercorn. In the time of Edward the Third, John de Meaux had claimed to have "wayf," the assize of bread and ale, and other privileges of a lord of a manor, and the property was called the manor of " Sutton, Stanefery, and Dripole," although quite distinct from the manors of the Suttons.

It is not probable that during the fifteenth century any of the persons owning these manors were very closely concerned with the affairs of the parish ; our knowledge of its history must therefore depend on the transactions of others. The master and chaplains of the College of St. James were then the only persons of importance actually resident in Sutton. Their revenue from tithes must have been very considerable, but their relation to the mother church of Wawne was unsatisfactory to themselves. The master used to appoint one of the chaplains to minister to the spiritual needs of the inhabitants, but these were required to repair to Wawne on the great festivals, and there to offer their oblations.

The enquiry of 1402, which has been alluded to, shewed how far the new church at Sutton had been used for parochial purposes, with or without reference to the mother church of Waghen. From its consecration, burials had taken place there to some extent. The masters and chaplains had been buried in their quire. Several laymen had been buried either in the nave or in the churchyard, according to their rank or their means. About the year 1352, Symon Owgram was buried before the

crucifix in the nave.* There is, however, reason to
think that these burials had been with the leave of
the vicar of Waghen, and subject to the payment of
his fees.

Baptisms had always been performed in the font of
Sutton, probably that which now exists. Peter
Dowson, Junior, had twelve children, his brother John
had as many. Peter Spencer's father, his brother, and
his three sisters had fifty children amongst them. All
these, with their fathers before them, had been
baptized at Sutton. But all persons dying in Sutton,
except the members of the College, must as a rule be
taken to Waghen for burial, and the offerings of wax
and money, and other things usually presented at
funerals, must be made to the vicar of Waghen. It
appears also that the inhabitants of Sutton, although
they had been baptized at the font there, preferred to
be buried with their forefathers at Waghen. The
master and chaplains were not content with their sub-
ordinate position, claiming after a time to bury all
the inhabitants of Sutton, Stanefery, Lopholme, and the
portion of Dripole who specially desired to be buried with
them, and all children whose parents desired it. Thereupon disputes arose. The Chancellor of York was, in
right of his office, the rector of Waghen, and was ready
to defend his own interests, as well as those of his
vicar there. Several enquiries into the matters in
dispute were held, beginning in 1402, and repeated at
intervals for more than fifty years. There were
decisions of one ecclesiastical authority after another,
appeals to Rome, further appeals and enquiries, and
an arbitration, ending, as it would seem, with a final
decision of the Archbishop of York, made in 1454.
The records of these proceedings, contained in a

* He was a person of some position. His name appears in the provost's book
of St. John of Beverley, under the year 1369, where it is said that Simon Ougrym
owes service to the court of the provost, for a sheepfold in Sutton which formerly
belonged to Simon Owgrym of Stanefery.

parchment book, written in Latin, belonging to York Minster, furnish interesting evidence as to the condition of the inhabitants of the parish in the first half of the fifteenth century.[*]

Two points come out clearly in these enquiries. A portion of the parish of Sutton was called Dripole, as I have proved from other evidence, and there was in the parish a hamlet called Lopholme, long since lost, but the site is, perhaps, not beyond recovery. Upon the Watson's Charity Estate there is a field of ancient enclosure, just beyond Stoneferry in the direction of Frog Hall, called "Loppam," and close to this field there are signs on the ground of foundations of houses. Here, on the edge of the West Carr, was doubtless the small hamlet of Lopholme, only two residents in which, Wm. and Thos. Watkin, are named in these enquiries. There were, however, families of the name of Lopholme then and afterwards living in Sutton and Stoneferry, and as late as the seventeenth century the name of Lopham or Loppam is found among the small farmers in the parish.

The first enquiry, held at York, lasted from the eleventh to the twentieth of October, 1402, Sunday included. The chief witnesses on the part of Sutton were the Dowsons, whose father leased the grange of Sutton from the monks of Meaux, Peter Dowson, Junior, was aged 68, John Dowson was aged 60, Peter Spencer, John Fyssher, Symon Tailiour, Thomas de Burton, Peter Carter, and others gave evidence. Those named had all been present, as well as a few women still alive, at the opening of the church fifty-three years before. There were others who testified to the recent practice as to burials, and to what they had heard from their elders. The younger men were John Wilkynson, John Clarkson, Henry Hobson, Nicholas Walde, John Stewenson Alison, Robt. Jonkynman,

---

[*] I have to thank the Rev. Canon Raine for a hint of the value of this book, and for facilitating its consultation.

John Sykes, Roger Watton, Wm. Wymplester, Wm. Burton, John Wandesford, Peter Sayer, John Semanson, Senr., John Bulphyn, and John Smyth.

Thomas de Burton, whose name appears in the Book of the Provosts of Beverley as holding a toft in Sutton in 1369, was present at the consecration. He said he had been a farmer (colonus et agricola) in Sutton for fifty years, and this would be the condition of the great bulk of the witnesses. Some, however, were of superior education and position. All who now gave evidence had been born or had lived in the parish from childhood.

The warden and his chaplains were not examined, but Richard Fenton, the Vicar of Sculcoates, gave evidence. He had known the neighbourhood for thirty-seven years, and well knew the former wardens. Amongst other things he remembered seeing, seventeen years previously, Richard, a Suffragan of the Archbishop, and Robert Dalton, Commissary, making a visitation of Sutton Chapel separately from Waghen.

Peter Dowson remembered the dedication of the Chapel and the burial of John de Sutton. He had seen the wardens of the college by themselves or their servants collect the tithes of Sutton, Stoneferry, and Lopholme. The Glebe consisted of an oxgang of arable land, containing 12 acres, with 12 or 14 acres of meadow in the fields of Sutton. In the Convocation of York, Sutton Chapel was separately assessed at twenty marks. The warden and chaplains had always been buried in the quire, and he had never heard of any claim for mortuary fees on the part of the Church of Waghen, of which fees he had been the collector. John Dogeson, uncle of the Dowsons, with John Maryot, Ralph Johnson, Wm. Schirwynd of Stoneferry, Wm. Damannasman, and many others, had been buried and still lay in the Church or Churchyard. William Pepyn, a former chaplain, had in his last illness received the viaticum and extreme unction from the parish Chaplain of Sutton. Of the younger witnesses, John Wandesford, aged 40, had been a servant in the college for six years. We may assume that he was related to William de Wandesford, one of the chaplains named in Thomas de Sutton's Charter of 1381. Thomas Wetwang and other chaplains bore Sutton names.

I do not see what came of this enquiry, but leaves are missing from the book. Fresh questions must, however, have arisen, for on the 19th January, 1428 (or the beginning of 1429 according to present reckoning), some composition or agreement was made as to the burials of parishioners of Sutton, which the master and chaplains were soon afterwards said to have evaded, and thereupon fresh proceedings were instituted against them in the Consistory Court at York. The Plaintiff, Robert Tyas, who had been the Vicar of Waghen since 1420, appointed William Dryffeld as his proctor, and Robert Marflete, the master or warden, who had been Vicar of Waghen from 1391 to 1413, with the chaplains of the college, who were defendants, appointed John Willyngham as their principal proctor. The enquiry began on the 10th December, 1429, and was adjourned from time to time. Witnesses were examined at York, at Sutton, and probably also at Waghen. The last of the witnesses was examined on the 5th May, 1430.

The evidence on the part of Waghen went to show that the master and chaplains of Sutton had buried the bodies of many adults and children contrary to the agreement of the 19th January, 1428. On the part of the college it was said that for sixty years and upwards, and "for time whereof the memory of man runneth not to the contrary," the chapel of Sutton had been a parish church, canonically dedicated, and had been adorned and decorated on the anniversary of its dedication. It had clergy and parishioners, baptismal font, a graveyard properly dedicated, and other signs and rights of a parish church, with free burial of parishioners, and oblations, by endowment of Alexander, Archbishop of York. It was also asserted that, by the custom of Holderness, an adult could be buried in any parish that he might choose, and that children could be buried wherever their parents might choose. From the 17th to the 22nd of January, 1430 (new style) Robert Alne, Examiner of the Court of York, sat in Sutton Chapel every day, and the following evidence was taken upon these and other parts of the case.

John Day, Chaplain of Halslam, with others, spoke as to the alleged custom of Holderness. He said that before Michaelmas last, Katherine, daughter of Wm. Brigham, of Ganstead, aged half a year, who had been out at nurse at Hedon, had died at Ganstead, her father not knowing of her death. Her grandfather, Wm. Twyer (who was then the representative of the family, anciently settled at Twyers, near Hedon, but who had bought Ganstead from the St. Quintin's), had caused the child to be buried at St. Sepulchre's Hospital, near Hedon, of which hospital his family were the founders and patrons.* John Alanson, of Ganstead, said he had himself buried the child. John Page, a servant of Wm. Twyer, went by his master's order to the Prioress of Swine, and obtained her licence to have the child buried at St. Sepulchre's Chapel. Another infant of Wm. Brigham, dying at Ganstead, had been buried in the same way. It was proved also that Thomas, the son of Wm. Terry, of Kyngeston-upon-Hull, who had been at nurse with Margaret, the wife of John Lambert, of Stoneferry, had been buried at "Kyngeston." Sir Robt. Hylton's child had died while at nurse with Joan, the wife of John Atkins, of

* Other witnesses say she died at Hedon. If the pedigree given by Poulson is accurate, William de la Twyer was her uncle. His son Robert married Constance, the daughter of George Salvain, and grand-daughter of Margery, one of the co-heirs of Thomas de Sutton. I have a charter by which Anthony St. Quintin of Harpham, and John Colman of Gawnsted, conveyed to this couple lands lying partly in Sutton, which they had received from William de la Twyer, no doubt for that purpose.

Stoneferry, and had been buried at Swine. These instances illustrate the habit of sending out children to nurse in those days of numerous births and great mortality. Other instances were given of such burials, the most important of which was the case of Alice Ryott, of Sutton, with five others who were named. These, with many more, were drowned in the Water of Hull, at Hull Ferry. Their bodies were taken out in the parish of Swine (that is in modern Drypool), and buried in their own parishes by the choice of their relatives. But upon the whole, there is room for suspicion that such burials were generally made by leave of the clergy of the parishes out of which the bodies were removed.

Some of the evidence shews the way in which surnames were then formed. John Hogeson said that his parents were Roger Watson, and Alice his wife. Hogeson, Hodgson, or Hochon, all which names were borne by witnesses, is the son of Hodge, or Roger, and Watson is the son of Walter. William Jakson spoke of John (or Jack) Adamman as his father.

John Hogeson had often heard from old Alice Sayer of the dedication of Sutton Chapel, at which she was present. Every year, as long as he could remember, on the feast of the dedication of the church in the autumn (between the feasts of the Nativity of the Blessed Virgin Mary and the Exaltation of the Holy Cross), the church had been solemnly decorated and adorned. A banner, with a little bell hanging from it, had also been displayed from a window of the belfry in token of the dedication. The chaplain standing in the pulpit immediately after the reading of the Gospel at mass on Sunday next before the dedication feast, gave out to the assembled parishioners the day on which the dedication feast would fall. He also counselled those who could conveniently come to service on that day to do so, and to see that all work forbidden on festival days should cease. Hogeson had often heard from his parents that John de Sutton, knight, whose body lies buried in the quire, built the nave "de novo," and that Thomas Sampson, Canon of York, and Rector of the church, built the quire "de novo."

Thomas Ogrym said that the walls of the church had been newly whitened fifteen years ago, before which time old crosses and characters were visible. As to the college, Thomas Wetwang spoke of a large and spacious rectory house, the residence of the master and chaplains.*

Hogeson said that the parochial chaplains had the Cure of souls in Sutton, Stoneferry, and Lopholme, and baptised and administered the Eucharist and the other sacraments and sacramentals. The masters of the college had all received the oblations of the parish, except that Robt. Tyas, the Vicar of Waghen, had received from every man or woman keeping house in Sutton, three farthings yearly, with a fourth part of the money and wax offered at Sutton for the dead.

Symon Bulfyn said he was present in Sutton churchyard when graves were dug, and saw the bones of very many persons who had been buried many years ago. He had often heard his mother say that she had seen fifteen corpses buried in the churchyard at the west end of the church, and John Silver, of Sutton, had often heard Symon Hyne, father of his wife, Alice, say that he had seen very many corpses buried in the churchyard at the west end of the church. John Hogeson, however, said that adults had, until recently, been buried at Waghen, "unless they chose otherwise." Symon Bulfyn's parents, and the parents of other witnesses, with some of their children, had been buried at Waghen. This was admitted to have been the common practice until the burial of a certain John Gardener at Sutton early in the previous year. John

---

* The Wetwangs, who must have come from the Wold village of that name, kept up their connection with Sutton until the latter part of last century.

Hogeson, speaking on the 17th January, thought he had been buried "a year ago and more," but others thought that his funeral had taken place in the previous spring. The date is important in reference to the great number of burials that had taken place since Gardener's funeral, which was about the date of the composition before mentioned.

"Dominus" Wm. Semanson, evidently a native of Sutton, now aged twenty-four, said that three years before this enquiry he was the parish clerk. He was now one of the chaplains, and in a few years later he became the master or warden. He gave evidence as to the burials that had taken place at Sutton, as to masses for the dead, and as to the manner of observing the consecration festival.

The people of Waghen had their own recollections and traditions. Some of their witnesses were clergy of local origin or experience. Thomas Foston, Dean of Beverley, was born at Foston. When seven years old he had been taken by his father to Waghen, and had lived there and at Sutton for six years. John Waghen, Vicar of Easington, of which the Abbot and Convent of Meaux were patrons, was born at Waghen, and, except when he was pursuing his studies, had lived at Easington and Waghen ever since. Thomas Poynton, of Beverley, was a native of Waghen. He had lived there for ten years with his father, and at Sutton with his uncle, Thomas Waghen, then the warden of the college, and afterwards while his own brother, John Poynton, was the warden. He had been a deacon in the choir of Sutton Chapel for three years. He said that Sutton Chapel was notoriously dependent upon Waghen. Indeed that this was so to a greater or less extent could hardly be questioned.

John Warde, the parish clerk of Waghen, could account for the recent neglect of the mother church, He said that the inhabitants of Sutton and the hamlets

therein used to bring their dead to Waghen to be
buried, but Robert Tyas, the vicar, used to lie in bed
until ten o'clock in the day, and not until that hour
could they get mass celebrated, so they had, as they
said, to bury their dead without any mass. For this
the Archbishop's vicar-general reprimanded the vicar,
enjoining him to be ready to say mass when dead were
expected from Sutton, and this he said he would
willingly do. John Haliday, of Waghen, said the
inhabitants of Sutton complained of the vicar absenting
himself when they brought their dead for burial. He
was, however, shewn to be a rather unsatisfactory
witness.

Many other men of Waghen gave evidence as to
the ancient and recent practice to much the same effect
as that of the people of Sutton. But what they of
Sutton thought natural and right, those interested
in Waghen thought entirely wrong, seriously de-
manding that all the bodies wrongfully buried at
Sutton should be exhumed and re-buried by the vicar
of Waghen, to whom all the mortuary fees should be
handed over. John Kexby, Chancellor, aged forty-
eight, was among the witnesses, making himself busier
than was quite prudent.

Then followed proceedings to nullify the effect of
this inquisition. It was alleged on the part of the
college that several of the witnesses were dependent
on the bounty of Chancellor Kexby and the Vicar of
Waghen, also that one of the witnesses was of bad
repute; perhaps also that he had distributed bribes.

On the 6th October, 1430, Wm. Smyth, of Stoneferry, said that last Wednesday he heard John
Halyday publicly acknowledge, in the presence of
others from Sutton and Waghen, that besides his
labour in riding to and fro, he paid out of his own
purse twenty shillings in the prosecution of the
present suit. Peter Skulkotes, of Stoneferry, said
that Halyday was publicly infamous, and that twenty

years ago he had hanged a man called John Mes-
syngham, at Richmond, on the gallows with his own
hands ; Skulkotes said also that he saw a paper book
used at the examination of the witnesses by Chancellor
Kexby, who said, in the English tongue, " Loke nowe
'at all thes wyttnes be askid als yis buke spekes."
The book contained a list of questions that had been
arranged beforehand, but it would have been more
regular if the Chancellor had refrained from meddling
in the examination.

Of the troop of children that had been present at
the consecration of the church in 1349 (some of whom
had lived to give evidence at the enquiry of 1402),
not one now survived.   But old Alice Sayer had not
been dead a year.   She and Katherine Dowson and
Margaret Spencer had talked about that event each to
her dying day, and though nobody troubled them for
their evidence while they lived, they had, as was
perhaps fitting, the last word through these witnesses
of 1430.

The funerals at Sutton during the year 1429, which
are given in detail, form a dismal catalogue.   It is not
recorded as a year of any great pestilence, but the
mortality here must have been appalling.   The list
of burials given at the opening of the enquiry on
the 10th of December, 1429, seems to grow as witness
after witness tells his story.   I have compiled the
following catalogue of adults and children belonging
to Sutton buried within twelve months.   It is a rather
long string of names, but there are several points of
interest in it as a register of burials during the year
1429 :—

Adults, or persons over twelve years of age :—

SUTTON.

Alice, wife of Peter Sayer.
Wm. Swaldale.
John, wife of Thomas Edmond.
Wm Cawman.

Wm Warner.
Katherine Warner.
Marjory, wife of John Alane.
Peter Spencer.
Elena, wife of Nicholas Bulfyn.
Elizabeth, wife of John Marshall.
Margaret, wife of John Doram.
John, son of   „   „
Agnes, daughter of Thomas Colyn.
Katherine Fyssher.
Matilda, wife of Wm. Both.
John Hobson, Senr.
Matilda, wife of Wm. Dowing.
Wm. Cok.
Peter, son of Wm. Hyne.
Seme, wife of John Twyer.

STONEFERRY.

Roger Dryby.
Amice, his daughter.
Margaret, daughter of John Sowter.
Joan, daughter of John Hall.

DRYPOLE.

John and Alice, son and daughter of Edmund Wynter.

Children under twelve.

SUTTON.

Isabella and Joan, daughters of Wm. Swaldale.
John and Willm., sons of Symon Waynflete.
John, Elena, and Katherine, children of Wm. Tropinell
Matilda, daughter of Wm. Cawman.
John and Joan, children of Symon Lowerans.
John and John, sons, and Matilda, daughter, of John Fyssher.
John, son of John or Wm. Taverner.
Agnes, daughter of Wm. Bothe.
Robert and Joan, children of John Lopholme.
Willm. and Margaret, children of John Stather.
Joan, daughter of John Smyth.
Willm., son of Robert Swaldale.
John and Alice, children of Wm. Wetwang.
Thomas, Peter, Alice, and Amicia, children of John Swaldale.
Edmund, Thomas, and Agnes, children of Thomas Colyne.
Katherine, daughter of Robert Watson.
Agnes, daughter of Wm. Cok.
John, son of Wm. Yole.
Willm. and Thomas, sons of Richard Syke (or Sykys).

Elena, daughter of John Baker.
Alice, daughter of John Hyne.
Robert, son of John Rychardson.
John, son of Peter Hogeson.
Willm., Symon, and Matilda, children of Wm. Hyne.
John, Alice, and Katherine, children of Symon Spencer.
Willm., Robert, Alice, and Margaret, children of John William-
    son.
Thomas, son of John Twyer.
Willm. and Matilda, children of John Watson.
Willm., son of John Alane.
Agnes, daughter of Thomas Spencer.
John and Alice, children of Thomas Tailour.
William and Alice, children of John Owgrym.
John and Nicholas, sons of Thomas Dawson.
Peter, son of Wm. Sayer.
John, son of Robert Wherledale.
Alice, daughter of Thomas Edmund.
Nicholas, son of Wm. Silver.
Joan, daughter of Thomas Burton.
Willm. and Alice, children of John Burthan.
John, son of John Hobson.
Agnes, daughter of Richard Stather.
Edmund and Alice, children of John Syle.

STONEFERRY.

John and Margaret, children of John Sowter.
Joan, daughter of John Robynson.
John, Thomas, Peter, Agnes, and Alice, children of Rd. Walde.
John and Thomas, sons of Wm. Gardener.
John, Willm., Margaret, Joan, and Matilda, children of Peter
    Owgrym.
Isabella, daughter of Peter Schakyll.
Richard and Isabella, children of John Lopholme.
Isabella, Agnes, Margaret, Alice, and Elena, children of John
    Hull.
John, Robert, and Cecily, children of John Kilpyn.
John, Willm., and Matilda, children of Robert Saunderson.
Alice and Beatrice, children of Thomas Skulkotes.
Katherine and Joan, children of Peter Rust.
John, Richard, Stephen, and Joan, children of John Watkyn.

DRYPOLE.

Seman, son of Edward Wynter.

Besides these, Henry, the son of John Burton of
Stoneferry, had been buried by his father's desire at

Waghen.   If more children or any adults had been
taken there since John Gardener's death we should
probably have had their names.

Upon the whole, it appears that besides the deaths
of adults, several of whom we should probably call
children, 25 families had each lost one child, 10 had
lost two, 6 had lost three, 3 had lost four, and 3
families had lost five children each.   The different
hamlets had suffered in the proportion following :—

	Adults.	Children.
Sutton Village - - -	20	71
Stoneferry - - - -	4	39
The portion of Drypool -	2	1
	26	111

Stoneferry had evidently suffered the most severely,
for if we may judge from the proportion of witnesses
examined, the number of households was comparatively small.   In the whole parish sixty-seven house-
holders had suffered bereavement and in some cases
parents as well as children had died.

This enormous mortality seems to have drawn no
comment from anyone at the enquiry.   By tradition
and by experience these people were accustomed to the
idea of a high and irregular death-rate, especially
amongst children.   There would be natural tears, soon
wiped away.   But when they got back into the rut of
their daily toil, and year after year brought fresh
miseries, they might even feel thankful that these little
ones had been taken away from the evil to come.*

The decision of Magister Richard Arnold, sub-dean
and official of the court of the Archbishop of York, in this
case has the appearance of a compromise.   Adopting,
to some extent, the alleged custom of Holderness, it

* In the ill-drained marshes by the Thames, which must have been precisely
similar to the lower parts of Sutton, children could hardly be reared.   The
survivors became acclimatized, but if they fetched wives from the higher ground these
were liable to be carried off by the malaria.   So says the local tradition.

recognises the right of the Vicar of Waghen to bury
the people of Sutton if, being entitled to choose, they
should not have chosen their place of sepulture elsewhere. But the Vicar's right to bury all the infants
was subject to no qualification. The burials of infants
at Sutton since the date of the composition or agreement of the previous year, had therefore been wrongly
done, and the bones of all persons wrongfully buried
must be exhumed and re-buried at Waghen, all the
oblations being paid to the Vicar. The warden and
chaplains, as defendants, must also pay the costs of the
suit.

The warden and chaplains appealed to the Court of
Rome, but before a decision was made, Symon Seller
had become the warden of the college, and Symon
Merflet had become the Vicar of Waghen. Symon
Seller was the warden from 1432 to 1443. The case
was considered by three auditors of the Apostolic
Palace, of whom Anthony de Vito (or Viro), Bishop of
Urbino, drew up an order reversing the sentence of the
Court of York, absolving the College from payment of
oblations, imposing silence on the Vicar of Waghen,
and condemning him in costs. This sentence was
confirmed by Francis de Cruyllis, and by Baptista de
Roma, two other auditors.

It was now the turn of the Vicar of Waghen to
move the Court of Rome, and a document was
obtained from John Lohier, LL.D., also an auditor of
the Apostolic Palace, and Gerard Folie, notary
public, setting out that when the sentence in favour of
the college was passed, the composition of the 19th
January, 1429, had not been produced, that Symon de
Merflet, the Vicar of Waghen, had not been defended,
and that Chancellor John Kexby had not intervened,
but must now be admitted to defend the appeal.

Thereupon the parties agreed to leave the whole
matter to the arbitration of John Kempe, Cardinal
Archbishop of York. He made his award on the 8th

April, 1447, by which time "Dominus" Wm. Semanson,
the Sutton boy, once the parish clerk, and afterwards
a chaplain, had become warden of the college. As to
the right of burial, the Archbishop confirmed the
sentence of the sub-dean of York, deciding that all
oblations in wax or money or other things given upon
burials, and all mortuaries and mortuary rights due
from the principal inhabitants of Sutton, at the feasts
of Pentecost, Sts. Peter and Paul, and All Saints,
belonged to the Mother Church of Waghen, and
condemning the college to restore the bodies and the
oblations.   He laid it down that the chapel or chantry
of Sutton, with the rectory house and the village and
hamlets, were in the parish of Waghen, and that the
chapel was formerly erected by consent for the increase
of devotion of the inhabitants, whereby they might
more easily and frequently attend divine offices, and
not be bound to go on all festivals to Waghen for
sacraments and sacramentals.   In recognition of this,
the wardens and chaplains must pay to the Rector or
Vicar of Waghen, thirty shillings and four pence at the
feasts of Pentecost and St. Martin-in-winter, yearly
for ever, according to the ordinance of Archbishop
William de la Zouch, dated on the morrow of St.
Lawrence, 1347.   The people of Sutton were bound to
pay all dues in their lifetime, and on their death, and to
contribute to the repair of Waghen Church.   Yet for
the sake of peace and amity, he directed that so long
as the warden and chaplains should obey this decree,
the bodies already wrongfully buried need not be exhumed nor the oblations refunded.

   But seven years afterwards the parties were again in
dispute as to burials and oblations, and the new
Archbishop (William Bothe), seems to have brought
about a fresh arbitration by Philip (Dayrell), Abbot of
Meaux, Sir John Melton, Lord of Swine, Robt. Tone,
Archdeacon of the East Riding, and John Marshall,
Residentiary of York Cathedral.   By this time Wm.

Moreton had succeeded Kexby as Chancellor, and as Rector of Waghen.

On the 11th of April, 1454, a meeting was called in Sutton Church by the ringing of a bell, just as a meeting is called there to this day. Thomas Burton, Wm. Ottringham, and John Swalldale of Sutton, acted as Procurators.

Among the men of Sutton were:—

> John Hogeson, Robt. Swalldale, Peter Hogeson, John Hobson, John Vergantte, John Bretane, John Dawson, Wm. Fisher, Symon Snaith, Wm. Dawson, Wm. Dowsing, Nicholas Spencer, John Smyth, Thomas Clerk, Wm. Burght, Wm. Watson, Robt. Lame, Wm. Coupar, Wm. Johnson, John Ganok, Peter Dawson, Robt. de Sikes, Wm. Jacson, John Borethan, Rd. Hyne, Thomas Edmonde, Robt. Whardale, John Richardson, Robt. Watson, John Silver, Thomas Lopholme, Robt. Jacson, Robt. Barker, and Wm. Stevenson.

From Stoneferry came:—

> John Lopholme, Wm. Surdevall, Thomas Sculcotes, Rd. Shakilles, Stephen Silver, Wm. Hochon, Rd. Frankich, Thomas Bernston, Robt. Saunderson, and Symon Shakilles.

The hamlet of Lopholme was represented by:

> Wm. and Thomas Watkyn.

Here, mingling with the Dowsons and the Hogesons, and other names of former generations, we now find such new names as Ganoc, which must have been taken from the monks' grange of Gannok, once leased to the Dowsons, also Vergantte and Whardale, names that we shall hear again.

At this meeting the parishioners formally consented to the election of the arbitrators. On the 8th May following, at a meeting similarly called in the church at Waghen, some sixty inhabitants agreed to the same arbitrators. The result of the arbitration was an award under which the master and chaplains were to pay to the Rector of Waghen, three shillings and four

9

pence, and to Symon Merflet, the Vicar, twenty
shillings yearly, so that the inhabitants of Sutton
might have the right of burial in Sutton Chapel
and graveyard.   These must also henceforth go
with their oblations to Waghen Church, and
besides their share of the repair of the nave and of
the ornaments and necessaries there, they must pay
four pounds as part of seven pounds ten shillings, the
cost of re-casting the bells.   They must also pay
yearly to the Rector and Vicar of Waghen, four pence
each, if demanded, as a sign of possession.

Thus, in 1454, the litigation which had outlasted
several successive masters of the college, Archbishops,
Chancellors, and their Vicars, with two generations of
parishioners, appears to have been finally settled.
The result was sufficiently favourable for the college,
and, as the reverence for their own church with its
comparatively splendid ceremonial grew, burials of
Sutton folk at Wawne would probably come to an end.
The duty of repairing to Wawne on days of high
festival, with the payment of oblations to the solitary
Vicar, would also in no very long time be forgotten.

At each of these enquiries questions were put as to
the precise boundaries of Sutton.   In 1402, they were
said to be Bilton Brigg on the east, Somergangedyke
and Drypoolgote on the south, with Fysshousegote
or Forthdyke on the north, and Northkerdyke or
Braunceholmedyke and "le Clowes" running to Bilton
Brigg.   The western boundary was of course the river
Hull.   In 1429, the boundary is said to run along
Forthdyke to Newland Hirne, and from thence by
Eastkerdyke to Bilton Brigg.   Thomas Paynton, who
had lived at Sutton as a youth, described part of the
boundary as beginning at Drypoolgote, extending by
certain running ditches to a little gate (portula), called
Billiegate, or Bilton Brigg, and thence by the Est-
Karr dike to Gaunsted Clow.   This is, I think, the
first document in which the North Carr is recognised.

The marr had probably shrunk so much that a tract of land had been laid dry which took that name.

It will be noticed that in all these proceedings no name appears that represents any of the descendants of the old lords of the manor. But, in 1458, Isabella Goddard, late wife of Richard Goddard, of Sutton, with Sir Ralph Bygod, Sir John Salvain, and William Bulmer, Esq., had the right of presenting to vacant chaplaincies in the college. It seems as if Isabella Goddard and perhaps also her husband had lived for a time on their share of the property at Sutton.

There was, about this time, in Sutton, a company—perhaps a guild connected with the church—that was able to give representations of the kind, that led in the next century to the performance of stage plays. In the Mayoralty of Hugh Clitheroe, 1442, the Mayor and Aldermen of Hull visited Sutton, "and were entertained by the Players of that place."

By the middle of the fifteenth century, the country, defeated and discredited abroad and at home, was entering upon the long struggle known as the Wars of the Roses. It may be that in the case of Sutton, the general misery of the times was not enhanced by any close contact with the strife. When Edward the Fourth returned from his last period of exile, it was in company with one who had a substantial interest in the parish, being the first person of high rank who was so connected with it. This was William, Lord Hastings, then the owner of the berewic, which was now called a manor.

It was in the spring of 1471 that Edward IV. landed at Ravernspurn, Hastings being his chief companion in his expedition for the recovery of the crown. He became his Chamberlain and a Knight of the Garter, remaining his most faithful adherent. When Edward was dead, and Richard, Duke of Gloucester, had determined to seize the crown, the first open step he took was to charge Hastings with

endeavouring, by witchcraft, to take his life. The
scene in the Tower of London on June 13th, 1483,
when Richard suddenly made his accusation, and
immediately ordered Hastings to be beheaded, is one
of the most striking in English history. In his will
Hastings mentions, amongst other manors, his manor
of Sutton-in-Holderness.

The inquisition as to his possessions (Inq. p.m.,
1 Richd. III., No. 31) was held Oct. 20th, 1484.
It states that he held, amongst other lands, the
manor of Sutton with its members. viz., Drypole
and Stoneferye, which manor was held of the Lord
of Holderness, as of the manor of Brystwyke, by
what service the jurors do not know. The peppercorn
tenure under St. John of Beverley appears to have
led to this uncertainty, but other questions crop up in
later documents, and I am not sure that they can all be
explained.

I have a Latin Charter dated at Sutton on the 22nd
May, 1484, by which Thomas Wharldale of Keying-
ham Marsh, grants to John Sparow of Sutton,
"generosus" or gentleman, and to William Burton of
Sutton, all his lands and tenements in Sutton, to hold
of the chief lords by the services due and accustomed.
The witnesses are Willm. Eland, Armiger or Esquire,
Willm. Bekwith, John Thomlynson, John Vele, Willm.
Lopholme, and John Vergraunte. We have here no
knights as in the older charters. Eland was from
Hull, where the family was then becoming prominent.
Bekwith bore a Hull name, and perhaps Vele also.
The other names we have met with in the old lists of
witnesses and of persons buried at Sutton.

THE REFORMATION PERIOD.

THE condition of the parish during the interval between the Wars of the Roses and the Reformation may, to some extent, be estimated. The free tenants on the manor, by degrees, became more independent. The troublesome system of "services" in labour and in farm produce, rendered by the free tenant to the lord of the manor, had grown less common, payment of amounts, often very small, in the form of rent being substituted. By this time the bondmen had become nominally free, and although the movements of the free labourer were restricted by law and by his circumstances, he would be the better for such freedom as he had.

The sub-division of the manor by its non-resident lords went on. There are signs that the owners of the larger shares were parting with portions of them, while the smaller owners were selling outright. Through these transactions we get some insight into the affairs of the parish.

In the year 1527 Cardinal Wolsey, Archbishop of York, acquired a share (stated in a document which will be given in the next chapter to have been a third) in the Sutton group of manors as part of the endowment of his college at Oxford, now called Christchurch. Upon his disgrace in 1529, this property was seized by the King, and was granted, June 14th,

1635, to Sir Marmaduke Constable of Everingham,
in whose family it still remained in the middle of the
seventeenth century. I believe that the lands connected with this share of the manor can be identified
as lying chiefly in Stoneferry, but members of the
Constable family held property in the parish that had
been acquired in other ways down to the reign of
George III.*

Before the Reformation the Salvains must have
parted with a good deal of the property that had
descended to them through the Mauleys. That
which remained to them in Sutton consisted of a sixth
part of the manorial rights, and of houses and lands,
in some of which their share was a sixth, while in
others it was a third, or a half. In some accounts this
share in the manor is said to be a ninth. Of the
demesne lands of the manor they had now only an
oxgang of tillage, with the meadows and pasturage
that belonged to it. In 1536, George Salvain sold his
interest in Sutton, Sudcotes, Barrow, Stanfery,
Dripole, and Roxton to Sir William Sydney, from
whom it was soon afterwards acquired in exchange by
Henry VIII. The King desired to grant the property
to the Corporation of Kingston-upon-Hull, in consideration of the assistance he had received from the
town at the time of the rebellion known as the
Pilgrimage of Grace. The transaction was, however,
incomplete at his death, and the actual grant was not
made until the 29th March, 1552, the sixth year of
Edward VI. In the description of this share in the
manor the following items, among others, are of
interest :—

* The original grant to Sir Marmaduke Constable, now in the possession of
Lord Herries at Everingham, is very handsomely engrossed, and has attached to it
an impression of the Great Seal. It is printed by Poulson (Hist. of Holderness,
vol. 1, p. 164) in a form somewhat abridged. There are difficulties in the way of
identifying this share with that of either of the three heiresses of Sir Thomas de
Sutton, but it seems probable that in the 17th century it represented the share
which Constance, the widow of Lord de Mauley, took into the family of Goddard.

The Abbot and Convent of "Mewlse" held lands and tenements, paying 3s. 4d. per annum.

The Master and Fellows of the College of Sutton held for a term of years the sixth part of a close called the Oxland, 19 beast-gates and their appurtenances in Bransholm field, 2½ beast-gates in the North lands, also one cottage and a half oxgang of land with the appurtenances, paying by the year 49s. 8d.

Stephen Knagg held for a term a sheepcot and a half oxgang of land in Sutton field, paying 14s.

There was a "Court and Lete" in the manor, and John Smith and Robert, his son, held by copy of the court roll a messuage and a half oxgang of land, paying 16s. 8d.

Among the tenants at will were the Master and Fellows of the College of St. James in respect of a sixth part of the Marland house, for which they paid 12d.

The Abbot and Convent of Meaux held the sixth part of a close called the Salts, paying yearly 6s. 8d.

Other items include pieces of meadow in the Ings and the Carr side meadow, beast-gates in the East Carr and in the New Ings at Stoneferry, and one half of a close called "Cowecroft."

John Loppham held the third part of a messuage called Spring Hill and of Spring Hill Close—probably the easternmost part of the old enclosed lands to the east of the church, where a spring still exists. There is, however, also a spring west of the church.

William Stubbs held a "selyon" of land in Stoneferry "in the Bothome," paying 10s. 1d.

John Kyddall and Rd. Loppam rented the sixth part of a piece of pasture called "the Rawe," paying 2s. 2d. yearly. This is the long strip of land lying between the ancient Foredike and Sutton dike, the existing portion of which is called "Roe bank," which is still a separate strip of ground running up from Soffham farm nearly to the river.

Rd. Broune held two acres of arable land in the "Fourd," which would be near to Foredike, paying 2s. yearly.

The "Castell Yng" was then vacant, but the usual rent, receivable by Salvain, was 3d.

The fishing and fowling belonging to a sixth part of the manor was worth to Salvain 5s. one year with another.

Robert Blassell held the sixth part of a "lathe" or barn, two stables and two gardens in Southcoates and Stoneferry.

Henry Bell held a messuage and a lathe, with a close and four acres of meadow, for 14s.

Richard Wilson rented three "commons" or grazing rights, each common being for eighty sheep and four horses. Such commons were held in respect of a house and a half oxgang of land. Very little has been heard of horses in earlier documents;

they would be bred for riding, and there would now be a demand for them for use in Hull.

The grant to the Corporation also includes the sixth part of the right to present the Master and five brethren of the College of St. James, valued at 30s. a year. The owners of shares in the manor had presented sometimes jointly, sometimes in turn.

John Gibson is named as the Bailiff of Sutton and the other lordships, whose yearly fee, granted to him for his life by George Salvain, was 31s.

Although serfdom, or bondage, must have been extinguished and practically forgotten, the careful scribe who drew up this document felt bound to follow the precedents handed down from ancient times. So the King was made to grant to the Corporation, not only the water-ways, markets, and a long list of other appurtenances, real or imaginary, but also the bondmen, and bondwomen, and villeins, with their children " then born, and in future to be born." This is, I think, the latest suggestion of the ancient condition of serfdom among our townsfolk.

The period over which this business extended coincided with the earlier of the series of transactions to which is given the name of the Reformation. By this time Henry VIII. had determined to seize upon the property and the whole organization of the church. The Articles of Religion, promulgated in 1536, laid down that the Bible and the three creeds were the sole grounds of faith, and that the seven sacraments were reduced to three, viz. :—Baptism, the Lord's Supper, and Penance. They condemned the old notions of purgatory, pardons, and masses for the dead. The ceremonies of the church were, however, hardly changed, and as transubstantiation and confession were still to be taught and practised, things may have gone on pretty well for the time. But the dissolution of the monasteries was at hand, and the suppression of chantries and religious guilds was to follow.

The monks of Meaux were dispersed on the 11th

December, 1539, upon the surrender of the Abbey to the King. Out of their revenues they had kept up the distribution of the "gate-alms," stipulated in their acquisitions of pasturage. Four pounds per annum was still expended by them, in this way, for the good of the soul of Sayer the Second, and three pounds for the good of the soul of Sayer the Third, who had been dead two hundred and fifty years.

It would be unfair to judge of the claim of these monks to the love and reverence of their neighbours by the errors, and failures, and bickerings so candidly confessed by themselves. The rugged surface of the pasture land where the foundations of the Abbey lie buried, and its deep enclosing moat, testify to the extent and importance of their buildings. The few remains that have been disinterred bear witness to the beauty of the pile now doomed to ruin and decay. But the daily routine of their services, their unrecorded charities, and the hospitality which the traveller would be sure to receive at their gate, would furnish them with a better title to public gratitude. It was, however, not in their religious or charitable aspect that they had been chiefly known at Sutton, but in their character as neighbours and competitors for land and pasturage. And, although their acquisitions had been long since checked, we cannot suppose that their disappearance from the parish was viewed with any particular regret.

Their property here, which they had managed to get recognized as a sort of manor, consisted chiefly of Southowscott and Hirncott, with all their new meadows and pasturage, which they appear to have kept in their own hands, and of the six and three-quarter oxgangs that remained to them of the gift of young Amandus. The Minister's Accounts in the Exchequer Augmentation Office give the details of this last mentioned property, which the monks seem to have let, either on lease or by the year, as follows :—

In Sutton.

	£	s.	d.
Free rent from Anthony Hylliard, for his land -		1	0

Messuage and 3¼ oxgangs of land, 26 acres, 2½
roods meadow, 9 gates in the East Carr, one
sheepcot with a croft, and one cottage with
appurtenances, and 9 gates in the East Carr
(every third year 10 gates), 7 gates in North
lands and 3 gates in Stoneferry New Ings (and
every third year one running-gate), leased to
Peter Snaith.   Rent payable at the feast of
St. Martin in winter (besides a "service" of
two hens) -   -   -   -   -   -   -   6 17 4
And for 2 "running-gates" in the same lands
which every third year lay waste or common   2   8

These particulars of grazing rights, which were in
certain cases held, and in other cases interrupted, every
third year, are the first evidences of the fallowing or
laying waste triennially of the arable lands between
the harvesting of the lent corn and the sowing of
wheat for next year's crop.   Even the meadowing of
certain lands, which I suppose lay open to the adjacent
tillage fields, was influenced by this periodical
fallowing.

	£	s.	d.
Messuage with croft and half oxgang of land let to Agnes Spencer, widow. Yearly rent (besides two hens) - - - · - -		18	10
Cottage and a rood of land let to John Yemars. Annual rent (besides two hens) - - -		6	0
Five acres meadow in Rysome Carr let to Peter Snaith. Annual rent (besides two hens) -		6	8
Farm house and oxgang of land with appurtences let to Ralph Sprott. Rent (besides two hens) - - - - - - -	2	4	2
Farm house and oxgang let to Richd. Hudson. Rent (besides two hens) - - -	1	5	0
Farm house and half oxgang with appurtenances let to Richd. Hartburn. Rent (besides two hens) - - - - - - -	1	0	4
Half an oxgang let to Stephen Knagge. Rent -	0	12	11

	£	s.	d.
Cottage and an acre of land let to John Sparke. Rent (besides two hens) - - - -	0	5	0
A piece of meadow called Syk-well let to John Sparke, lying waste or common every third year - - - - - - - -	0	3	4

The total rent was 14 2 3.

STONEFERRY, in the parish of Sutton.

	£	s.	d.
Half an oxgang with appurtenances let to William Druffelde. Rent - - - - -	0	19	6
Cottage and two acres meadow let to John Thomson, senr., for - - - - - -	0	8	5

Total rent 1 7 11.

DRIPOLE, in the parish of Sutton.

	£	s.	d.
Farm and two acres of land, 19s ; and a close called Magnusale, 60s., leased to Agnes Squyer, widow, at - - - - -	3	19	0

The perquisite of sixteen hens, the last remnant of the "services" rendered in ancient times by tenants to their lords, was by no means overlooked. It was now leased under the king's seal to Launcelett Alford for two shillings and eight pence per annum or two pence per hen. This driblet of a rental introduces the name of a family that was to be powerful in the parish for a century to come.

Lancelot Alford came from Holt in the county of Denbigh. His coming into Holderness seems to have been induced by the traffic in church lands then being actively carried on. On the 20th November, 1540, he had a grant of Meaux Abbey, with lands including Southowscott, Hirncott, the meadows in Soffham and the Ings, and the pasturage in the West Carr, the Salts, and elsewhere in Sutton. Two sheepcots belonging to the abbey called Billicot and Redcot went with the pasturage. In Brown's sketch survey of the road between Hull and Hedon (Lansd. MS.) Redcot is shown to be on the south side of the Holderness Road, not far from the place where it is joined by the Ings Road. Unless there was another Redcot in Southcoates this must be the sheepcot that had belonged to the Abbey, of the gift of Richard de Otringham.

But more important persons were to be connected with these lands. In 1549, John Dudley, Viscount Lisle, who in the earliest days of Edward VI. was created Earl of Warwick, a Knight of the Garter, and Lord High Admiral, obtained these lands with many others in an exchange with the king. Soon afterwards he caused himself to be created Duke of Northumberland, and in the beginning of Queen Mary's reign lost his head, unpitied, on the failure of his attempt to obtain the crown for his daughter-in-law, Lady Jane Grey. His grant of the Sutton lands was subject to the lease to Alford, whose family continued to hold the property under a succession of persons of high position until the middle of the seventeenth century.

The Priory of Swine was dissolved on the 30th September, 1540. Amongst its possessions were thirty-seven acres of meadow in " Lez Dales in Sutton Inge," worth £2 9s. 4d. per annum or sixteen pence per acre. A century before this time the rate was about a shilling. The nuns held also Drypool Grange with the lands that belonged to it. The property was granted in the first instance to Sir Richard Gresham, by the year 1553 it was again in the hands of the crown, for in that year it was granted by Queen Mary to Sir John Constable.

The Carthusian Priory at Hull was dissolved on the 9th December, 1536. Amongst its possessions were lands in " Stanefery, Sutton, Lopham, and Drypoole," worth £11 9s. 6d. per annum. This property had descended from Benedict de Sculcoates through William de Seintluce, the Grays of Rotherfield and the De-la-Poles. It was held afterwards chiefly by members of the family of Alured, who were for a long time closely connected with Hedon and Hull.

The College of St. James was the last of these

religious communities to be dissolved. When, in 1547, the young king, Edward VI., succeeded his father, the changes in religion and Church ceremonies still went on apace. Pictures and images were ordered to be removed from churches, the mass was abolished and communion substituted. The prayer-book in English was introduced. Priests were then allowed to marry, and under the new *régime* it might seem that no useful purpose was any longer served by the Master and Fellows of the college. They were dispossessed accordingly, the rectory with its barns and stables, the glebe, the tithes, great and small, and all that they had, being taken into the hands of the king. Some small annuity out of the endowment would be allowed to each of the members. The stipend of the parochial curate was secured out of the same fund. It would be fixed at the amount which had been usually allowed by the Masters or Wardens, which was not more than sixteen pounds, but perhaps only ten pounds, per annum. He would, however, have also his fees from the parishioners, and there appears to have been on his part some claim to a small portion of the lands which the college had held. Thomas Whyte who, in 1540, had been presented by the King to the third chantry, was the parochial curate. The King also took possession of a cottage held by the churchwardens, and formerly given "for the perpetual observance of an anniversary in the church of Sutton." This was granted (Pat. Roll, 1 Mary, part 5) to Joan Constable, widow, and John Constable, of Burton Constable, in consideration of £500 15s. 7½d. paid by them to Edward VI. for this amongst other property formerly belonging to religious houses.

It is not quite certain that the duties of the members of such communities as this were actually performed by them. The Provost and Fellows of the college of St. John at Beverley had made no pretence of personally carrying out their

religious obligations in connexion with the minster.
There is, however, no evidence of such neglect on the
part of the college of St. James. It is probable that
the members continued to be selected as of old, from
the sons of neighbours or from the local clergy, that
they lived regularly in their spacious rectory house,
and were publicly buried with the solemn mass within
their quire.

On the 22nd August, 1547,—the first year of
Edward VI.—the king, by patent, confirmed to Sir
Michael Stanhope six grants of religious houses,
amongst them the college of St. James, to be held as
of the king's manor of Beverley, subject to the rents
and payments which had been paid to Henry VIII.*
Sir Michael Stanhope was the brother-in-law of the
Protector Somerset, and the steward of the Seigniory
of Holderness. Upon the fall of Somerset in 1552,
Stanhope was attainted of high treason for opposing
the ambition of Dudley, Duke of Northumberland,
and was executed. His widow's jointure out of his
forfeited possessions was acquired by the Crown (Pat.
Roll 1 and 2, Philip and Mary, part 2) in exchange
for other property.

But though everything that the College had
possessed would seem to have been confiscated, there
still remained a chance of wringing something more
out of their former benefice. Commissioners having
been appointed to make a survey of Church goods,
Sutton Church was duly visited. The curate, Thomas
Whyte, was still officiating under the altered conditions
of the period, when on the 23rd August, 1552, a deed
(see Exchequer Augmentation Office Books, vol. 515)
was drawn up between "Sir William Babthorpe, Sir
Robert Constable, Sir Rauff Ellerkare, Knightes, John
Ogleffeld and Lancelot Oldforde,† Esquires, the King's

---

* This grant had been made 17th July by Mag. Walter Bayne, chaplain, Custos
of the Chapel of St. James and of the Collegiate Church of Sutton. He does not
appear in the list of Wardens, but was probably appointed in order that he might
make this grant.   † Lancelot Alford of Meaux Abbey.

Commissioners, and Thomas Whyt, curate, Richard Harman and John Browne, churchwardens, Thomas P'sone, Steven Hoge, inhabitants," which deed catalogues the following list of goods used in the services :—

> " Imprimis, one Challes of silver, 2 bells, and one hand-bell.
> Itm. one suyt of vestmentes of whyt Rowyd Sairsnet, with all thinges belonging theirto.
> Itm. one paire of orgains, one old cope, one corporax of dornix.
> Itm. one Pixe of Latyn, one old surples.
> Itm. 3 altar clothes, one crosse, one crysmaterye of latyn, one sacryng bell, and 2 crewettes.
> Itm. 2 old whyt vestmentes with albes, stoill, and fannells, 2 Paxis of woode." *

The organ is an evidence of the scale on which the services had been performed, as to the rest there is not much that would be worth confiscating. I think we may feel sure that after this visit the church was left bare of all saleable goods.

In these changes, there would no doubt be many in the parish who clung to the form of worship in which they had been brought up, and regretted the disappearance of the Master and Fellows from their midst, but others would have learned to look upon their more solemn services as superstitious or idolatrous, and in the troubles of the years which followed, all that I have collected of their history would soon be clean forgotten.

The subsequent ownership of the lands of these religious communities will be detailed so far as it illustrates the agricultural customs of the seventeenth and eighteenth centuries.

* The Chalice was the Sacramental Cup, it was covered with the Corporal. The Pyx contained the consecrated bread, it was of latten or fine brass. The vestments were for use chiefly at Mass. The Chrysmatory contained the consecrated oil or chrysm used in sacraments and at ordinations. The Fanon or Maniple, a long strip of cloth like the stole, was attached to the left wrist of the priest. The Pax was a tablet bearing a sacred picture ; during the Mass it was presented to the principal clergy that they might give it the kiss of Peace. The Albe was a long white vestment worn under the others.

QUEEN ELIZABETH TO QUEEN ANNE.

PART I.

THE Reformation, while leaving untouched the routine of the farmer and labourer, gave another impulse to the changes that for a century and a half had been going on in the ownership of the land. The monks, and nuns, and collegiate priests, were now swept away. The short-lived tenure of Cardinal Wolsey had ended, and the ancient Holderness family of Constable had taken his place. From one cause or another, Hastings, Salvain, Goddard, Fairfax, Bigod, Bulmer, and Stapylton, had disappeared. These had all belonged, more or less, to the old order, and had carried down the traditions of the mediæval life. Their successors, the Dudleys, Greshams, and Stanhopes, with other non-resident grantees or speculators in manors, and the Daltons, Alfords, Alureds, and Trusloves, who were gentry or merchants, chiefly of local origin, had little or no connection with the ancient families. They belonged to the new order of social life and thought. These and their contemporaries were, however, strictly conservative of all distinctions in social rank. After the new noblemen came the Baronet, the Knight, the Armiger or Esquire, and the Generosus or Gentleman, standing out well in front of the yeomen and farmers, who, with the labourers, were the practical tillers of the soil.

When the government became settled under
Elizabeth, there were many who began to use the
wealth which they had acquired by commerce in
gathering together again the estates that had been
dispersed, owing to the breaking up of the old families.
To these must be added the hosts of speculative
capitalists and of courtiers, who, upon one consideration
or another, obtained grants of the church lands.   Such
of these lands as were not already under lease were
now let to farmers or small gentry.   But the King and
his successors were sorely in want of money, and
enormous sums were raised by granting, for ready cash,
long leases to capitalists who would collect the rents
from the annual tenants and smaller lessees.   In the
course of these arrangements monastic lands were often
bought back by the Crown, and combined into groups
so as to facilitate the traffic.   I shall give in this
chapter a sufficient number of instances to show how
these matters were managed in Sutton, and we shall
gather from these and other sources some idea of the
kind of people that lived here or were influential in
the neighbourhood.

More interesting, however, than these traffickings, is
the subject of the division of the land amongst the
small freeholders and farmers.   The common people
still worked as their forefathers had done, under the
system that had descended to them with no great
modification from the ancient village community.   But
as the details of the agricultural arrangements are
intricate and extend over a long period, I shall give
them in a separate chapter under the heading of " Old-
fashioned Farms."

The estates, once belonging to the Suttons, that had
been acquired by Cardinal Wolsey as an endowment
for his College in Oxford are described in the following extracts from a document dated September 16th,
1649, in the time of Sir Philip Constable.   It is
entitled " Surveys of most part of Sir Marmaduke Con-

10

stable's estate." The portion that relates to Sutton, Southcoats, Atwick, and Rollstone, no doubt includes as much of the share of one of the three heiresses of Sir Thomas de Sutton as remained at the date when it was drawn up. It will be observed that certain of the tenants are liable not only for substantial rents in money, but for the ancient "services" in capons to be annually delivered to the lord of the manor. The other tenants are liable only for "Free Rents" of very insignificant amounts in respect of lands that are called their own.* These were freeholds of inheritance.

LANDS IN HOLDERNESS.

	The severall Rentalls of Lands in Atwick, Sutton, Sutcotes, Summergangs, Stoneffery and Rouston in Holdernes as ffolloweth, viz. :—	There yearely rents.			There rent Capons.
		£	s.	d.	
The Rentall of Atwicke.	George Brand, lateMr. Hunts	15	0	0	
	Richard Wetherells, late Francis Keyleys - - -	09	0	0	
	Raiph Person - - -	11	0	0	
	Totall	35	0	0	
The Rentall of Stoneffery. †	Thomas Hay of Stoneffery -	02	13	4	2
	John Crosse - - -	10	01	08	2
	William Watson - - -	01	14	08	2
	Steven Snaith - - -	02	00	00	2
	Totall is	16	09	08	
The Rentall of Rouston. ‡	Mr. Trusley - -	04	00	00	

* I am indebted to the Right Honorable Marmaduke Constable Maxwell, Lord Herries, for permission to make use of some of his family records relating to this property.

† In MS. erroneously called Atwicke.

‡ Rolleston or Rowlston is returned in Domesday as Roolfestone, a soke of Mappleton. It is written Rowton, Rouston, Roston, and Roxton, in documents of the sixteenth and seventeenth centuries. Edward Truslove, the son of Edward Truslove of Mappleton, married Alice, daughter and co-heir of Thomas Mayne of Rolleston. Their son, Mayne Truslove, is the "Mr. Trusley" above mentioned. This property, the lordship over which had been acquired by the Suttons, de-

		£ s. d.	
The Rentall of Sutton, Sutcots, and Summer-games.	Richard Wright for his owne and John Squires - -	06 10 00	4
	Mr. Miller for his grassing in Sutton and Sutcotes, with Sir Philip Constable's part of the Royalties and Perquisites of Courts in Sutton and Sutcotes - - -	15 05 08	
	James Johnson - - -	03 06 08	2
	William Gibson for his ffarme in Sutton - - - -	02 13 04	2
	Thomas Bachous - - -	01 06 08	2
	Anthony Meadley - - -	01 00 00	2
	Widdow Stevenson - -	00 03 04	2
	Raiph Sowden late William Kides - - -	04 15 00	2
	Robert Miles late Richard Lophames - - -	02 13 04	2
	Robert Harpham - - -	00 12 00	
	Thomas Harrison - - -	03 10 06	2
	Michaell Richardson - -	12 00 00	2
	Totall is	53 16 06	

Free Rents belonging Sutton.

	£ s. d.
Payd by the bylawmen off Sutton ffor the West Raw being our owne land - -	00 01 05½q *
Payd by Richard Hudson ffor Thornton House it being Mr. Langdale's land - -	00 00 4½
The heires of Peacock payd by John Richard of Sutton for his owne land - -	00 05 01 q
The heires of Ingram † payd by George Harwood of Hull - - - -	00 00 02½q
The heires of Hilliard which were Sophers now Josua Blades of Hull - - -	00 00 2⅓

scended through the heiress of the Trusloves to the family of Brough of Rowlston Hall.   It now belongs to Lieut.-Col. Haworth-Booth, of Hull Bank Hall, to whose mother it was left by her aunt, the widow of the last of the Broughs.

* For quadrans = a farthing.

† Probably of the same family as the Owgrams, formerly of Stoneferry.

	£ s. d.
Carr side payd by the Bylaw-men of Sutton - - -	oo oo o2
Charter House payd by Robert Woofe out of Robert —— lands - -	oo oi o2½q
Payd by the gisters * of Sumergangs - - -	oo oi o5½
Totall is	oo o9 o5 oo

Out Payments.

Payd ffor a ffree Rent for all the lands in Holdernes yearely at Michælmas -   oo ii oo

And soe the whole yearely Rents and ffree Rents of all the said lands in Holdernes due to Sir Phillip Constable, deducting the xi^s thereout payd ffor a ffree rentis *de claro ultra* the Rent capons   109 o4 o7 Sir Philip Constable is a third Lord in Sutton and Sut-cotes, and hath a third part thorow all there, none knowing their owne. And in the other places he hath one † the particulars in the Rentall thereof expressed

The expression "the West Raw being our owne land," seems to indicate that a share at least in the old disused road or bank between Foredike and Sutton-dike was held by Constable as a freehold within the manor. This will more clearly appear under the names of Thomas Watson and George Bromflete, who within a few years became successively owners of this portion of the manor.

We have seen that John Dudley, Duke of Northumberland, became the superior lessee of the Abbey of Meaux, with its meadows and

---

* Those who superintended the ajistment or stocking of the pastures. The same as " Bylawmen " in Sutton.

† Oné = only.

pasturage in Sutton.   In the third year of Elizabeth, he having died ingloriously, his son, Robert Dudley, Knight of the Garter, Keeper of the Horse, and afterwards Earl of Leicester, received a grant of the same lands, subject to Lancelot Alford's lease for twenty-one years, and to a lease in reversion for a like term, granted to Sir John Bourne, one of the Queen's principal secretaries.   We need not suppose that Sutton saw anything of the splendid courtier Leicester, who, though his father had been beheaded for a traitor, and his grandfather had been beheaded for a knave, and though he himself was under strong suspicion of crimes that deserved a like fate, remained for life the favourite of the Queen, and even kept the esteem of many of the most scrupulous men of his time.   Nor would Sir Christopher Hatton, who succeeded him, nor the Consorts of the Stuart Kings, on whom these lands were successively settled, trouble themselves much about the property, so long as they received punctually the rents payable by their under-lessees.

The farms that had belonged to Meaux Abbey, but which were kept separate from the pasturage, continued to be let upon leases until 1609.   On the Patent Roll for 7th James I., there are grants by writ of Privy Seal of many properties in different counties to Sir Baptist Hicks, a rich merchant and an Alderman of London,* with several others who had together paid into the Exchequer £75,000, also to other companies, consisting partly of the same, men who had advanced £67,000.   Amongst these properties are the farms mentioned in the last chapter, formed out of the six and three-quarter oxgangs which the monks had kept of the legacy of Amandus, the son of Sayer, and in respect of which the Alfords claimed the old tribute of hens.

The new gentry attracted towards Sutton by the dispersal of the manorial and monastic lands, remained

* The first Viscount Camden.

here until the latter part of the seventeenth century. Their personal history and their family connections are of some interest, and their wills and other records afford much information as to the way in which their lands were held by the farmers of two or three centuries ago. I shall therefore group these details under the names of the families that were most influential in the parish.

The Alfords and Trusloves.   Lancelot Alford, Esquire, of Meaux Abbey and of Beverley, whose early acquisition of monastic lands has been noticed, died in 156⅔, and was buried in Beverley Minster. He had acquired amongst other property the piece of old enclosed land adjoining Marfleet, called the Oxlands, which is probably the same as "Cothecroft," named in some of the old charters.   By his will (proved at York, 5 Aug., 1563), he left, amongst many other legacies, to his brother Peter of Sutton, twenty pounds, and to John Truslove of Wawne, twenty pounds ; to Thomas, Earl of Northumberland, ten stud mares ; and to "my lady his wife," four colts.*   Each man of his kindred, present at his funeral, was to have a gown, a hood, a coat and a cap of black cloth, and every woman a black gown.   His menservants were to have coats of black cloth, also some of his workmen at Wawne, "and they with the same gownes on their backs to bear Torches at my funeralls."   He left his "oxe lands" and his other lands in Sutton to his nephew, John Alford, but his nephew Lancelot, then at school at Beverley, was his executor and principal legatee.   They were the sons of his brother John, who lived at Holt.

Peter Alford of Sutton died in 1566.   His will directs that he shall be buried in the chancel of the church.   Amongst his legacies are a young

---

* After the death of Dudley, Duke of Northumberland, the earldom of North-umberland was revived in favour of Thomas Percy, 1st May, 1557.   Earl Thomas was beheaded in 1572, for treason against Elizabeth, and died asserting the Pope's supremacy.   Lancelot Alford, although he did not scruple to hold church lands, would not be without sympathy with the form of religion in which he had been reared.   He had a brother, "Sir" William Alford, a priest, to whom he left two silver bowls.

horse called "a colte stagge," of a brown bay colour
with two white feet.   He left to his godson, Edward
Truslove, a young cow called "a halflinge whye,"
to John Truslove's wife, a feather bed, a pair of
sheets, and a pair of blankets.   In disposing of
his sheep, he left to each of John Truslove's children
"two yowes," and to another person "one yowe
hogge." A gray "meare" called Bonny was left to
another of his friends.   The happy notion of distributing household goods and farm stock, as tokens of
remembrance, amongst relatives and friends is
observed in most wills of this period.

Lancelot Alford, the younger, of Meaux Abbey,
succeeded also to the property of his brother John.
On the 15th May, 1596, a lease of the meadows and
pasturage which the abbey had held in Sutton, with
certain lands in Meaux, was granted direct from the
Crown to himself, his son William, and to Margaret,
William's daughter, for their lives.   In 1603, when
James I. was making his first progress towards London,
Lancelot Alford was one of the crowd of country
gentlemen who assembled at York to receive him,
and he was one of a considerable number who then
received the honour of knighthood.   In 1608, Sir
Lancelot Alford was a member of Parliament for
Beverley.   His son, Sir William, who had also been
knighted early in the reign of James I., administered
to his estate 15th Sept., 1616.

Sir William Alford was High Sheriff of Yorkshire in 1618, and was elected member of Parliament for Beverley in 1625 and 1627.   Having married
Ann, the daughter and heiress of Sir William
Knowles, of Bilton, he lived there, and would be a
near neighbour of his friends and under-tenants in
Sutton.

The last of the Alford leases lasted beyond
the middle of the seventeenth Century.   Margaret,
the daughter of Sir William Alford, had married

Sir R. Strickland, of Sizergh in Cumberland, and
held this property as the surviving lessee.   Her sister
Dorothy was married to Thomas Grantham, and lived at
Meaux Abbey, which her father owned and had settled
upon her.   Thomas Grantham rented the meadows and
pasturage in Meaux and Sutton.   The rent payable
to the Crown for the whole was £20 19s. 6d., with £6
for a heriot on the death of either of the lessees, but the
actual value in rent receivable by the Alfords was
£244 15s. od.   In the account of rents, the sixteen
hens receivable from eight of the farmers in Sutton in
respect of the six and threequarter oxgangs of land that
had belonged to the monks were by no means forgotten.
I shall give below the comparative values of the meadows and pasturage in this lease as they stood in 1596
and 1674 respectively.   Meanwhile, it will be interesting to learn something about the owners and their
tenants, and the system of managing the common
pastures under the Byelawmen of Sutton.

In 1653, when dame Margaret Strickland was the
only surviving lessee, the lands being let to her
brother-in-law, Thomas Grantham, a case was pending
in the Court of Exchequer between him, as the
complainant, and William Dalton, gentleman, with
Thomas Brocke, Robert Miles, William Munby, John
Johnson, Thomas Hodgson, Edward Plummer, and
Roger Baley the defendants.   Dalton was then the
chief resident in Sutton, the rest were farmers, and the
dispute was as to the extent to which Thomas
Grantham could take advantage of the very extensive
pasturage in the West Carr and the open arable fields,
which had been enjoyed by the monks, and had been
granted to the Alfords.   The defendants insisted that,
by the custom of the manor, no man ought to enjoy
any house-common, land-common, or grass-common,
except an inhabitant " down-lying and up-rising " in the
parish.   That this was the general rule appears to
have been admitted, but Grantham relied upon the

lease from the Crown as over-riding this custom. Evidence was taken by commission at the house of Tristram Nettleton at Wawne, 19th Oct., 1653 (Exchequer Commission, Michs. term 1653. Yorks. 22.) when several old men then or formerly living in Sutton were examined.

The complainants' witnesses agreed that Sir William Alford had stocked the West Carr sometimes with five or six hundred sheep, and as many as twenty horses, and had underlet this pasturage to other persons who, however, appear to have lived in Sutton. His horses were sometimes impounded by the Byelawmen when they "drove" the West Carr, because the horses had not been shown to them when they were turned in. They were, however, always released without paying "pounsell." Stephen Snaith, probably the leading farmer in Sutton, said that, on complaint having been made about twenty years ago to Sir William Alford in respect of his horses, he said he had right to only eight horse-gates "which belonged to Crabcoate-close * in the manor," and blamed his servant for putting in seventeen, as wrong was thereby done to the inhabitants. He wished the excess to be impounded that those who put them in might suffer, and the horses were thereupon removed. The Alfords and their undertenants had also turned their stock out into the Carrside and North Fields in average time.

It seems clear that the Alfords had stocked the pasturage more or less, though they were non-resident, but it was suggested by the defendants that they were too important to be kept in check by the inhabitants. One witness called by the defendants, said that Sir Lancelot and Sir William Alford "were ancient and potent men of great power, and, in their lifetime, most of the inhabitants of Sutton were poor men of mean and small estate." But Lancelot

* The old name of the narrow strip of meadow between Hirncott and Southowscott is Crab-close.

Truslove, then of Beverley, said that the Alfords were knights and honest gentlemen in the country, and the inhabitants were some poor and some rich men, and he was an impartial witness called by both parties.

I suspect that the result was unfavourable to Grantham's claim, for twenty-one years afterwards little or no evidence could be got as to his having turned sheep into the West Carr or the arable fields. The times were, however, very bad, and it is questionable whether the pasturage was worth anything to the owners of common rights, who had no arable land that would enable them to turn the pasturage to account.

The Alford lease must have expired on the death of Lady Strickland soon after this evidence was taken. In 1674, the lands in Meaux and Sutton were held by Mrs. Cornewallis, a widow, whose husband had held them under Queen Catherine, the wife of Charles the Second. A survey made on the 16th February, 1674, by Sir Robert Hildyard, Knight and Baronet, Sir Hugh Bethell, Knight, and Charles Vaux, Gentleman,* by direction of John Hall, Esq., Her Majesty's Surveyor-General, enables us to compare the values of these properties in 1596, and in 1674. The chief portion of the Sutton property was the two neighbouring pieces of enclosed land called South-house Cott and Hern Cott, which the monks had so eagerly sought to acquire and to keep.

In 1598, the "garth or piece of pasture ground where formerly stood a house called Southhouse-coat," containing an acre, was valued at 16s. per annum, and the three other closes, measuring 32 acres, were valued at £25 12s. od. But in 1674 the whole was worth only £21 10s. od. In 1598 the two closes "where Hern-coat lately stood," measuring 27 acres, were worth £21 12s. od., but in 1674 they were worth only £15. William Munbie and Mr. Cocke, whose descendants became landowners in Sutton, appear as under-tenants.

* Town Clerk of Hull, and steward of the Manor of Sutton.

Notwithstanding the idea conveyed at both these dates that South House Cott had disappeared, it is shewn in Joseph Osborne's map of the river Hull, made in 1668, as a house with two stacks of chimneys. It was probably ruinous while in the hands of lessees under the Crown.

> The sheepcot in the Ings called Redd-Coat, or Red-Cott, with pasturage for 760 sheep in the West Carr, was valued in 1598 at £19. In 1674 no information could be got that it had been let for twenty years past or at all. But the Red-Cott garth now let for 10s.
>
> There were 42 acres of meadow spread about in the Carr fields in "Sougham," valued in 1598 at £21 5s. 0d., worth in 1674 only £12 12s. 0d.
>
> A sheepcot called Billy Coat, or Billicott was "decayed and gone" in 1598, and valued at nothing, but in 1674 the "coat-garth" was let for 13s. 4d.
>
> Allotments of meadow in the Ings, amounting to 59 acres, valued in 1598 at 10s. per acre, were worth 9s. in 1674.
>
> Pasturage for 300 sheep in a common in Sutton fields was valued in 1598 at £7 10s. 0d., but nothing could be learned about this item in 1674.
>
> The pasturage for 300 sheep in Sutton Sads, or Salts, was worth £25 in 1598, but only £20 in 1674.
>
> The perquisites of sixteen hens were worth 8d. per hen in 1598, but only 4d. in 1674. This is the last entry that I have found of payments or "services" in kind.

An entry occurs in the survey of 1674 of four hundred sheepgates in Summergames, which were forgotten to be given in. Upon account of the charge of the highways thereupon, they had not been stocked by Mr. Grantham for many years, nor by Mr. Cornewallis since his lease began. Among the out-goings to which the property was liable in 1674, was a year's assessment for lands in Sutton, £4 ; the constable's tax, £1 0s. 10d. ; the overseers of the poor, £1 0s. 10d. ; and for dressing or cleaning out the fleets or ditches belonging to the Salts and meadows of Sutton, £4.

The Alfords were connected by marriage with the Holderness family of Truslove or Truslowe, branches of which held good estates at Mappleton, and in other places, one branch being, for a time, closely connected with Sutton. They had been for many years in possession of a leasehold property called Keingley, close to the ferry at Wawne. In 1559, Katherine Truslow of "Waughan," widow, left to one friend a "gimber lamb," and to another, a red petticoat, which she had worn commonly on holy days.

Edward Truslove, Gentleman, whose will was made 13th September, 1609, and proved 30th January following, lived in the Rectory House at Sutton, but kept in his hands the lease of Keingley. He left to his wife (Frances, the daughter of Edward Alford), his interest in the Rectory of Sutton, as he held it from Sir Richard Mompesson and Lady Elizabeth, his wife. He left to his wife also the lease of Keingley, with reversion to his son John. Amongst other legacies to his wife, were half the household stuff in his house at Sutton, certain horses and draught oxen, his greatest silver salt, his greatest silver bowl, and his gilded bowl standing upon "Artemes of Lyons." Between two of his daughters he left his chamber at London with the goods there. One daughter got twenty kine and a bull, and another had the lease of his lands in Sutton, which he bought of Francis Hunt. A child, not yet born, was to have (if a boy) lands in Sutton, bought of Richard Wray, late belonging to Thomas Hodgsonn or Hutchinson.

The lease of the Rectory was no doubt granted by Mompesson, but, under the date of 1601, there is a fine which records the acquisition by Queen Elizabeth from Richard Mompesson, Esquire, and wife, of the site of the late College of Sutton, lands in Sutton, the Rectory, and all the tithes of the same. From an entry upon the Patent Roll of the 7th year of James I., it seems that this property had been held by Lancelot Alford, Esquire, and by his nephew John Alford. There, probably, Peter Alford lived.

We have here another instance of the grouping of many such lands together in order to raise large sums of money for the use of the King. It is a grant (at the petition of Sir William Ryder, Sir Baptist Hicks, and several of their associates who had paid large sums into the Exchequer) to Francis Morrice and Francis Philips of London, Gentlemen, of properties in several counties. Amongst them is the manor of the Rectory of the church or chapel of Sutton, with the site of the college and Mansion house of the Collegiate Church of Sutton, "formerly in the holding of Lancelot Alford, and now or lately in the holding of John Alford," also all glebe, tithes, and other commodities in Sutton, Sudcotes, Marfleete or elsewhere. The annual value is set down at £25 19s. 4d.* beyond the following annual payments :

To the parish of Sutton for collection of tithes - £0	6	8
To the curate of Sutton as salary - - - 10	0	0
To the Archbishop for a perpetual pension - - 0 13		4
To the Dean and Chapter of York do. - - 0	6	8
To the Vicar of Wawne for oblations - - - 0 01		0

£11 16 8

This grant was sealed September 25th, 1609, about the date of the death of Edward Truslove. The value of the curacy at this time is noteworthy.

Edward Truslove was evidently a man of good position, having his "chamber" in London, and counting the Alfords among his relations and chief friends. His widow married Lancelot, one of the Mappleton Truslove's, † and they left Sutton, probably for Kengley, which young John Truslove was to inherit. Of John Truslove's family we shall hear again in connexion with Stoneferry.

* This was, I assume, the amount payable by the underlessee, who would collect a much larger sum.

† Lancelot, the brother of Mayne Truslove, was living at Beverley in 1653. He was then about 67 years of age, and had been for 42 years away from Sutton, where he had lived for 24 years.

The Daltons.   The man who did most in gathering together the fragments of the ancient manors in Sutton was Thomas Dalton, thrice Mayor of Hull, a " Merchante of the Staple and Venturer." His ancestors for three generations had been eminent merchants and Mayors of Hull, and his descendants were to reach these and higher dignities. In 1563-1564, he bought of Sir Henry Gate, certain lands in Sculcoates, Sutton, Stoneferry and Drypool, part of the possessions of the dissolved Carthusian Monastery in Sculcoates, the ownership of which we have traced from Benedict de Sculcoates, the contemporary of Sywardus de Sutton.*

In 1564, he bought from Thomas Fairfax and Thomas Boynton, their shares in the Manors of Sutton and Rowstone, with twenty messuages and twenty cottages in Stoneferry and Drypool. In 1565, he bought from Henry Hastings, Earl of Huntingdon, " The Manor of Sutton," and twenty-four messuages and a windmill in Sutton and Stoneferry. This was the ancient berewic of St. John of Beverley, mentioned in Domesday, and now, the ancient manor and the berewic were again getting, to some extent, into the hands of the same proprietor.

In 1568, Dalton bought from Sir John Constable, four messuages and three cottages in Sutton, Stoneferry, and elsewhere. In 1569, he bought of Matthew Quintin, " five parts of a sixth part" of the manor of Sutton and Sutcoates, sixteen messuages, eight cottages, and free fishing in the Marr and Fyllyng, in all which St. Quintin had a life interest. † In 1565,

---

* This, and the following items, relating to the Tudor period, are taken from the Yorkshire Fines, compiled by Mr. Collins, and printed by the Yorkshire Archæological Society. Areas and numbers are only given in general terms sufficiently large but with no approach to accuracy.

† The Fyllyng, or Filling, was a piece of water in which nets could still be drawn for fish when the Marr was diminished by drainage. The Corporation of Hull regularly exercised their manorial right of fishing in it until the open fields and carrs were enclosed in 1768.

Henry Curdeux acquired from Thomas Grey one-eighth part of the manors of Sutton and Sudcoates, and of twenty messuages and fourteen cottages in Sutton, Drypool, and Stoneferry, and free fishing in the Marr and Fyllyng. In 1547, Dalton bought from Curdeux lands which would be part or the whole of this property.

Thomas Dalton is described as of Hull and Sutton. Besides the Hastings Manor or Berewic, he seems to have acquired a large share in the Manor of Sutton, and although he had other houses, may have occupied at some time a manor house upon one of these properties. He died in 1590, and was buried in the chancel of Holy Trinity Church at Hull, where a tombstone containing a rude representation of himself with his two wives and their children, testifies to his piety and charity.

Within a few years after his death, his sons, Robert and Philip, were conveying small portions of the Sutton property, but Robert Dalton and his descendants continued to hold a very substantial estate. He married Elizabeth, the daughter and co-heir of Ralph Constable, of North Park in Burstwick, and died in 1626. The Hastings Manor is said (Inq. Ct. of Wards, Bdle. 46, No. 97) to have been held under Constable. His son, Thomas Dalton "of Swine," died in 1639, holding the Hastings Manor under the King (62, No. 23) and the other Sutton properties.

John Dalton, Esquire, "of Swine, etc.," the son of Thomas, was a man of wealth and position, whose importance has scarcely been recognised by local historians. He entered his pedigree at Dugdale's visitation in 1665, he then being forty-two years old and unmarried. He kept up the family connexion with the Constables by marrying Mary, the daughter of the Earl of Cardigan, and widow of John Constable, Viscount Dunbar of Burton Constable. He owned, amongst other properties away from Sutton, the

Berewic or Manor of Nuttles in Burstwick, and lived there in considerable style.

In 1668, he bought of the Hull Corporation their sixth part of the Castle Hill and Ring, and the Hall Court Walls, which he had previously rented of them. In 1675, he bought of the Corporation the sixth part of Spring Hill House and Close, and he also acquired their moiety of the Mair or Mayer Close, which, if in Sutton, would extend down to the Marr. There are still two or three springs in the grounds sloping from the village down to the East Carr.

John Dalton and George Bromflete are said by Poulson to have been joint lords of the manor, but they were really owners of separate portions of it. Bromflete acquired a share in the manor under the will of his uncle, Thomas Watson of Stoneferry, and none of the owners of shares, except the Corporation of Hull, John Dalton, and George Bromflete, seem to have thought fit to assert their rights. In 1676, Dalton and Bromflete granted licence to the Mayor and Burgesses for setting up stakes and posts on the margin of the river for mooring vessels that were drawn above the North Bridge. In the Corporation Records the place is called Sutton-side, but this space between the bank and the stream was commonly called the Growths, a name that has been changed into the Groves, and now applies to the whole district between the river and the Sutton Drain. In 1692, the Corporation, with Dalton and Bromflete, challenged the right of the Byelaw-men of Sutton, who managed the pasturage, to collect the rents of certain cottages that had been built upon the waste.

John Dalton of Nuttles, Esquire, who, in his will, makes no mention of Swine, died in 1685. He bequeathed Nuttles, with other properties, to his wife, "Lady Mary Viscountess Dowager Dunbar," for her life. Amongst these were four farms in Sutton and Stoneferry, two of which were let at ten pounds, and two at twenty pounds a year. Besides the reversion of these estates, he left to his brother Thomas properties which he described as "my mannor of Hastinges and all my other mannors and parcells of mannors in Sutton and Stoneferry with all my lands tenements and hereditaments in Sutton and Stoneferry and also the inheritance of all my lands and rights in Bransholm." Cattle-gates in Bransholm are distributed amongst the smaller legatees, Mary Andrews getting ten gates for her life, "in case she comes (continues?) to be my Lady's Chambermayd." The will was proved at York by Thomas Dalton, the executor, Oct. 21, 1685, and the Viscountess, who was named as executrix, must have died about that time, for her will was proved three weeks afterwards.

With Thomas, the brother and heir of John Dalton, this branch of the family came to an end. By his will, proved 12 January, 1700, he left his estates, including his Hastings Manor and the other manors and lands in Sutton, with one exception, to his wife Elizabeth (Wytham) and her heirs for ever, "she paying one hundred pounds to Jane Wytham, my sister," who was his sister-in-law. To his servant, John Champney, he left his farm in Sutton called Headley Farm. Champney was probably a clerk or assistant.

Thus the property accumulated by the Daltons of this branch was carried into the family of Wytham or Witham of Cliffe, in the North Riding. Except the Hastings Manor, it was retained by them until it was sold to Mr. Thomas Broadley in 1768.

There was, however, also a family of Dalton actually resident in Sutton during the seventeenth century. As far back as 1598, William Dalton, of a collateral branch, was buying messuages and cottages, and his branch lived in the village in the condition of gentry for at least three generations. It will be remembered that Agnes, one of the co-heirs of Sir Thomas de Sutton, had married Sir Ralph Bulmer, and held one third of the manor. It appears that though this branch of the Daltons did not make much claim to manorial privileges, they held this share of the manor or a considerable portion of it. It was called " Boomers or Bulmers," when their property was sold in the earlier part of the eighteenth century. In 1618, Edward Dalton of Sutton, Gentleman, left to his son William, then a minor, "one great press and one little cupboard " standing in the hall of his house, and desired to be buried in the Church. In 1635, Edward, the son of William Dalton, "Generosus," was buried at Sutton. In 1658, Mr. William Dalton, Gentleman, was buried at Sutton. In 1667, William Dalton, Esquire, of Hull, Counsellor at Law, directed by will that he should be buried in the Church at Sutton. After this time the family appears to have become dispersed ; their lands being sold bit by bit down to the early part of the eighteenth century, when the manor and the remaining lands were disposed of.

The Alureds. In 1557, and again in 1559, Thomas Alured was elected a Member of Parliament for Hull. In 1561, he was Mayor. His acquisitions of land in Sutton were chiefly in or near to the Ings, and were parts of the lands of the dissolved priories of Swine and Sculcoates. In the 16th year of Elizabeth, 1574, John Alured held meadows in the Ings, and Thomas Alured held four acres in Prioress dale, with five acres in the Grimes abutting on Summergangs. In the reign of James I., Henry Alured held a bercaria or sheepcot called Suinlathes in the Ings, next to Summergangs, in or near to Hedoncroft, which the nuns of Swine had acquired in the 13th century from Sayer the third.

From the time of Elizabeth down to the time of George the Second, there were at least three or four families, besides those whom I have named, living in the parish as well-to-do people. They owned houses of a superior kind, with two or more oxgangs of land,

which they cultivated like the yeomen and farmers
around them. They must have had other occupations
or means of living. Some of them were connected
with shipping or mercantile affairs in Hull, where
they had handsome houses. In relation to Sutton,
however, they are simply described as "gentlemen," and that term is rarely omitted in deeds,
registers, or wills. In less formal documents the
prefix " Mr " distinguishes them from the yeomanry
and peasant farmers. Members of the families of
Blaydes, Cock, and Munby, held property and lived
here in this way. The lands of other owners who did
not actually live in the parish can also be identified.

William de Bursblades acquired, by his marriage with
Margaret Appleyard of Burstwick, some share in the
manors of Sutton, with Bransholm, Sudcoats, Marfleet,
and Drypool, and died in 1591. He is mentioned in
old deeds as "Gulielmus Blaydes de Sutton." Joseph
Blades of Sutton was Mayor of Hull in 1636. James
Blaydes of Sutton married Ann, the sister of Andrew
Marvel. In the eighteenth century the representatives
of the family, who called themselves shipwrights, lived
in fine houses in Hull and at Paull. Benjamin Blaydes,
who received an allotment when the parish was
enclosed in 1768, was an Alderman and twice Mayor
of Hull. He is described as lord of the manors of
Sutton, Paull, Thorngumbald, and Dimblington, but
his share in the manor of Sutton could not be very
considerable.

Early in the seventeenth century, we get another
glimpse of Magnusdaile, the little estate which the
monks had contrived to create, and struggled to retain.
On the 25th June, in the fifth year of James I., the
King, by letters patent, let to Peter Orrell, of South
Cave, one close called Magnus Daile "in Dripole
within the parish of Sutton late to the monastery of
Melsa, alias Meaux, sometime belonging," on lease for
forty years at the rent of sixty shillings, at which rent

it had been usually let, with sixteen shillings more
"for increase for the price of one sheep." By an
indenture, dated the 10th April, 1627, this close, with
the buildings thereon and all appurtenances, was
conveyed by Walter Orrell of Magnus daile, the son
of Peter, to William Popple of Hull, "Master and
Mariner," for a payment of one hundred and fifty-eight
pounds. In 1656, William Popple, Alderman of Hull,
bequeathed to his son Edmund "that house and
tenement and close wherein it standeth called Mauns-
dale or Magnusdale then in the occupation of Peter
Tocke and Richard Tocke, together with two acres
and a half of meadow in Sutton Ings in a place called
Larkin (or Parkin) Nooke." The freehold must have
been acquired by Alderman Popple ; it was afterwards
held by the Hodgsons.

John Truslove and the Watsons. In October, 1650,
John Truslove of Keingley, Wawne, the son, or
grandson, of Edward Truslove of Sutton, married, at
Drypool Church, Elizabeth, the daughter of Thomas
and Margaret Watson of Stoneferry. Thomas Watson
had died three years before, desiring to be buried near
to his mother in Sutton Church, and John Spoffard,
the former minister, was to have twenty-two shillings
for his funeral sermon.* He left two pounds to be
divided amongst poor widows in Sutton and Stoneferry,
"and them y* hath decreped husbandes y* cannot labor."
Besides other small legacies, he left to his son-in-law,
Robert Bromflete, four pounds ten shillings, and also
a hundred pounds in full of his wife's portion, and to
his son, Thomas, "the paceing 'earing filly." In 1661,
his widow followed him, and wished to be buried near
to her husband. Though they seem to have been of
good position, their wills give no indication of wealth.
But their son, Thomas Watson, Gentleman, lived at the
White House in Stoneferry, and, dying in 1665, left a

* John Spoffard signed the parish registers as curate from 1625 to 1633. He had
a son, John, baptised 16th April, 1626.

considerable estate. There is sufficient reason for believing that this property was the share of one of the heiresses of Sir Thomas de Sutton, probably Constance, which had been held by Cardinal Wolsey, and the Constables. Amongst other legacies, he left to his nephew, George Brumflete, the land called " West Raw," with all the Royalties of Courts, privileges, etc., thereto belonging. He wished to be buried in the Church near to his seat. His most trusted executor was his friend Charles Vaux, the Town Clerk of Hull, who was also a landowner in Stoneferry. He may have acquired his estate by trade at Hull. The bulk of his property was settled on his widow for life, without any further directions as to its disposal. It was therefore divided between his sisters as " shift lands," Elizabeth, the wife of John Truslove, receiving a considerable share. On 1st August, 1676, " Johannes Truslove Generosus de Stoneferry " was buried at Sutton.* The only legacies mentioned in his will are twenty shillings to each of his daughters and forty shillings to each of their husbands. The residue is left to his wife. He desired to be buried in the Church near his own seat. His widow (described in her will as Elizabeth Truslove of Hull) survived until 1690, and divided her White House farm between her children and grandchildren in three shares, which shares were bought in 1698 by Mrs. Anne Watson and her mother, and now form part of the Watson's Charity Estate. Elizabeth Truslove left the remainder of her lands between her two daughters, Margaret Dickinson and Frances Stather, and, in 1709, Margaret's share in this part also was bought by Ann Watson, who lived at the White House until her death in 1721.† Elizabeth Truslove left to her daughter, Margaret

---

* Another John Truslove was churchwarden, 1684-5. There were Trusloves in Wawne eighty years later.

† The White House was the principal house in Stoneferry. The very small portion that remains is the oldest structure in the parish except the Church. I shall have more to say about it.

Dickinson, a messuage and close in Drypool, which messuage had been lately demolished, and the ground taken from her upon the making of the citadel or fortifications near Drypool. She also desired to be buried in Sutton Church.

These old wills disclose one feature of curious interest. With very few exceptions, every testator arranges for burial within the Church. John Truslove and his wife, her brother, father, mother, and grandmother, with four generations of the resident Daltons, lie there no doubt, as well as John and Thomas de Sutton, with yeomen like John Hodgson and Nicholas Squire, and a hundred wardens and chaplains of the college.* There also lie six generations of the leading parishioners, who, since John Truslove's time, have played their parts and have passed away. The thought of them seems to connect us with those old times, and to enhance the solemnity of the place. But let us not forget their more humble contemporaries in the churchyard, whose labours are unrecorded though the fruits of them cannot be altogether lost.

NOTE.—In the last chapter I expressed some uncertainty as to the Manor which had descended in the family of Hastings, and had been held originally under the Archbishops as of their College of St. John of Beverley by the service, in 6 Henry IV., of a peppercorn, but which was said, in the first Richard III., to be under the lord of Holderness, by a service unknown. It appears that the family of Hastings held one or more shares in the Manor of the Suttons, in addition to the berewic, and this may account for the discrepancy. There is a Fine (York 3, Rich^d II., No. 56) by which Ralf de Hastings, Chivaler, the

---

* Simon Sellar, the warden, who died in 1443, desired to be buried in the churchyard against his mother's grave.

husband of Alice de Meaux, acquired from Thomas
Ughtred, Chivaler, for 100 marks of silver, a third part
of the Manor of Sutton, which is said to be of his
inheritance.   There were 9 messuages, 5 oxgangs, and
30 acres of land, 11 acres 1 rood of meadow, the fishing
of Sutton Marr and Swine Marr, and the ferry of the
water of Hull.   The tenants were William Bulfyne and
several others.   It may be that the Hastings family
retained this or some portion of it.   In 1548-9 (Yorkshire Fine), Francis, Earl of Huntingdon, acquired from
Thomas Saunders and wife, and John Proud and wife,
the manor of Sutton, with 20 messuages and 10
cottages with lands, 100 acres of land covered with
water, free fishing in the water called the Marre and
two fairs in Sutton.*   It is not certain that this was
retained in the family, but early in the reign of
James I., Marmaduke Constable, of Wassand, held
lands (Inq. p.m., 5 Jas. I., p^t 2, No. 121), which
comprised 2 messuages 40 acres of tillage, 10 acres of
meadow, and 20 acres of pasture in Sutton and Stoneferry of the King, and "de heredibus de Hastinges."
This appears to be distinct from the Manor of Sutton
"known as Haistinges," held in 1626 by Robert
Dalton of Sir Henry Constable of his Manor of
Burstwick, and in 1639 by Thomas Dalton of the
King as of his Honour of Albemarle.

The family of Hogge was for many years resident
in Stoneferry and in Marfleet.   In 1554, Stephen
Hogge left 3s. 4d. towards the maintenance of Stoneferry Clowe, and the like sum towards " the reparinge
of the gutters or slackes for dryving the water owte of
the lordshipp."   To his wife Sibill he left his part of
the Manor of Sutton to hold for fifteen years.   It was
then to go to his son Peter.   His son Stephen got all
" my two parts of the house in Stoneferry, wherein I
now inhabit," with two parts of Cowe close, and two
parts of three quarters land arable, with the meadow

* Sutton Feast on St. James' Day may be one of these.

appertaining thereto, and my lease which I have of Sir Marmaduke Constable. A child, then expected, was to-have, if a son, the "chimneye land, five acres of meadow in Stockdailes, a quarter of land arable, called Lordes land, a piece of ground called Lopham, with the common, and another common called Bowffin Common, and the leases of them." Failing such a child his son Edward was to have the chimneye land, Peter was to have Lopham, and Stephen would take Lordes land with the meadow. Robert Hogge, of Marflete, was appointed his attorney to execute deeds on his purchase from Mr. Constable of Clif.

Bowffin is no doubt Bulfyn, a Sutton name. The chimney land was close to Marfleet, where the Oxlands farm now is. These lands of Stephen Hogge appear to have been held from the Constables.

QUEEN ELIZABETH TO QUEEN ANNE.

Part II.

Floods over the low grounds.—The drains and their outfalls.—Scheme for a new drain.—Sutton during the Civil War.—The embankments cut.—Soldiers quartered.—Quakerism in Sutton.—Persecution of the Ellikers and their brethren.—A Quaker burial-ground.—The Parish Registers.—Arthur Harpur's gift to the poor.—Churchwardens' Accounts.—The Dog-Whipper and the Constable.—The " Visited " people.

THE condition of the lower lands in the parish, at the end of the reign of Elizabeth, may be inferred from an entry under the year 1596, in the register of the parish of Drypool.

> " Dinis the daughter of Wadworth of Stoneferie was baptized here in the water time the VI of March when they could not well pas to Sutton."

A record like this may remind us that, since the reclamation, eight hundred years ago, large areas of the Carrs and other low grounds were no better than marshes, except in dry seasons. Indeed the existence of three-fourths of the parish has always depended on the banks and drains, with the cloughs through which the waters ought to discharge into the Humber and the Hull. Any serious neglect of these outlets would soon reproduce the great tidal hollow, the Isle of Holderness, and the ancient Sudtone, with the scattered holms just showing above the water and mud. This state of things has actually been brought about to an alarming extent more than once.

Poulson gives a long list of orders and enactments respecting the ditches and cloughs Sometimes the chief outlet for drainage was sought southward into the Humber, sometimes westward into " Hull Water," every drain in Sutton having had its current reversed

Flows

once or oftener. Yet the improvement was always
small and difficult to maintain. Whenever the water
came down too plentifully from Benningholm, the Carr
drains and ditches would fill, Sutton Marr would rise
and spread, Ankedam and Langsike would flood the
lands between Sutton and Stoneferry, and the water
which ought to have gone into Swine Marr would run
deep over the roads and fields near the Salts.

It was the duty of some person or public body to
maintain each bank and drain, the great cloughs,
the stocks under the roads and the " weeriers," which
protected the banks at particular spots. Neglect was
visited with penalties, proportioned to the seriousness
of the offence. I can only give here a few extracts
from scattered records relating to the drainage, which
happen to bring out interesting facts, or to identify
some doubtful or forgotten locality.

An order of " the Queen's Magesty's Commissioners
of Sewers" made in 1602, directs that

> "Foord Dyke from Lowlands Nooke to Helpster at
> Grainings and soe to the Fish house Clow" shall be dressed,
> wood cut out of the banks, the falls of earth cast out, widened
> from Lowlands Nooke to the Grainings, and the stones cast out
> from under Foredike bridge.

This nooke, which is often mentioned, is the angle
formed by Foredike at the place now called Fox.
Helpster, or Helpston, appears to have been the name
then borne by the old Sutton dike cut along the West
Carr by Sayer the Second. This auxiliary watercourse
began twenty perches westward of Foredike bridge,
where the Sutton drain now takes off the water of
Foredike. Grainings was the name for the "fork," at
the junction of the two dikes; it is scarcely yet
obliterated.

At a Session of Sewers, held at Hedon in 1633,
it was found that a sewer in Ganstead, which had
formerly discharged its water into Swine Marr, had
been neglected, so that the water spread itself over the

Armitage, opposite to Salts house. The highways were thus made impassable, and very dangerous to travellers going from Hedon to Hull, or to Sutton. It was therefore ordered that the ancient watercourse should be reinstated. John Burnsall, in his account of Holderness, says that the Armitage was a noted place for a great confluence of water in winter time, lately made passable in the midst of winter. The Byelaw-men of Sutton were partly responsible for the condition of Cogham Clute, one of several banked watercourses that conveyed the floodwater through the low ground by the Salts.

An undated copy of a list of penalties, compiled about 1650, seems to refer to every watercourse in the parish that had to be maintained as a drain. The following items are of interest :—

> The sewer from Fairholm to the "Leade" of Cowlands (or Lowlands), and Thirty Acres, "and soe to the old Willm⁵, and soe to Dowmanlodge, and soe to the Foredike," is to be dressed with scythe and rake, and ground-scoured under a penalty of six and eight pence for every cord undone.*
>
> The New-dike in the West Carr is to be sufficiently dressed under the like penalty. New-dike Clow is to be maintained under the heavy penalty of £500.
>
> The banks at Fishhouse Raw are to be raised under a penalty of twenty shillings per cord.

The Old Williams was a piece of water in the Carr, in which the old manorial right of fishing was publicly exercised, until the Carrs were enclosed in 1768. Dowmanlodge was named from its owner, Dolman, pronounced Dowman. Persons whose names are written in each of these ways, appear as landowners in Sutton. A lodge appears to have been a shelter for cattle, one that was in or near to East Field is frequently mentioned in deeds. Newdike was a very important outlet made for Foredike, running diagonally into the river between Fish-house and Frog Hall. It is now barely to be traced. Fishhouse Raw is the

* A cord was a length of twenty-one feet.

narrow strip left between Foredike and Sutton-dyke, also called "West Raw." Another piece of land near the Salts was called a Raw, a sewer being named as running between the Raw-side and the Bilton and Marfleet closes.*

> Foredike from Cowland to "Helpston Grainings, and soe to New-dike," is to be well dressed "with sithe, and rake, and spade and shovell" before midsummer, under paine of twenty three shillings and four pence.
> Sutton "Helpston" bank from New-dike end to "grainings" is to be raised.
> The "Fillings Goate" is to be well dressed.
> The "Leade Stocke" at Stoneferry, where the road crosses Antholme dike, is to be maintained by the Byelawmen of Sutton under a penalty of three pounds, six shillings and eight pence.

It will be remembered that, in descriptions of portions of the manor, rights of fishing were always claimed in respect of the "Marre and Fyllyng." We shall hear again of the pieces of water that were so fished by those who claimed to be the lords of the manor.

The name "Goate," for an artificial watercourse, is the same as "Gout," which is equivalent to the French "Egout," a drain or sewer. Gouts Dike Drain, which was made to carry the water from the East Carr by Salts to Summergangs, is now called "Gold dike drain." But the name as applied to these Carr drains became corrupted to Coate or Coat, creating some confusion between names derived from ditches and those derived from Cots for sheep or cattle.

Amongst other orders made about 1650, the assignees of Sir William Alford are to repair the banks between the New Clow in West Carr and South-house-coate, which is Frog Hall. The Alfords had succeeded to the old liability of the monks of Meaux for the repair of the river bank here. Weeriers had to be maintained for the protection of the banks at Southfield, below Stoneferry, by the assignees of Mr. John Alured and by Edward Hogg ; at Maunsdaile

* I think this Raw was a part of Marfleet Lane.

Bridge by Elizabeth Wright, and by other landowners elsewhere. Maunsdaile Clow is to be maintained under a penalty of only £40, which does not shew that it was of very great importance—the main outlets for the drainage being then at New Dike Clough, and at Marfleet. The drain beginning at " Chimney Lands Nooke," close to the Oxlands, and running between Summergangs and Sutton Ings, as far as the new sewer at Maunsdaile, and on to Maunsdaile Clow, is to be dressed and ground-scoured, and Summergangs bridge is to be maintained. A manuscript map in the possession of Alderman Symons, dated 1668, indicates " Mausdell Clow." When in the seventh year of William III., the Corporation of Hull leased their Sutton lands to Thomas Atkinson, they included three roods of pasture in Drypool Field, near " Moundscale Clough." From it this field got the name of the Cloughfield. The modern Ordnance map shews the remains of a ditch running by the side of the Flax and Cotton mills called Mounsdale Drain, the last visible memorial of the Magnusdaile estate of Meaux Abbey. .

In June, 1708, the jury of the Middle Baliwick of Holderness, after viewing the Summergangs dike, presented, amongst others, Mrs. Ann Watson, of Stoneferry, who afterwards founded Watson's Charity, " for 30 cordes of dike undressed," for which she was threatened with a fine of a pound. And in June, Mr. Henry Cocke, of a family that had then risen to importance, was also presented with others for negligence of the like kind.

But notwithstanding stringent regulations, and the provision of new drains and cloughs, it was evident that the drainage of the Carrs in Sutton and the townships beyond required some more effectual treatment. On the 24th March, 1674, Sir Joseph Ashe who then held the Manor of Wawne, had submitted to the Mayor and Aldermen of Hull, with the other owners of portions of the Manor of Sutton, and the freeholders, a proposition to cut a new drain from Foredike to the River Hull. Though this foreshadowed the scheme afterwards carried out as the Sutton Drain which discharges into the river near to the North Bridge, it was not quite the same. They proposed to make use of the existing outlet into the river at Magnusdaile, as appears from a report made on the 8th October, 1677, by five aldermen of Hull who had been ordered to consider the matter. They had met Sir Robert Hildyard, Henry Constable, Esq., John Dalton, Esq., and others at Malmesdale Clow; they thought, however, that the project would be prejudicial. They believed that one level near Sutton might be "dreaned" by a new cut through Sutton Field going through part of Sutton Ings and through Summergames into Humber betwixt Marfleet and Drypool. Thus Sir Joseph Ashe's scheme was shelved for the time.

Early in 1639, soldiers were being quartered in all the villages round Hull. In April, 1642, the gates had been shut against King Charles. Soon afterwards he was threatening to attack the town, and strong precautionary measures were necessary. On the evening of the 12th July, the Governor, Sir John Hotham, opened the sluices and cut the banks of the Humber and the river so that the whole country round was inundated. The roads were covered and the hay crop spoiled. The tillage lay too high for inundation, but all the grass lands would lie waste for some time after the water was drained away. The damage done was incredible, and though the Parliament promised to pay compensation, little or nothing could be got from them even by their friends. But the neighbourhood generally was in favour of the King, and for many months all the villages round Hull were plundered by the soldiery.

On the 29th June, 1643, the Governor, Sir John Hotham, was deposed upon detection of his intended

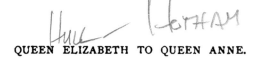

treachery, but immediately escaped. Riding out by the Beverley Road he struck off from Newland towards the river at Stoneferry, but there was no boat to take him across, and he had to proceed to Beverley, where he was captured. On the following day, an assessment of seven pounds laid upon Sutton was brought into Hull by some soldiers. On the 10th July, the Committee of Defence ordered that such of young Hotham's men and horse as had come into Hull (he also having turned traitor to the Parliament) should march to the quarters of Sir Thomas Fairfax and Sir Henry Fowler at Sutton and Stoneferry, to be employed by them.* We may imagine the condition of village and hamlet, filled as they were, more or less, for years with soldiers whom they would have to maintain with but slender hope of recompense.

About the middle of the seventeenth century "the people commonly called Quakers" became notorious, not only because of their protests against the licentiousness of the age, but on account of the persecution to which they were subjected. Hull was one of the centres of this persecution, there were several Quaker families in Sutton, and members of the sect seem to have been scattered over the country side. There is a curious reference to them in a letter written in 1682, by John Watkinson, who was then overseer of works at the Citadel. He asks leave to visit his farm in the country, and says "I shall suffer to my great prejudice iff I be not ther, by neglect of servants and the unlawful deceits of the quakers, of which sorte of people ther is a greate many in our parish." The precise nature of the mischief here indicated may not be so clear to us as it must have been to him and his correspondent, but there can be no doubt that, to many persons, their conduct was offensive in the highest degree. It was offensive to the Presbyterians of the Commonwealth, but still more so to the

* The Hothams were executed in London in the following year.

Churchmen of the Restoration. The Quakers preferred the illegal meeting in the house of a brother to
all the services of the church. They would pay
neither church rates nor tithes. They would take no
oath nor would they remove their hats upon their
rather frequent appearances in Court. They called
the church a Steeplehouse, treated the parson to home-
truths, and called the justice a liar to his face. They
did not take any great pains to make themselves
agreeable to their ungodly neighbours, and they took
no pains whatever to avoid the punishment of their
offences. The penalties actually inflicted upon
Quakers in and near to Hull were set down in minute
detail by Joseph Besse in his " Sufferings of the
Quakers," and there are books in the possession of the
Society of Friends in Hull which give the sufferings
in this locality in greater detail.*

There could be no difficulty in recognising the
Quakers, for they affected a peculiar garb. If they
appeared in the streets of Hull the constables would,
without ceremony, beat them with an oaken cudgel or
a knotted stick until the blood flowed, their limbs
were maimed, or the stick broke. If the justice
before whom they were haled did not think them
worth more serious notice he would turn them out to
the mob that was waiting to pelt them out of the town.
At one time a number of them were locked up for
twenty hours un-fed in a bare room in Hull, and others
were kept for weeks in quarters so filthy as to
jeopardise their lives. The more serious cases were
passed on from one parish constable to another till
they got to York, where the prison in the Castle was
full of their brethren, and there was reasonable
apprehension that they might not leave it alive.

In the year 1659, because William Elliker of Sutton

* I have to express my acknowledgments to the officers of the Society for
permission to consult these books, and to Dr. A. B. Wilson-Barkworth for the
information in his possession on the subject.

refused to pay eight shillings and sixpence towards the repairing of the steeple-house, he was visited by Richard Blaker and George Wetwand, steeple-house officers, with Peter Tock, constable, who seized a bacon flitch which was sold for twenty-six shillings, also two chines worth one shilling and sixpence. On the thirteenth day of twelfth month 1660, William Elliker, Laurence Elliker, and Thomas Elliker, of one family and brethren, Edward Barker, John Twyman, and John Plummer, all of Sutton, with seven others, being peaceably met together at Sutton to wait upon the Lord, the constables of the town came without any warrant and commanded them to depart, and so forthwith had them to Hull before Anthony Gillbe, Deputy Governor, who refused to meddle with them. Then they brought them before Hugh Lister, who said if they would take the oath of allegiance they might have their liberty, but they refused to swear ; then he dismissed them for the time. But on the fifth day of the same week, upon a warrant issued by him, they were brought before him and Robert Hildyard, who tendered them the oath, and on their refusing to swear, committed them to York Castle. On the second day of second month, 1661, one of them, Peter Calf or Caiph, died ; the rest were released a week afterwards.

The Ellikers were constant sufferers. In the same year they, with Grace Richardson, Ann Burne, Edward Barker, John Twyman, and John Barron, all of Sutton, suffered by the seizure of their goods for steeple-house rates amounting generally to no more than three shillings, and goods worth thrice the sum demanded were taken from them. These small amounts seem to indicate that the sufferers were not of the farming class, but rather of the class of labourers or small traders living probably close to Hull. Peter Tock, or Tocke, the constable, belonged to that part of the Parish. But William Elliker, whose church-

12

rate amounted to eight shillings and sixpence, appears to have been an exception. In 1664 he shared with two others the tenancy of the pasture ground of South-house cott under Mrs. Cornewallis at a rent of twenty-one pounds, ten shillings.

The manuscripts above-mentioned exceed Joseph Besse's Book in Quaker-like precision. According to their account, Constable Richard Bishop used his cudgel with all the strength he had "fetching the stroke over his shoulder as a man doth when he is hewing down a tree." They give more indications of Quakerism in the class of farmers, as the following details will show :—

In 1660, Thomas Clarkson, of "Pfarom House" suffered for being peaceably met with others. If he lived at Fairholm beyond Bransholm, he was a farmer of good position. In the same year, John Twinam, refusing to swear at ye Towne Court of Sutton, Charles Vaux, being Steward, fined him 5s., for which he had taken from him five putber dishes worth ten shillings, by John West the Bailife. In 1664, John Barron lost a yearling calf worth £1, 6s. 8d., for the same cause. Wm. Elliker denying to pay John Renholds one shilling and fourpence, for Clarke wages, as he calls it, Goslin Richardson took two sheep worth 10s., and returned nothing again. Others suffered the loss of sheep for the same offence, but pewter dishes were commonly taken.

In 1663, William and Thomas Elleker, being summoned by William Cannum, Steeple-house Warden, to go to the Steeple-house on ye first day, and refusing, William Canum, and Thomas Hodgson, by a warrant, had them before Hugh Lister, who demanded twelve pence apiece, and they refusing to pay it, he granted a warrant for the Wardens to levy twelve pence apiece, for which they took a pan worth 5s., of which "they would 'a Returned threepence." Others who refused in like manner to go to Church on Sunday lost pans or pewter dishes of similar value, all refusing to touch the trifling sums offered to be returned.

In 1665, William and Lowrance Elleker, being peacably met together at a meeting in Sutton amongst the Lord's people, had to go to York Castle for seven days, with a threat of banishment.*

* There must have been much division in families over these questions. At Easington, William Blashell, as constable, was seizing cows, worth three pounds, from farmers who refused to bear arms or to pay taxes for maintenance of arms, and Francis Blashell, a frequent sufferer, lost a cow for refusing to pay the clerk. The journeys of George Fox through Holderness, recorded with many interesting details in his diary, will account for the strong footing which his Society gained here.

The Quakers had certain burial grounds used exclusively for their own people. One of these was in the parish of Sutton, where the curious may still find it wedged in amongst the houses off Hodgson Street, in the Groves. Of three flat stones that remain, the oldest is thus inscribed, " Here lyeth the body of Eliz., the wife of Ant⁰· Wells, of Kingston-upon-Hull, merchant, who departed this life the 28th day of the 6th month, 1676." That which is most recent belongs to a very different time, commemorating Leonard West, a resident in Hull, most highly respected, who died in 1854.

The curate or minister duly entered in the register all burials in Sutton, wherever they took place. On the 24th September, 1678, the wife of Thomas Richardson, of Wyton, was buried in the Quakers' burial place, James Huntley making the grave, and being witness of the burial. No affidavit that she had been wrapped in woollen according to the law, then newly passed, was brought in, but it had by mistake been sent to Swine. The burial-place was in the portion of Sutton then called Drypool, and the party responsible must have assumed that the burial ground was in the Swine portion of Drypool. On the 19th February, " Johannes Plummer de Hull Bank" in Cottingham was buried " in loco usarpato a populo vulgo dicto Quakers." In 1679, George Huntingdon, of the parish of St. Trinity, was buried " in the Quakers' burying place near Hull, in the parish of Sutton." In the same year, Isabel Elliker, of Sutton, widow, and Edward Barker (of Marton), were there buried, and the wife of William Bacchus is said to have been buried " in Sepulterio Quakerorio." With these the entries of such burials end, probably because the Quakers had begun to keep proper registers of their own. In 1680, " William Reeder of Hull Bricklayer of the parish of Sa. trennites was buered in yᵉ buering place in Stonefery in the parish of Sutton, May 15th."

If he were the same as the Quaker, William Reader,
Bricklayer, of Hull, who in 1660 was taken at a
meeting at Fishlock, near Pontefract, and sent to
prison, this entry may really refer to the Quaker
burial ground in the Groves.

There was, however, somewhere between Stoneferry and Hull, another burial ground provided for the
inhabitants of that district, from which, upon account
of the floods, access to Sutton was always difficult and
sometimes impracticable.   In 1680, the daughter of
John Gibson, of Drypole, was buried in the burying
place at the " Oute housses" in the parish of Sutton;
Richard Tocke, who rented Alderman Popple's
land at Magnusdayle, appears in the register as of
the " oute houesiss."   Other entries relate to
"the buering place of Stonefery" or a burying
place in the parish of Sutton, as distinct from the
Churchyard.

The parish registers begin in 1558, and are at first
kept in Latin.   In 1626, Johannes Spofford, curate,
makes the first entry in English.   In 1633, Dakins
Fletcher, "Minister," begins to sign the registers,
making his entries in English.   During the seventeenth
century, Latin and English alternate, and mix in a
curious way, the English being usually worse than
the Latin.   In 1636, the minister and churchwardens
sign together.

Dakins Fletcher was one of those ministers who
managed to keep their livings through the Commonwealth.   In 1649, a survey of church lands was made,
when Christopher Broadripp of Somersetshire, was
found to be the impropriator of the tithes, Richard
Alexander farming or receiving them for his benefit.
Mr. Dakins Fletcher had for his salary out of the
tithes sixteen pounds.   The value to the impropriator
was one hundred and forty pounds.   There were lands
of the value of twenty-six pounds in the hands of the
impropriator, who would not admit that they belonged

to the parson. In 1654, Thomas Renton of Stoneferry, yeoman, left five shillings to the "pastor," Mr.
Dakins Fletcher.

During the Commonwealth the registers were kept
by a person duly appointed and sworn in before a
Justice of the Peace. In 1653, John Dickinson was
sworn before Robert Overton. In 1654, John
Reynolds was sworn before Hugh Bethell. Marriages
were performed by the Justices of the Peace. From
1654 to 1656, Hugh Bethell signs the register in proof
that he has married the parties after three askings.
The Restoration of Charles the Second took place in
1660, and soon afterwards " Dak. Fletcher " again
begins to sign the register. In 1674, "Dakins
Fletcher, vic. de. Sutton " was buried. In 1678,
" Georgius Wilson de Sutton" was said to be a hundred
years old. In the year 1666, an Act of Parliament,
intended principally for the encouragement of the
woollen   manufactures,   required   that   all   bodies
buried should be wrapped in a woollen material
only, and by an Act of 1678, affidavits had to be
brought to the Clergy within eight days testifying that
this had been done.*

There was some irregularity in the entries about
this period. The Register for 1681 begins with " a
note of all such as were buried since yᵉ first of August,
1678, according or contrary to yᵉ late Act of Parliament for burying in Woollen." The first note is this,
"Christopher Holmes a stranger, father to Thomas
Holmes of Stonefery, buried August yᵉ 26th, 1678.
An Affidavit was brought in August yᵉ 30th." The
obligation to bury in woollen continued nominally until
the year 1814.

* The following is a copy of such an Affidavit that was presented in an Essex
parish :—
" Richard Sweeting of Greenstead in the County of Essex maketh Oath that
Susan Sweeting of Greenstead in the County of Essex lately deceased was not put
in, wrapt, wound up, or buried but in sheep's wool only, according to the Act dated
the 28th day of May in the two and thirtieth year of the reign etc. and was buried
the same week, anno dni 1680."

This interference with the habits and inclinations of the people in a matter so important as the burial of their dead, gave intense dissatisfaction.   The rich were accustomed to wrap their deceased relatives in fine linen, and to deck them with gilded and silvered ornaments.   The prevention of such waste was one excuse for the new enactment.

In 1679, " Johannes Reynolds, Clericus Parochianus de Sutton " (the parish clerk) was buried on November the third.   Six days later, Anna Reynolds, widow, was buried.   After several burials during this and the following month, we find the entry, " Henricus Carvile, Clericus de Sutton, Sepultus January Septi."   The burials in 1679 were forty-one, a number so large that we must suspect a visitation of the plague.

The most interesting testamentary record that we have is a copy of the bequest of Arthur Harpur, which is bound up with the oldest volume of the registers. It was made early in the reign of Charles the First, when similar endowments were common, and runs as follows :—

Laus Deo, September 11, 1631.

The bequest of Mr. Arthur Harpur with directions to the Minister, Churchwardens, and Overseers of the poore of y⁰ Parish of Sutton in Holdernes, within the County of Yorke, for 12 Bybles & foure pounds in money towards the yearly relief of the poore there inhabiting.

(1)   First it is desired yᵗ the 12 Bybles be bestowed in 12 of y⁰ poorest families within the parish and that in every such family there be one yᵗ can distinctly reade the same to the rest of the family, and yᵗ, at the least once every day, there be read two Psalms and a chapter wᶜʰ I entreat the minister for y⁰ time being and his successors to see duly performed as they may conveniently.

(2)   Secondly that upon the death or removal of any such family out of the parish that the Bybles there remaining may be delivered to some other poore family as aforesaid.

(3)   Thirdly that the Minister and Churchwardens at the least once a yeare, will take view of all these Bybles and see that they be not negligently and carelessly wasted or spoyled, but that they may be preserved to posterityes (as nere as may be) that God

may have glory and his people much comfort in the reading of those Divine Scriptures for the benefit of their poore soules.

Thus much for the Bybles.

Now for the foure pounds

(1) First for the foure pounds in money to be yearly bestowed for the relief of yᵉ poore. It is desired that there may be provided every Sabath day in the forenoon 12 peny loaves of sweet and good bread of wheat to be sett in some convenient place in the Church by the Clark of the Parish, who for his care and paines therein is to have the advantage of every doozen of bread and 12ᵈ· yearly which bread is to be given after morning prayers and sermon to 12 of yᵉ most aged and impotent persons, and not to such as are young and able to labour, and take paines, and that the bread may not be used alone upon the 12 persons but' may be removed according to the necessityes of yᵉ other poore within the parish as you in your wisdomes and godly care shall think most meet. And further, that no person living in any notorious shame, after three admonitions by the Minister and Churchwardens, be suffered to have any benefitt of this poore gift.

(2) Secondly. If any of these poore appointed for the same, being of strength and health, shall absent themselves any Sabbath day from divine service and sermon (notice taken thereof and warning given twice at the least of any such person) that then that bread to be taken from them and given to such other person or persons as will diligently and conscionably repaire to the Church every Saboth day. Always provided yᵗ if any such person or persons shall be sick or lame and not able to come to divine service or sermon that then the Clarke of yᵉ parish shall cause yᵉ said bread so appointed to be sent unto them and they excused from coming to Church till God restore their health.

Now whereas the Act of Parliament and publicke Authority comande that in remembrance of God's great mercy and deliverance of this whole land from yᵗ monstrous and horrible treason of those bloudy papists Garnett and his Confederates in the Gunpowder plott every fift day of November everie good subject to God and the King should repaire to yᵉ parish Church and there hear Divine Service and Sermon wᵗʰ publique thanksgiving for the great mercy never to be forgotten. My desire is yᵗ after such a thanksgiving and worshipp of God there may be provided for 40 poore children a small dinner for which shall be allowed thirteen shillings and foure pence and for a dinner for yᵉ Minister Churchwardens and Overseers of yᵉ poore sixe shillings eight pence and to yᵉ preacher for his sermon that day sixe shillings eight pence. And it is further desired that after such dinner or repast the Minister before yᵉ children rise from

yᵉ table do read some psalme of thanksgiving and yᵗ those poore
children may sing it after him as a testimony of God's deliverance
yt day to his church and children.   And thus, hoping this poore
mite may bring glory to God, good to his poore church and
comfort to the poore soules of this my native soyle and playce of
byrth, I comend you all to the blessed protection.   In whom· I
rest in the surest bond.

    Your poore friend and loving countryman during life

                                        ARTHUR HARPUR.

After payment of these sums there would remain in
every ordinary year a balance of four pence, which
would provide for the occurrence of an additional
Sunday in some years.   But nothing is now known of
Arthur Harpur's gift, so carefully apportioned.

If we remember that this gift was made only twenty-
six years after the Gunpowder Plot, the tone of the
document will cause no surprise.   There is something
touching in the idea of this solemn feast by which the
donor expected to burn into the minds of future
generations in Sutton the memory of that dark con-
spiracy, in which the Wrights of Plowland, who might
almost be called neighbours, were so deeply implicated.

In the reign of Queen Anne the churchwardens'
accounts give many illustrations of the life of the
parish.   One of the churchwardens was elected by
the town of Sutton, and the other by the town of
Stoneferry.   Each collected his church rate, for doing
which he charged five shillings, and presented his
separate account.   Several of the items of expenditure
were simply shared between them.   The accounts
shew that the bells were rung on the Queen's birthday
and on the anniversary of the Gunpowder Plot,
when the ringers were paid six or eight shillings.   A
few years later it was agreed in parish meeting that
the churchwardens should pay every year, on the 5th
November to four ringers, two shillings per man,
and should be allowed to spend ten shillings and no
more.   In 1710, eighteenpence was spent "upon
treating some strange ministers."   In 1711, three

shillings were spent " on the two rejoicing days." In
1712, seventeen shillings were paid for bread and wine
at "the three Communions." In 1714, one of the
wardens charges for " Breed and Wine at Meeclemas,"
and the other has " Breed and Wine at tow times."
It appears that the celebrations being limited to
three, the churchwarden of Sutton was responsible for
two of them.

In several years there is mention of that ancient
officer, the Dog-whipper ; two shillings per annum being
paid to him by each churchwarden. Such entries as,
" to Wm. Dove for Whipping Doggs," " Will Doofe
for wiping doogs," and " Will Dufe 2ˢ," occur. When
all the farms in Sutton were in the village near to
the Church, every dog who missed his master on
Sunday would know where he was, and would insist
on joining him. But in addition to the duty of
struggling to prevent such intruders, the dog-whipper
had to awaken those parishioners who fell asleep
during the sermon. The anxiety of testators for the
provision of this particular portion of the service does
not seem to have been universally appreciated.*

In 1712, the sum of seven shillings and a penny was
spent " when Peace was proclaimed and at some other
times." This would be the peace afterwards ratified
at Utrecht, which has been called " just and honorable,"
but which Chatham some years afterwards called " the
indelible reproach of the past generation." These
people, however, had had their days of fasting as well
as days of rejoicing, and were tired of the war, so that a
peace of any kind might seem to them well worth a
cup of ale and a peal on the bells. There are charges

---

* It was the duty of the churchwardens to compel stragglers to go to Church,
and the constable would assist them. Sabbath-breakers and profane swearers
would be fined or set in the stocks. The constables' tax was not levied for
nothing. The constable was the visible arm of the Law. He would seize
strangers after nightfall, examine servants suspected of having run away, see that
no strangers were entertained, put a vagrant in the stocks (unless he had a pass)
or get him whipped, and search out " papist recusants," of whom there are some
traces in Sutton.

for repairs of the bells, of the lead roofs, windows, and seats, for "Luances," or refreshments for workmen, and money spent with neighbours when works were in hand.

In the autumn of 1665, the plague of London extended to many parts of the country, and no doubt to Sutton. Upon September the 6th, a day of humiliation "for the Visited people" was observed, when four shillings and three pence was collected. This was repeated in the five following weeks, when the collections varied from three and four pence to four pence. Briefs were frequently sent round by public authority directing collections to be made for a great variety of purposes, most usually for distant churches, frequently for sufferers by fire, sometimes for particular individuals, once for keeping up the trade of fishing. In 1661 a collection was made for the persecuted Christians in Lithuania, when "three shillings and nine pence halfpenny farthing" was given. But for more important objects, collections were sometimes made by "house-row" when twice or thrice the amounts obtained in church were received. During many years such collections were regularly paid to an official receiver in Hull.

These records in the parish chest are among the few relics that remain to us of those days which yet are not so very far off. No buildings now existing in the parish, except the Church and a fragment of the White House, at Stoneferry, were seen by any of the persons whose names and deeds have so far been recorded in these pages. The castle mound and moat down in the Carr and certain ancient banks and watercourses are survivals of a far earlier time. But the general face of the parish has been changed almost beyond recognition since the days of "good Queen Anne."

OLD-FASHIONED FARMS.

THE particulars which I have collected in relation
to certain farms have, so far, been mingled with
other items of parochial history. They have been
given sometimes on account of the special interest
which they possessed, sometimes on account of the
interest attaching to their owners. Towards the end
of the seventeenth century the details of the composition of many of these farms begin to be recorded so as
to shew what they really were. We may thus learn
how they were occupied by the tenants and yeomen,
where he who carried the scythe and reaping hook
would find his master's patches of meadow and his
strips of harvest, and where the tenant's team of oxen
would tramp over the clods of the summer fallow. I
have promised to give to this subject a separate
chapter.

The ancient agricultural system under which the
village community was held together by a close
partnership in ploughland, meadow and pasture, has
already been described. I have pointed out that the
curving selions or lands of the ancient tillage may still
be recognised on each side of the road which runs from
Foredike Bridge through the town towards Bilton.
There is no reason to think that the tillage materially
changed in extent from remote times down to the
reign of George III. Until that time all the farmers
still lived huddled together in Sutton, or else in the

more spacious enclosures of Stoneferry. Their narrow
ploughlands lay scattered over the three great common
fields. But these ploughlands had probably undergone
considerable change in shape since their first allotment
in the very far off past.

There is reason to believe that the tillage was
originally laid out in straight selions, or "lands" as
they are now called, all being usually of equal width.
They were arranged in distinct groups, each group
being distinguished by a particular name. Such
names as Yarlshou, Watelands, and Scotlandes have
been given in earlier chapters. The length of each
land was usually about one-eighth of a mile, which,
being the length of a furrow, may have given rise to
the term "furlong." Their width from centre to
centre would be about thirty-three feet. But the
cultivated portions of the lands did not quite touch
each other. There was originally always a strip of
grass, which might be from three feet to six feet in
breadth, between each ploughed land and that next to
it on either side. This tended to prevent the en-
croachment of one man upon the land of his neighbours. It also provided excellent grazing for the
cattle when they were turned out upon the fallows or
the stubbles, and a place on which they could lie.
The grass strips were generally called "balks," which
appears to have been their usual name in Holderness.
In Keyingham there were "grass balks and marstalls"
in the common fields. In the Carr-side in Sutton
there was "a swange of grass" called Mastall.*

In a small grass field to the south-west of the homestead at Low Bransholm, the existing lands are alternately eighteen feet and nine feet in breadth. This
may be a piece of ancient ploughland laid down to
grass before the balks became narrowed by encroach-

* In Lincolnshire the grass strip was called a "mere-furrow" or "marfur,"
and in a particular parish there was a penalty for diminishing the marfur by the
plough.

ment ; but there is an excellent specimen of the lands with their separating balks in a grass field in Bilton to the south side of the high road and not far from Salts House. From one cause or another the balks, with such rare exceptions as these, have been added to the cultivated lands.

Whatever may have been the case originally, the lands are not now all of equal breadth, and, in every group of ten or a dozen, one or two are usually

A GRASS BALK.

narrower than the rest. There may be also one or two of excessive breadth. In certain parishes it has been proved that all the lands which belonged to the glebe were narrow, and it has been thought that the parson was not so vigilant in looking after his rights as his parishioners would be who were ploughing their own ground. It is, however, quite possible that these lands were made narrower in the original adjustment of the glebe. The larger strips have sometimes been thought to be those belonging to the lord of the manor, whose servants would take unusual care of the boundaries of his lands.*

It will be noticed that the lands are now far from being straight, they are, in fact, very decidedly bent, with a double curvature into the shape of the letter " S " reversed.† This has always caused much curiosity amongst farmers, though, until quite recently, it escaped the attention of writers upon ancient agriculture. By a curious chance, the poet Mason, whose family property lay in Sutton, has noticed in his poem *The English Garden*, the double curvature of the lands in the tillage fields. Having in his mind what Hogarth called the Line of Beauty, he draws attention to

> "that peculiar curve,
> Alike averse to crooked and to straight,
> Where sweet Simplicity resides ; which Grace
> And Beauty call their own ; whose lambent flow
> Charms us at once with symmetry and ease.
> 'Tis Nature's curve ; instinctively she bids
> Her tribes of being trace it. Down the slope
> Of yon wide field, see with its gradual sweep
> The ploughing steers their fallow ridges swell."

Upon the whole, the best explanation of this curved form of the lands is that the ancient ploughland being cultivated by means of oxen yoked to a heavy plough, the unwieldy team, turning round on arriving at the end of each furrow, would tend, little by little, to produce this curvature. If the habit were to turn round to the left, each end of every land would, in the course of centuries, acquire a perceptible bend to the left such as we now see. The objections to this explanation are the great extent to which this bend has been carried, and the necessity of believing that

* In a certain parish all the lands belonging to a particular family were distinctly wider than the rest. The explanation given by a neighbour was that the members of that family were " very good ploughmen." If these " good ploughmen " managed to nibble even a small fraction of an inch from the grass balks each time they ploughed, the gain would in a few years be very substantial.

† See the plan of selions and balks on page 16.

not only the ploughed lands have thus become so bent, but also the balks between them, which were never ploughed. Besides this I have pointed out that at present the practice of ploughmen is to turn, not to the left, but to the right; and also that, though on the Continent the lands generally curve to the left as with us, there are districts in which they curve to the right, a thing never seen in this country. Still the explanation given above seems much more probable than any other, and I think it is correct.[*]

The division of the land into oxgangs was very strictly preserved in Sutton as long as it remained unenclosed. Much has been written about the variable size of the ancient carucate, and of the oxgang, which was an eighth part of a carucate, but in Sutton the oxgang certainly contained as nearly as possible fifteen acres of arable land with the appurtenances in meadows and in pasturage. The homestead was also an appurtenance, for it was valueless apart from the land. I have shewn that, from very early times, the arable land must have remained unaltered in quantity, being spread over all the higher portions of the ancient manor, while the older meadows and pasturage formed a margin extending to the surrounding tide-covered hollow. The several shares in these ancient meadows appear to have remained permanently attached to the particular oxgangs to which they had always belonged. From the numerous records which I have printed of gifts and purchases of land in the Ings and other reclaimed portions of the parish, it will be seen that the portions of these newer meadows attached to the several oxgangs must, in later times, have varied greatly in quantity. The rights of turning out animals to graze in the pastures were also dealt with

[*] In a paper on this subject written for the British Archæological Association, I have suggested that if the ploughmen of two districts turn their oxen in different directions upon arriving at the end of the furrow, they probably belong to tribes or races that have had little communication with each other since the time when they began to use oxen in the plough.

to a small extent, but these rights were in general kept very equally divided by apportionments made amongst the owners of houses and lands.

From his village homestead the farmer had to go out into the tillage fields and the meadows and identify the strips and patches of his scattered farm. There were farmers who occupied more farms than one, and there were yeomen who rented farms belonging to other persons ; but there is good evidence to prove that in the sixteenth and seventeenth centuries the ordinary size of a farm in Sutton was half an oxgang, or seven and a half acres of tillage, with a large share of meadow and pasturage. Some farms might consist of one or even two oxgangs, and the tendency would be to increase their size by purchase. In any case the tillage of each farm was pretty equally divided between the three open arable fields : the East Field, the North-Carr Field, and the West or Carr-side Field. Thus the owner of half an oxgang would have five lands widely scattered over each field. Upon one of them he might have a toft or toftstead, a small piece of enclosed ground with some rude building for con-venience in working the land.

It was necessary for all to cultivate their lands on one system. When the East field was fallow one of the other fields would be growing a crop of wheat, and the third would be growing the spring corn in patches of oats, barley, beans, and peas. In Sutton the ancient system of the manorial plough drawn by the oxen of different tenants must have come to an end at a very early period ; for, according to the apportionment made in the time of Sayer the Fourth, the owner of only half an oxgang would have such plenty of meadow and pasturage that he could easily provide enough oxen for a plough of his own. The actual quantities of grass and pasturage in proportion to the tillage will be clearly shewn in the details which I shall give of the separate farms.

The management of the meadows would present little difficulty except that many of the isolated pieces would be far away from the homestead. But the common occupation of the pasturage was intolerably awkward and irritating. It could only exist under troublesome but necessary restrictions, and subject to the constant interference of the Manor Court. Three kinds of grazing rights are mentioned in the old documents relating to Sutton. To each half oxgang was attached a " Land Common," which gave the right of turning out fifty sheep and eight large cattle upon the commonable places. To each farmstead was attached a " House Common," which gave the right of turning out thirty sheep and eight large cattle. In addition to this there were a few better pastures where the grazing was limited to the owners of " beast-gates " or rights to turn out oxen. Some of these, particularly in Bransholm, seem to have been parts of the demesne lands of the Lord of the Manor. Other portions, as in the Salts, had been possessed by the monks of Meaux. Most of the farms seem to have had a few of these separate grazing rights for oxen or horses. These animals were called " great-mouths " to distinguish them from the sheep.

The pasturage was under the management of Byelawmen or " Jesters," * who employed stockmen or grassmen, and the cattle could only be turned out where and when the Byelawmen might direct. Every manor court might take steps to prevent fraud and trespass and overstocking. Wool-gathering, an industry akin to gleaning, could, as a rule, only be done when the shepherd was present to see that wool was not " gathered " off the backs of the sheep. There were pastures into which large cattle might not be turned, but in general five or six sheep could be substituted for one " great-mouth." As regards the West Carr, it appears probable that the possessor of rights of pastur-

* Ajisters.

age there could only exercise those rights so long as
he was a resident in the parish "down-lying and up-
rising," but Sir William Alford had let his pasturage
there to residents. The ordinary rule, however, in
common pastures was that the stock must belong to
the man who turned it out to graze. We have seen
that the monks of Meaux were severely punished for
turning strangers' sheep into the Salts.

A few tattered scraps of paper at the Hull Town
Hall contain copies of proceedings at the manor courts
in Sutton ; there are many more relating to Summergangs. The chief offences dealt with seem to have
been the turning out of more cattle or sheep than the
farmer had the right to turn out, permitting geese to
stray in the cornfields, and turning horses or oxen into
places where sheep only were allowed. But in spite of
fines and reproofs such offences were constantly
recurring.

It happens, fortunately, that there are records, some
of which have already been given, extending back for
two or three centuries, which shew the sizes of the
farms in Sutton, their proportion of meadow and
pasturage, and by whom they were held.

By the end of the seventeenth century, few traces
remained of the names by which the groups of selions
and the flats of meadow had been known during the
Middle Ages. The old names had lost their signifi-
cance. New occupiers and fresh incidents had been
commemorated by the application of new names to the
lands. These names are recorded in many family
deeds, and by entries of deeds and wills in the East
Riding Register.

In the Middle Ages, the hill or holm nearest to
Bilton, was called Billshull and Billill. In later times
the name of Billin, or Billing, seems to have been applied
to it. Great Hill is probably the hill nearer to Sutton
town, on which some modern residences have been
built, but the descriptions are not clear. The hill

nearest to Wawne, which most probably gave its name to the Sefholm meadows, was in the sixteenth century sometimes called Soffham Hill, but more frequently Nordail or Nordale, a name that must have been taken from the adjacent meadows, and after being corrupted into Noddle, has gone out of practical use. A hill called the Marr Hill, sloping down to the North Carr, is that on which the windmill recently stood. The high ground at the West end of the town which is cut through by the railway was called the Runhill or Runnil in eighteenth-century descriptions of the ploughed lands that extended down to Leads Common and to the Ings.

Though I cannot in all cases fix the precise locality, the lists of names given below will convey some idea of the positions of the lands to which they were attached. In this and other detailed descriptions of lands the East Field must be understood to include the whole of the tillage lying to the east of Sutton village on both sides of the Bilton Road. The North, or North Carr Field extends along the north-eastern side of the Wawne road, and also includes three-fourths of the tillage on Soffham or Nordall Hill on the opposite side of that road. The Carr-side or West Field extends from the old enclosed land on the south side of the village as far as Nordall.

TILLAGE.

In the East Field :—
 The Larkes dyke. Next the East Carr?
 Syke-well. Next the Ings? Landsyke was here.
 Stainhood, or Stonehead Balk, going down to Risam Carr.
 The Whole, or Hoale, against the Northlands. There was also
  meadow in the Whole.
 The Salts gate.
 The Little Balk going down to Risam Carr.
 The High-end lands.
 Broadland. On north side of Bilton Road.
 The Mill-hill. Perhaps the site of a corn mill just outside

the East end of the town, the existence of which I see
strong reason to infer.   Tillage near here ran from the
Bilton road down to the Ings dyke.

The Mill Slack.   A water course near the mill.

The Milnbridge.

Hinding Hill.

Billings Balk.

Hoalebutt, or Holeabut-Flatt.

Stinging Hill.

Esops, on Hunger Hill.   ·

Stockhole.   Near Gold dike Stock?

Hall Garth, or Holgarth Walls.

In the North Carr Field :—

Nordale head-land.   On west side of Wawne road.

The Marr Hill.   Where Sutton Mill was afterwards built.   One
side extending to North Carr dike.

The Mill.   Built in 1715.   Had half acre of land 1764.

North Carr dyke.   ·

The Parting-of-the-field Balk.   Between North Carr and Carr-
side fields.

Forde—the tillage nearest to Foredike bridge.

North Daile Stoope.

Half mile.   Half mile from the town?

Meast Hill.

Glasthill Nook.

In the Carr-side Field :—

The Storke.

Crook't mare, or mear, Balk.   Near the present road to Soffham.

Crookmarr-headland.

The Runhill, or Runnil.   The hill on which the railway station
stands.

Mr. Cock's Kiln's Nook.   On the south side of the Runnil,
behind his homestead.

Claypit Head.   At the back of Mr. Henry Cock's Barn.

The Leads balk.   Down by 'Tween-dykes road.

A swange of grass called Mastall, Mastill, or Marstall.

Pennyhill Flatt.   6 acres 3 stengs of tillage belonging to Henry
Cock, against his garth and barn.   ·

Nordall Slack.

Stock Rundel.

There was, besides, a tenement with an oxgang of land or a
"Plowland," called Byrsall, or Byrsill, lands belonging to
the owner of the glebe, and which would be spread over the
three fields.

MEADOW.

In the Ings :—
  Parkin Nooke.
  Burnt Skins.
  Blewstone.
  Little Folly.   A pighill of an acre owned by Mr. Henry
      Cock.
  The Causey.   The road from Hull towards Bilton?
  Head-dale.   Near Salts.
  Sideing.   Ancient enclosure ; part of Belle Field.
  Pighill called Benington Coate.   Abutting on Leads Common.
  Egghill.   Near to the Mill Bridge.
  Oxland-dale.
  A Fall called 30 Acres.
  Mr. Atkinson's bridge.
  Dunkindale.   In the South Ings.
  Thurnham Coat Garth.   A little close or pighill adjoining
      Summergangs.
  Ewland Gate.
  Dother Syke.   Near Castard Gate.
  The Garth-ends.   Behind the farmsteads on east side of Stone-
      ferry town street.
  The Raw.   Probably Marfleet Lane.
  Rawson Pighill.
  Castard Acre.
  Bessy Bell Bridge.
  Summergangs Gate.
  Summergangs Far Gate.
  Gothing.
  Mowbrey Dale.
  Chimney land.
  Stockdailles.

In the Carr-side, including Soffham Meadows :—
  A pighill at Summergangs side.
  The Butts in Antim (Antholme ?) Nooking.
      Do.   in dutin nook.
  The Shorts.
  Anthony Johnson's pighill, or pickell.
  The footbridge.
  The Stock balk.
  The Gairs.   Near Footbridge.
  Capes' Acre in Soffham.
  Walter Snaith Coat.
  The Parson Gate.
  Norden's Croft.
  Pepperwell.

In Risholm Carr :—
The Cooper Piece.
The Lodge.
Mowbray Dale.
Great Hill bridge.
Parramore Pitt.
There were also meadows called :—
Scodales and
Blaydes' ten acres.
Boat Grass, Boad-gross or Broadgrass.   In Sutton Side, or
   Sucker Side, near the East Field and in Bransholm.   Also
   at the Salts End, and in the Shorts, near Sydings.
There was a close called Gyme or Guime Close—to the north of
   Stoneferry and to the south of the West Carr—also
   closes in Sutton called The Hill, or Thrush Hill, and
   Mustard Hill.
Beast Gates in Hope Ferry (John Hope was a small landowner)
   at Bransholm, New England, Rougham, Old Ings, and
   Cowland.

In 1695, in the reign of William III., the Corporation of Hull let on lease for three years, at fourteen pounds a year, the bulk of their Sutton property, which was Salvain's share in the manor.   Thomas Atkinson, their tenant, was a yeoman and a prominent man in the parish.   His holding comprised the "newly built messuage or Mannor House in the Highgate," which stood to the east of Elm Tree House, with a half oxgang of land, "arable meadow and pasture," also another half oxgang separately described.

The Half-oxgang, with its appurtenances belonging to the Manor House of the Corporation, consisted of the following items :—

		Acres.	Roods.	Poles.
Tillage in the West Field	- - -	2	0	20
,, ,, East Field	- -	3	0	0
,, ,, North Field	- -	2	3	0
	A.	7	3	20
Meadow in Ings	- - - - -	3	2	0
,, Rysome Carr	- - -	1	2	0
,, Carr Side Meadow	- -	1	3	20
	A.	6	3	20

Pasturage for 2½ beasts in the East Carr and Common of pasture for three beasts in Stoneferry New Field (new Ings). Two Commons which belonged to the Manor House and its half-oxgang—*i.e.*, a house common for 30 sheep and 8 cattle, and a land common for 50 sheep and 8 cattle.

Two rods of " Boadgrasse " in Suttonside nigh Castle Hill.*
Three acres of pasture in Stoneferry Westcroft.
Five roods in Drypool field nigh " Moundscale " Clough.
One half acre in Stoneferry Southfield.

The other half oxgang consisted of :—

	Acres.	Roods.	Poles.
Tillage in North Carr Field - - -	2	2	0
., West Carr Field - - -	2	2	0
„ East Field at Suttorside - -	2	2	0
A. 7	2	0

	Acres.	Roods.	Poles.
Meadow in Carr Side - - - -	3	0	20
„ Pepperwell - - - -	0	1	20
„ Carr Side in Walter Snaith Coat	1	1	0
„ Beyond the Parson gate - -	0	1	20
„ Beyond the Shorts - - -	0	1	20
„ Against Norden's Croft - -	1	0	0
„ Beyond Soffham Hill - -	0	3	0
„ In the Casterd Gate - -	1	0	0
„ In a place called Seven Stengs†	0	1	0
„ In Parramore Pitt in Rysome Carr	1	0	0
„ Over the great Hill in Rysome Carr - - - - -	0	1	0
A. 7	1	0

Two beast-gates in Norlands, two in Bransholm, two and a half in the East Carr—"with the appurtenances."

I suppose the appurtenances would comprise a "land-common." Nothing is said of a house with its right of common.

* Boadgrasse, Boatgrasse, or Broadgrasse was, It hink, unenclosed pasture land, probably part of the ancient demesne. It lay down in the Carrs, and may originally have been approached by boat.
† A steng is the old name for a rood : it is often used in these documents.

Other Corporation leases in 1735 and 1750 mention the following items :—

> Two acres of arable land at or near "Fryer-dyke ;" five acres of meadow at the Garth ends ; half an acre in the Scodales ; two and a half on east side of "Blaydes' ten acres ;" two four-acres dales, one on each side of the highway leading to Bilton (from Hull) ; one steng and a half of meadow at Carr Side, in a place called Soffham ; and two acres of tillage near "Feerdike Bridge."

By that time the old Forthdyk had come to be so called, and that represents the local pronunciation now.   Fryer-dyke, mentioned above, and also in relation to the possessions of the Carthusians of Hull, appears to be the same.   The "Garth ends" was the usual description of meadow lands in the Ings at the back of the farms on the east side of the town-street of Stoneferry.

In 1674, the name of William Munbie appears as tenant under Mrs. Cornewalleys, of Hyrncoate, at a rent of fifteen pounds, and he, with Mr. Cocke, rented meadow in "Sougham" at twelve pounds per annum.   Both these names were then coming into prominence.

Early in the eighteenth century, William Munby, Gentleman, who had married Ann, the daughter of John Cock of Sutton, Gentleman, was in possession in right of his wife of three farms, the first of which is a perfect example of a farm of one oxgang. It had been bought of Thomas Markham, and consisted of

Messuage with garth or close,

						Acres.	Stengs.
Tillage in the East Field		-	-	-	-	5	0
„ „ „ West or Carr Side Field			-	-	5	0
„ „ „ North Carr Field			-	-	5	0
					A.	15	0

Meadow Land—

	Acres.	Stengs.
In the Ings nigh Underdale Pighill * - -	2	1
,, ,, ,, ,, Hy. Tiffin's Pighill - -	2	1
,, ,, ,, between Underdale and James Wallis's Pighill - - - - -	0	1½
At Stoneferry Garth end - - - - -	1	0
At New Ings - - - - - - -	0	2
In Carr side near the Pighills of the Corporation of Hull - - - -	0	3
Nigh Footbridge, a Pighill and meadow - -	1	1
In Sopham - - - - - - -	1	1
More in Sopham - - - - - -	0	3
In Rysom Carr - - - - -	1	1
Near Great Hill Bridge - - - - -	1	1
Nigh Great Hill - - - - - -	0	1
A.	13	0½

Five Beast gates in the East Carr.
One House Common.
Two Land Commons.

The following lands had been bought of Edward Thewlass and wife :—

Seven and a half acres in the fields, with a close of meadow or pasture in the Side Ings containing three and a half acres and one Land Common.

This appears to have been a half oxgang without a house. The "Sydings," which was the piece of old enclosed land at Belle Field, may have had upon it such buildings as were necessary for the cultivation of this land, but it would not be entitled to a House Common.

The third of these farms furnishes an instance of the breaking up of the strict division of land into oxgangs. Lands purchased from Sir William Dalton are thus described :—

* The local name for a Pightil—a small enclosure. In a list of lands in Marfleet in the reign of Philip and Mary, two Pightells are set down as worth a rent of 2s. 4d. each.—*Poulson.* In 1755, Underdale was called Autherdale Pighill, Joseph Auther having rented it some years previously. Names were always changing in this way.

"That half oxgang of land containing 20½ acres arable meadow and pasturage," viz.—

		Acres.
Tillage in the East Field - - - - - -		4
„ „ „ West Field - - - - -		4
„ „ „ Carr Side Field - - - - -		3½
„ „ „ Clough Field - - - - -		⅛
„ „ „ South Field - - - - -		⅛
		A. 12½ *

Meadow Land—

	Acres.	Stengs.
In the Ings at Parkins Nooke - - - -	3	3⅓
„ „ „ „ Wm. Francis' Garth end - -	1	0
„ „ „ nigh Mr. Gunby's Pighill - -	0	3
In new Ings - - - - - - -	0	1½
In Carr Side Ings late Mr. Henry Cock's (deceased) Sheepcot - - - -	0	3
In Sopham (called Cape's Acre) - - -	1	0
More in Sopham - - - - - -	1	1
	A. 9	0 †

Leonard Chamberlaine, draper in the Market Place at Hull, was a landowner in Sutton. In his will, dated 1716, by which he founded Chamberlaine's Charity, he describes his property as consisting of two farms, the one in Stoneferry, the other in Sutton; both occupied by Robert Parrott, containing two houses and three closes. There were also fourteen acres and a half of meadow in the Ings, a Pighill, and four gates in Sutton New Ings, and four Commons in Sutton. At Sutton there was a farm house and garth, with a Land Common and a House Common, and also a Pighill, which adjoined land of Mr. Henry Cocke; and three garths where three houses had formerly stood, adjoining the farm house, with three commons belonging to them. The farm lands were as follows :—

* Apart from the land in the Clough Field and in the South Field of Stoneferry, there were here 11¼ acres, or three-quarters of an oxgang.

† With this property went a small amount of pasturage in Southcoates, where pasturage was reckoned by the Noble. "Two nobles of grass, ancient rent for six beast gates." Three beast gates were valued at a noble, which was six shillings and eight pence.

	Acres.	Roods.	Poles.
In the East Field - - - - -	3	1	0
„ „ North Field - - - - -	3	2	20
„ „ Carr Side Field - - - -	3	0	0
A.	9	3	20

	Acres.	Roods.	Poles.
In the Ings—meadow ground - - -	4	1	0
„ „ Carr Side Meadow - - -	1	0	0
„ „ Rysom Carr - - - - -	0	3	0

There were also two roods of Boat grasse in a place called "Suckerside," and two gates and a half in the East Carr.

One of Chamberlaine's executors was Ralph Peacock, sail maker, a deacon in the Presbyterian congregation in Hull. In 1709, he bought from one Dolman two properties, which respectively shew the composition of a half-oxgang farm, and a farm of one oxgang and a half. These, with other lands, descended to his daughters, one of whom had married the Reverend John Witter, the minister of the congregation. Mary Witter, widow, held her share at the enclosure of the common fields in 1768.

The smaller of the two farms is said, in an abstract of title, to consist of—

"One farm house with ye Garth, Back-side, Barn, Stable, and buildings," tenanted by Matthew Ward, comprising :—

	Acres.	Stengs.
Tillage in East Field - - - - -	2	3
„ North Carr Field - - - -	2	0
„ Carr Side Field - - - -	2	2
A.	7	1

	Acres.	Stengs.
Meadow in the Ings - - - - -	9	1

4¼ pasture gates in North Lands.
2¼ „ „ East Carr.
1 House Common.
1 Land Common.

The larger "farm and farmhold," tenanted by John Wallis, comprised a house with barns and other outbuildings, garth, and "onsett," with

							Acres.	Stengs.
Tillage in East Field	-	-	-	-			9	1
„ North Carr Field	-	-	-				6	3
„ Carr Side Field	-	-	-				7	3½
						A.	23	3½

Meadow in the Ings	-	-	-	17 acres	3	rouths.
„ Carr Side Meadow	-			7 „	2½	stengs.
„ Rysom Carr -	-	-		1 „	1½	„
			A.	26	3	

The pasturage consisted of :—
7¾ Gates in East Carr.
1½ „ Salts.
3 Land Commons.
1 House Common.

But such details as these give no clue to the actual
positions in the fields of the half-acre selions or lands
which made up the tillage, nor of the particular pieces
of grass as they lay in the sections of the meadows.
No doubt every farmer knew the lands which he
farmed, and his neighbours would know them also,
but it very often happened that the owner was quite
dependent upon his tenant for such information. If a
farmer held lands under two landlords, or if he were a
yeoman and farmed for several years the land of
another owner as well as his own land, the distinction
between them would cease to be remembered, except
by the farmer himself.

To prevent accidents the lawyers drew up minute
descriptions of the scattered farms as they "lay
dispersedly" in the open fields and meadows. Many
such descriptions, evidently taken down from the lips
of the farmers, are to be found in conveyances and
settlements, but more particularly in the volumes of
the Register of Deeds for the East Riding at
Beverley. From these sources we may learn the
names of all important parts of the parish as they were

known before they became obliterated through the
enclosure of the open fields.

Among the old manorial lands belonging to Thomas
Watson of Stoneferry, which came into the family of
his sister, Elizabeth Truslove, was a farm which
seems to have consisted of an oxgang and a half, but
which was divided between two of Mrs. Truslove's
daughters. The share (three-quarters of an oxgang),
received by Frances Stather, was dispersed in this
way:—

In the East Field :—

  One acre at Mill Slack lying on the north side of lands of Madam
    Dalton.
  Half an acre at the town end of Stoneferry (should be Sutton) at
    the east side of Matthew Lengs going down to the Larkes.
  A steng and a half going down to the Garbridge* abutting on
    the lands of Mr. Wilson on the west side of Geo. Wetwang.
  A half acre going down to Rysome Carr near the Engine Hill
    lying west on the lands of Anthony Johnson.
  An acre over Billin running down against Holgarth Walls lying
    on the south side of lands of the said Mr. Dalton.

In the North Carr Field :—

  One half acre near the town end of Stoneferry (Sutton) adjoining
    on the lands late of Mr. Cᵣ. Gunbie at the upper end.
  One acre at the beginning of Nordall, lying west of lands then
    late of Mr. Brodrip.
  One "three steng" near the headland lying west on the land of
    Mr. Dalton.
  One acre near Feard Dyke, the lesser end thereof running to the
    North Carr, the broad end thereof running to Carr Side.

In the Carr Side Field :—

  One half acre, being the fourth off Lead Balk "stinting" on a
    steng of Jnº Treasures.
  One acre at Stock lying on the east side of the lands of Mr.
    Dalton.
  Half an acre of land lying west at the upper end of the lands of
    Mr. Bromfleet.
  Half an acre at Nordall Slack† at the upper end of Matthew
    Leng.

      * Carr-bridge?
    † Where the road now leads to Soffham farmhouse.

The grass lands consisted of :—
Half a steng of meadow, half lower end west of Barbara
  Naylor.
One acre and steng, half in the Shorts.
Five Carr-gates and a quarter in the East Carr.
One common, half Land Commons.
Two rood of Boat Grass at Long Garbridge.
With the appurtenances.*

The appurtenances include a right to stock the commons where there was no "stint," of which Leads Common between Sutton and Stoneferry was, I think, an example.

In the early part of the eighteenth century, Samuel Dalton of Beverley, gentleman, and after him, his children and grandchildren were parting with shares in the properties that had descended to them from the second branch of the Daltons. The portions which lay in Sutton included the manor called "Boomers or Bulmers," the share of Sir Thomas de Sutton's daughter Agnes, with houses and lands generally described in such terms as these :—

Messuages, etc., with two garths adjoining, two house commons, 7½ acres and half a steng, arable in the Fields of Sutton with one land common. One pighill, and 3 acres 3 stengs meadow in the Ings, 2 acres 3 roods in Carrside, 4 beast-gates in the Northlands, 2½ in East Carr, 2 beastgates and 1 foot in Bransome, with common pasture in Bransome, East Carr, and Salts, late in tenure of Hannah Hart, now Ann Munby, widow.

The details of tillage and meadow are given thus :—

In the East Field half an acre, the Mill-Slack on High-end, half an acre, the fifth land, the little balk going down to Rysome Carr ; half a steng, the fourth (or the further) of the four going down to Rysome Carr ; half an acre from the headland to the Northlands in the Whole, half a steng at the Saltsgate.

* Frances Stather's share above described went to her descendants of the name of Cowart. The other portion had been acquired by Mrs. Ann Watson in 1709.

In the North-Field half an acre behind the Marr Hill abutting on the North Carr Dyke, one acre upon Nordale going from the highway to the said dyke. In the Carrside Field, a three steng at the Runnell at Mr. Cock's kilns nook, adjoining nine lands of Mr. Cock on east, a steng and a half lying next to the Leads Balk, half an acre going up directly against the mill.[*]

In the Ings one acre and a half of meadow nigh to Mr Atkinson's bridge.

In the Carr side a three steng of meadow running by Anthony Johnson's pighill, half an acre at the foot-bridge, abutting on the lands of Mr. Munby, in the Gairs, lands of Charles Scrivener on east and Elizabeth Witty on west, and one acre at Stork Balk abutting on lands of Mr. Munby and the College [†] on east.

In Rysom Carr one acre at the Cooper piece going from East Carr dike to three half stengs of William Clappison, one steng at the Great Hill abutting a steng of Thomas Watson's and Mr. Munby's on east and Charles Scrivener on west, and one steng at the Lodge between Richard Hodgson and Thomas Morton.

Other conveyances by the Daltons describe parts of the old enclosed lands by the river in Stoneferry that probably descended to them from the lords of the manor. They comprise a pasture of twelve acres called the Intake; an arable field of nine acres called the Little Field; a field of twenty-seven acres called South Field, with lands in the Clough Field and in Sutton Ings. All these lands, which lay to the south of Stoneferry, became part of the estate got together by Mr. Thomas Broadley, and transmitted to his descendants.

In 1742, Martha Lacy, of Hull, daughter and heir of Henry Cock, late of Sutton, gent., deceased, conveyed to Hugh Blades, of Hull, shipwright, the farmhouse on the south side of the High Street, with forty-five acres of land. There were

in the East Field, near Town Side, one and a half acres; five and a half acres near Blindwell; half an acre near Stinging Hill; four acres, called Esops, on Hunger Hill; half an acre and

[*] That is exactly opposite to the site of Sutton Mill, built in 1715.
[†] This was a few years before Ann Watson's death. The College here meant must have been the dissolved College of St. James.

one steng near Cooper piece ; half an acre running near Stockhole ; one steng at Hall Garth Walls ; half an acre, the fifth
land or thereabouts from Sidings ; half a steng at Skyewell
Side ; half an acre up the Salts, with three stengs and two
pieces of land near the Billing Balk.　In the North Carr field,
at Marr Hill, half an acre against the mill ; two and a half acres
a little from the mill ; one acre next long balk ; land next Meast
Hill ; land next Glasshill Nook ;　land against Parting Field
Balk ; land in the Carr Side Field at back of barn, and near
Claypit head, and land west of Millbalk ; land against Crookmar-
headland ; and land near Stock Rundel.　In the Ings there was
land (to wit) at Castard acre, at Dodder Syke ; land in Bessy
Bell Bridge ; one shifting at Stoneferry Garth Ends ; lands near
Summergamsgate ;　land near Marfleet Row ; * and lands in
Gothing Mowbrey dale.

The following catalogue of lands composing a very
small farm conveyed by Beauley and Nettleton to
Thomas Wetwang, of Stoneferry, in 1713, contains
some peculiar names, and also one case of changeable
ownership, which reminds us of the earliest system of
allotment of lands in an ancient manor :—

A garth where a messuage formerly stood at the east end of
the town of Sutton, and two butts of arable land at back
containing one acre, extending down to the Larkes Dyke.
Common for 8 beasts and 30 sheep.　A quarter oxgang arable
land dispersed in several fields.　In the east field 1½ acre, i.e.,
two lands part thereof called two three-stengs, one running over
a hill called Billing Hill, and the other into Syke Well.　In
North Carr Field 1½ acre, i.e., one land containing half an acre
which runs against the town-end, one other land called a Steng
being first part of Nordall head-land, one other Steng in the
Feaud,† running down to the Carr side, and one other land
being half an acre, running up to Nordall head-land, and down
in the Feaud.　In the Carr-side field 2½ acres lying in two
lands called two three-stengs running down into the Carr-side,
one against the Storke, and the other up Nordall, and half a
common to the said land belonging.　And 5 acres, 3 stengs
meadow in Ings, one acre running over the Cawsey adjoining
Bilton Common, one three-stengs (other part thereof), one end
running against the Row, the other end against the Head Dale ;
and 4 acres, the remainder thereof running over the Cawsey,
one end extending to Sideing, and the other one running to

* Marfleet Raw.　　　　† Féa-ud = Forde.

Chimney lands. And also one Pighill containing about half an acre lying in the Ings abutting on the Leads, and formerly called Benington Coate. One cow-gate and a calf-gate in the East Carr, also 1½ acre meadow lying in Rysom Carr, and half a five steng lying at the Carr Side to be had and taken every other year—*i.e.,* "when Wetwang has the 1½ in Carr-side, Mr. Broadley has the 1½ acre in Rysom Carr, and the half five steng in Carr-side"—and *vice versa.*

Some of the transactions of which I have given the details were mortgages, and not absolute sales. I am, however, not now dealing with such questions, but with the names used to describe the localities in which the lands were dispersed over the open fields. If such reading as this should prove tedious, as perhaps it may, it will shew all the more clearly the complicated system under which our great-grandfathers carried on their farming operations; a system which they had inherited from an unknown antiquity, and against which they rebelled by no means too soon.

OUR GREAT-GRANDFATHERS' DAYS.

I F the period which we have now reached may seem to lack the charm of antiquity; if the items of the chronicle are comparatively trivial, the middle portion of the eighteenth century must nevertheless have for us an importance and a charm of its own.

The reign of George II.—1727 to 1760—covers the generation immediately before the enclosure of the open fields, which is the only event of really grand importance that has happened in the parish since its lower grounds were freed from the ebb and flow of the sea. In that period considerable portions of the land were already owned and occupied by families that are still connected with it, or that are well remembered.

The generation then living was the last to know Sutton in its ancient aspect as it was known to the lords of the undivided manor, their free tenants and their serfs, and the last to understand the farming arrangements which have been herein described. It is no very great while since all this came to an end; there are many persons still living who have talked with people that could remember the ancient system; yet it is remarkably little that tradition has handed down to us. Among the oldest people that I knew fifty years ago, one had been told of a great open field, and another had heard of disputes over the harvesting

of crops on adjacent lands.   Fortunately we have
records of various kinds to shew what was going on,
and who were influencing the affairs of the parish
in those days.

In 1716 Leonard Chamberlaine left the farms
already described, chiefly for the benefit of the poor of
Sutton and Stoneferry.   Presbyterian though he was,
he made no distinction on account of religious profession, stipulating only as to some of his gifts that
they should be distributed among "sober and good
Christians and such as want relief."   He left also eight
shillings per annum for a sermon to be preached on
Sutton Feast Day, which sum has never been claimed,
and five pounds to a schoolmaster for teaching twenty
of the poorest children "of what persuasion or
denomination soever" to read in English.   Chamberlaine's Charity is still managed by trustees connected
with the chapel near Bowlalley Lane, the congregation
of which became Unitarian about a century ago.   The
English Presbyterians had, however, taken a line of
their own, and the new name probably indicated their
old belief.   In 1800 and again in 1804 a portion of the
funds was spent in building almshouses in Sutton for
ten poor women, usually widows, each of whom receives
a weekly pension.

The acquisition by Mrs. Ann Watson, the widow of
Abraham Watson, of property in Stoneferry has already
been mentioned.   Her maiden name was Headon,
the name of an old family in Holderness.   I can see
no connexion between her and the Watsons of Stoneferry, but from some cause she, with her mother, began
in 1698 the formation of an estate there, chiefly out of
the property left by Thomas Watson, which had been
inherited by his sister, Elizabeth Truslove.*   In that
year they bought a house with lands from Mrs. Trus-

---

* Thomas Watson had settled a jointure out of his lands upon his wife, and
had left her a life interest in other lands, making no devise of any remainder.   As
he had no children, these lands, on the death of his widow, were divided between
his sisters as " shift-lands."

love's descendants, and in 1709 Mrs. Watson bought a further portion of the same estate. Mrs. Watson lived at Stoneferry in the large house called White House, which formerly stood on the west side of the town street between Antholme dike and the lane that leads to the old landing-place on the river. A small portion of it remains, which I have alluded to as the oldest specimen of building in the parish except the church. I do not doubt that it was the house which Thomas Watson mentioned in his will as "my house in Stoneferry where I now dwell," and it most probably occupied the site held in 1564 by Stephen Hogge, under Sir Marmaduke Constable, to which he alludes in his will as "two parts of the house in Stoneferrye wherein I now inhabit," and "two parts of a close called cowe close."

Mrs. Ann Watson's will, by which she founded a very important charitable trust, furnishes incidentally many interesting particulars as to her house and lands, and other possessions. She left amongst her friends her plain gold ring, with a "posie" or motto in it, her gold ring without a posie, her clothes of woollen, linen, and silk, and a pair of silver candlesticks and snuffers. Her heirlooms and pictures in her house were to be continued there for ever for ornaments and benefits to the house. Her house, called White House, the north end of cow-house, and the close it stood in, were for ever to be appropriated to a college or dwelling for clergymen's widows and clergymen's daughters, old maids, and for a school for teaching children.

She seems to have been making extensive alterations to fit it for its intended occupants. The great parlour, with the closet and half a room that was in the kitchen, was to be a dwelling for one of these ladies. Another lady was to have the chamber over the great parlour and the Hall chamber. The chamber over the parlour opposite was appointed for the schoolmistress. The two garrets over the last named chamber and great chamber were for the fourth lady. The kitchen was to be in common. They were to have the north end of the cow-house, and each of them might keep a cow if she should think it convenient. They were to use the little close as they might think fit. Her farm tenants were to have the "Stand-Heck-Garth" and free entrance and exit to and from the barn and stables. Any excess of profits was to be used for better maintenance of the inmates, and "for procuring themselves to be carried on horseback to church, when they could not otherwise get there, to attend all opportunities of divine service and preaching there." But she contemplated some more substantial increase in the value of the endowment, and provided that the other half of the room within the kitchen and the two chambers over that room and the kitchen should be a dwelling for one more inmate. And whereas she had added "two other dwellings new built to the said College or Almshouse," each dwelling of one "low" room, chamber, and garret, as soon as fitted, should be a dwelling for another inmate as there might be occasion. The low room would be a ground floor room.

Ten girls, who could read, were to be taught by the school dame to knit, spin, and sew. The girls were to be the children of poor inhabitants in need of such assistance, and were to help the ladies in their domestic affairs, and each was to receive twopence per week. The children were to go to Sutton Church on St. James' Day, and every Sunday when there should be service and sermon, and to be catechised when there should be catechising. The minister of Sutton was to have five pounds for the service and sermon on St. James' Day. The school dame was to read prayers on Wednesdays and Fridays. Each of the inmates was to receive five pounds per annum, the school dame being paid five pounds more.

All this indicates a large house. Each of the chief

rooms was large enough to be divided into two, so as to make a sitting-room and bedroom. There was a third storey of habitable garrets. The small portion now remaining consists of a low room with a chamber over; the floor of the chamber is carried on a beam and joists all bearing a good moulding on the angles. There was originally a wide fireplace, but within the opening a more modern fireplace has been constructed. It may be that this was done by Mrs. Watson, or even by the Trusloves or Thomas Watson. The floor-timbers and the wide fireplace look as old as the time of Stephen Hogge. Another portion of the White House now

OLD FIREPLACE.

forms part of the stable and granary; the rest, which stood between these two portions, has been destroyed. The old building was abandoned as a residence about seventy years ago, when the existing house was built.

Early in the eighteenth century new names were appearing amongst the chief landowners, replacing nearly every one of the old names. As I have done in former chapters, I shall here give the more important events under the names of those landowners who were most influential in the parish.

The Masons and Pooles. In 1710, Hugh Mason, Collector of Customs in the Port of Hull, acquired the

ancient possessions of the College of St. James, which
had been for many years in the family of Brodrepp.
The descriptions in the East Riding Register, and in
private documents, include the following items :

> A tenement with the appurtenances called Byrsall lands,
> formerly occupied by Fox, now by Brodrepp, a cottage and an
> oxgang of land, or "one plowland," called Byrsill in Sutton
> and Sudcoates, occupied by Joan Todd, with other properties in
> Sudcoates. The Rectory of the church and chapel of Sutton,
> with the Scite of the Colledge of St. James and the rectory or
> mansion of the said collegiate church of Sutton, and the mansion
> or dwellinghouse, barns, stables, orchards, garden, and premises,
> as well within as without the precincts of the scite, and 7
> commons to the mansion house belonging, formerly in the tenure
> of Lancellot Alford, and then or late in the tenure or occupation
> of John Alford or his assigns, and all glebe land and all manner
> of tithes of corn, grain, hay, wool, lamb, flax, hemp, and cattle,
> and all other titheable things, commodities, advantages,
> emoluments, and hereditaments whatsoever belonging to the
> Rectory.   There were 487 acres of enclosed land, 786 acres
> Ings meadow, and 251 acres of meadow in Carr-side and
> Rysome Carr subject to tithe.
>
> Of the land there were 33 acres in Carr-side meadow, one
> close of 30 acres called Great Oxlands (there was a Little
> Oxlands in Southcoats) and 30 acres of tillage in the three
> fields, with beast gates in different pastures.   Mention is also
> made of Oblations, Obventions, Easter Dues, and Smoke
> Money, and a mortgage made in 1727 includes 30 acres of land
> covered with water.

The Oxlands pasture juts in between the parishes
of Marfleet and Drypool at "Chimney lands nook,"
which name must have been applied to land in or near
the Oxlands.   The "land covered with water" was
probably a loose estimate of land behind the churchyard, which was still in a condition of marsh or marr.
The mention here for the first time of Byrsall lands
opens a curious question, the details of which I
obtained too late for insertion under the name of
Alford.   I have stated on page 151 that Lancelot the
younger succeeded to the property of his brother John,
but the Rectory property, left by the elder Lancelot to
John and his heirs, with the remainder to the younger

Lancelot, seems to have actually descended to the heir of
John.   I will not attempt to unravel the complications of
the leases and underleases to Alford, Mompesson,
Edward Truslove, and the associates of Sir Baptist
Hicks.   It may be enough to say that in 1634 Henry
Alford and his undertenants appear to have been in
actual possession of the property that had belonged to
the College, for, in that year, a suit in the Court of
Exchequer was brought by Katherine, Mary, and
Margaret Davye, whose father had inherited certain
lands in Sutton and Southcoats from Dame Katherine
Moore "after her death and the death of Sir Richard
Mompesson, her husband."   Dame Katherine had
bought the lands from Morrice and Philips, who in
1609 got the grant from the Crown.   The following
particulars are taken from the records of the Special
Commission, Nos. 5773, York, 10th Chas. I., and
5779, 5780, 5784, and 5822, 11th Chas. I.

Henry Alford was said to hold wrongful possession of a
tenement called "Bersilland, alias Horton Farm, or King's
Hold Land (at 6s. 8d. yearly rent), a cottage in Sutton (at 4s.
yearly rent), a bovate of land called Bersilland, alias Oxlands
(at 26s. 8d. yearly rent)" with lands and pasturage in Sudcotes.
Alford, who claimed the Rectory, said that though these lands
were not specially granted in the demise from Queen Elizabeth
to his ancestors, they were included in the general words.
Before the Commission Stephen Snaith, of Stoneferry, said he
had often heard from his brother Richard, who was servant to
Edward Truslove, that the Rectory had no land except a steng
in the Carr-side Field, which was evidently an error, as the
particulars given on pp. 106 and 135 shew.   The Court found
that Bersilland and the other lands had been granted and held
distinct and separate from the Rectory, though the Alfords had
held them with the Rectory lands for several years, and had paid
the rent in one sum.   A new Commission was therefore ordered
to set out these lands so that they might be given up to the
sisters Davye, and the Commissioners met on the 1st April,
1635.   They set out the Sudcotes properties and the cottage in
Sutton town, but according to the report of two of them,
Watkinson and Moore, they failed to find Bersilland, which
had been said to lie in Sutton and Sudcotes, nobody
remembering the name.   They found, moreover, that the

plaintiffs were in possession of lands in Sudcotes beyond those to which they could shew a title, and they suggest that Bersilland was amongst them. They complain of the other Commissioners, Wakeman and Burgesse, because they desired to set out as Bersilland an oxgang dispersed in the common fields, and another oxgang which was part of the Oxlands (a piece of pasture of 30 acres belonging to different owners), and when they could not have their way they went off, carrying the Commission with them.

And so the matter seems to have ended in heat and doubt, but Brodrepp conveyed to Mason the shadowy Byrsillands, wherever they might be.

The "Scite" of the College of St. James, the original "Mansion House" of which appears to have been destroyed, must have been on or near to the rough ground in "the Hills" on the west of the churchyard, near to the place where the old workhouse now stands. There was a more modern mansion, with extensive buildings, yards, and orchards, which I suppose to have been occupied by Edward Truslove, and these were distinct from the tithe homestead with its mansion that lay to the east of the churchyard.* In 1736, the tithes were "farmed" under Hugh Mason by George Heath. In 1755 the tithe farmer was Mary Pearson.

In 1718, the fee-farm-rent of £20 19s. 4d., which was formerly paid to the crown out of the Rectory, was payable to Hugh Smithson, of Tottenham. It was inherited by his great-nephew, Sir Hugh Smithson, of Stanwick, who married the heiress of the Percys, and was created Duke of Northumberland.

About this time the Daltons of the second branch

---

* I have found no clear description of the site of the College, but there was no room for it or for any complete residence between the tithe farm and the church. In 1731, Hugh Mason acquired from his son and heir, William, his interest in "the cross or east end of the capital messuage or Mansion House," with the great tithe barn and half the fore yard and back yard and part of stable with land behind, and conveyed them, with the tithes in trust, to Charles Poole. This is the land now immediately adjoining the churchyard on its east side, and, in 1755, it is described (Register, Book X., No. 551,) as lying between William Winship's farm (the Hastings Manor) and "the orchard belonging the Mansion House of Mrs. Mason." The orchard must now form part of the churchyard.

were disposing of their property which formed the remains of Bulmer's share of the manor. In 1723, Hugh Mason bought of Samuel Dalton, of Beverley, the Hill Close, containing six acres abutting on the High Street, and extending back to the Carr. It abutted to the west on the way leading down to the Carr where the church school stands, and to the east on the lands of Hugh Mason, that is on the ground formerly belonging to the College of St. James. In 1734, Hugh Mason bought for £141, of Samuel Dalton, a dwelling House in the High Street of Sutton with meadow lands and pasturage, also Mr. Dalton's part of the manor of Boomer or Bulmer with Court Leete, and with rights of hunting, hawking, and fishing. This portion was eight-ninths of Bulmer's third part of the manor.

Of Hugh Mason's family, one daughter married Charles Poole, a Captain in the Royal Navy, and another married Arthur Robinson. Neither of his sons-in-law survived him, but each left a son bearing his father's names, and both these sons were for many years intimately connected with the parish. His eldest son, the Rev. William Mason, was appointed, in 1722, the Vicar of Holy Trinity, Hull. In his lifetime, Hugh Mason settled his tithe homestead, with the tithes and certain of his lands, upon his nephew, Charles Poole the younger, upon trust for the benefit of the family.

Hugh Mason died in 1739, leaving to his son William the eight parts in nine of Bulmer's manor with the lands west of the church acquired from Dalton, and the oblations and smoke money amounting to about thirty shillings a year payable at Easter. William succeeded also to the portion of the rectory lands not attached to the tithe homestead, and to the advowson or right of presentation to the curacy of Sutton to which he presented his sister's son, the Rev. Arthur Robinson. He died, in 1753, of an "infectious

fever "* and was buried in Sutton Church, leaving a
son, the Rev. William Mason, whose name is always
associated with that of his friend, the poet Gray.

William Mason, the poet, was born in Hull in 1725.
At Cambridge he made the acquaintance of Gray,
with whom he became on terms of the most intimate
friendship.   He had himself a considerable faculty for
writing verse, which after being freely criticised by his
fastidious friend, was good enough to secure for him a
high position amongst the poets of his age.   It is
pleasing in style and admirable in its general tone, and
if some of the finer passages were suggested, or even
supplied, by Gray, we who gain by the result need not
cavil at the process.   His father's will left him joint
executor, and he was to share the goods with the
widow.   Mrs. Mary Mason was a third wife with a
young daughter.   The landed property was left to her
for her life, with remainder to her step-son and his heirs,
and then to his half-sister.   In a letter to Gray,
Mason, while lamenting the loss of a most affectionate
father, complains that with such a will he could raise
no money on his reversion.   As he had not yet taken
Holy Orders, and, so far as we can see, had no regular
income, it does seem odd that his father, with whom
he had been on the best terms, should have left him
no substantial legacy.   He describes his affairs as
"perplexed," but they rapidly improved.

In the following year, 1754, having taken orders, he
was presented to the valuable living of Aston, near
Rotherham.   In 1756, he was made a prebendary of
York Cathedral.   In 1762, he became Precentor and
Canon, the combined income from these two appointments being four hundred pounds a year.   In 1768, he
came into the reversion of the ground "near Hull," on
which the Charterhouse had stood, and on which Mason

---

* So writes William Mason the younger. It must have been a pestilence. His
stepmother and his own man-servant were down with it, but recovered. His
father's man-servant died of it.   His life-long friend, the Rev. Marmaduke
Pricket, also died of it.

Street is now the principal thoroughfare. Gray playfully congratulated him on his preferments, rejoicing to see his insatiable mouth stopped, and his anxious periwig at rest and slumbering in a stall.

He was not of a slumberous disposition, as Gray very well knew, and although he hated York, he attended to his duties as precentor in a way which must have set an example to the ordinary ecclesiastics of that day. He was an excellent musician, and while he went on writing poetry as if he expected to make a living by it, he found time to produce an " Essay, historial and critical, on English Church music," and to compose a *Te Deum*, with other sacred pieces, including a setting of the anthem, " Lord of all power and might," which is still an important item in cathedral music. He is credited with some improvement which helped to produce, out of the imperfect instrument of his day, the modern pianoforte. At forty he married Miss Sherman, of Hull, whose death from consumption within two years left him inconsolable, and gave occasion to one of the most touching epitaphs in the language. He occupied himself in his seclusion at Aston by writing his poem, " The English Garden," which will probably live as a record of the art of landscape gardening in his day, and in making his parsonage famous for the taste and beauty of its surroundings. It was not until 1772 that he succeeded to his paternal estate, and the patronage of the living of Sutton, which he had one opportunity of exercising.

He is usually called " the amiable poet Mason," a distinction which is justified by the general tenor of his writings, by the simplicity of his character, at least in youth, by the warmth of his friendship, and by the cheerfulness that distinguishes his correspondence. He was, however, a man of strong convictions, and sturdy rather than compliant. He did not hesitate to sacrifice his court chaplaincy rather than stifle his Whig principles, which were then intolerable at court. If Gray made

merry with him in his early youth, nicknaming him as
was the habit of the time, he shewed a regard for his
" dear Scroddles " almost fatherly, and ended by
leaving to him all his papers, together with a handsome
legacy.   He was one of the correspondents of Horace
Walpole.

His death, in 1797, at the age of seventy-two,
resulted from a slight accident to his leg, which came
in contact with the step of his carriage.   A handsome
monument in Westminster Abbey, near to that of his
friend Gray, suitably commemorates him, but his
position as a man of letters is best indicated by something like a hundred entries in the catalogue of the
British Museum, which, for one reason or another,
stand against his name.

In the settlement of Hugh Mason's affairs, his
grandson, Charles Poole, a merchant of considerable
position in Hull, and evidently the chief man of
business in the family, purchased the tithes with the
tithe-farm on the east side of the churchyard, and other
lands in Sutton.   He afterwards bought other properties in the parish, amongst which was a farm that had
been part of the property of the Hon. Elizabeth
Willoughby, of Birdsall.   He had managed the Yorkshire estates of Miss Jane Wilkinson, and, in
consideration of this service, she left at her death in
1769 her property in Sutton to her worthy friend
Charles Poole.   It consisted of a brick house, with
barn, stable, and garth in the High Street on the west
side of Elm Tree House, the land on which the
stationmaster's house now stands, and 76 acres of tillage
and grass lands.   He was at this period the most
influential man in the parish.

Mr. Thomas Broadley.   In 1737 and 1738 Mr.
Broadley, whose name already appeared amongst the
owners of farm lands, was acquiring property in Stoneferry, one portion of which, being part of the old
enclosure, lay by the river bank and was traversed by

the ancient road to Hull. The road is nearly obliterated, and the fields called the Intack, Little Field, and South Field are now scarcely distinguishable : upon these accounts this acquisition is interesting. Another of his purchases was Crab Close, the long, narrow strip of land that had always separated South-house-cott from Hirn-cott, and had, I think, been kept in the hands of the old lords of the manor as an access from their pasturage in the West Carr to the river. In 1752 he bought from Jewet Cowart, the great-great-grandson of Elizabeth Truslove, the lands which had belonged to her, and had not been acquired by Mrs. Ann Watson. But the most important of Thomas Broadley's acquisitions was made in 1768 while the common fields were being enclosed.

We have seen how the estates of the elder branch of the Daltons, except, perhaps, the Hastings manor, were carried by Elizabeth Witham, the widow of the last of those Daltons, and afterwards the wife of Robert Dolman, into the family of Witham, of Cliffe. Her grandnephew, Matthew Henry Witham, having succeeded to this Sutton property, together with Nuttles and other estates, found himself, through family charges and expenses, unable to keep up his position, and applied to parliament for powers to enable his trustees to sell some of his estates. The full details are frankly disclosed in the Witham Estates' Act of the seventh year of George III.

The Sutton property of the Withams, bought by Mr. Broadley, consisted of the manor of Sutton and Stoneferry, with several other parts of manors in the lordship of Sutton with farms and lands, and the cottage or farm called Castle Hill Farm, also four cottages, together with the sites of three other cottages lately demolished, 7 ½ acres of meadow in Sutton

* Called White House farm, though the White House itself had been acquired by Mrs. Watson.

Ings, 102 pasture gates in Bransholm pasture, and tenements erected on the waste of the manor at "Bridge-foot, otherwise Witham." This eastern entrance to the town of Hull appears to have taken its name from the family that held these important shares in the manor. The purchase included the ancient moated mound called Castle Hill, and Mr. Broadley now became the most prominent amongst those who claimed to be lords of the manor. Other large acquisitions made by his family will be noticed in a later chapter.

The appearance of the towns of Sutton and Stoneferry during this period, and the condition of their inhabitants, may be gathered from a variety of sources, some of which I have already used in describing the farms and the family concerns of their owners.

From the steeple of the church the whole area surrounding the long low ridge that formed the ancient Sudtone would then be seen as a level green plain, without a fence or house, or even a tree except such as had sprung up by the sides of the old watercourses. There were indeed the few ancient enclosures called "pighills," which represented the ancient sheepcots. The three tillage fields upon the higher ground would be easily distinguishable, one of them growing a crop of wheat, another bearing patches of barley, oats, beans, and peas, and the third lying in "clotts" or fallow. These fields were dotted with the tofts and toftsteads so often mentioned.

The village lay almost exactly within its present limits, the farmsteads inconveniently crowded together. There would be a few houses occupied by the village tradesmen, the blacksmith, wheelwright, shoemaker, tailor, and weaver. There was one inn, if no more, and, probably, a general shop. There was at least one man who got his living partially by fishing with boats and nets in the larger ditches and pools of water. There could not be many cottages. The tenant of one of the small farms that I have described would generally find his family sufficient for its cultivation. Very few yeomen or farmers who owned their farms were then left. Most of these farms had been sold long before by the descendants of the old free tenants.

The farmstead at the corner of the Stoneferry Road, with one or two small farms or cottages adjoining, belonged to Mr. Thomas Broadley. Then came a farmstead belonging to Mr. John Cock's daughter, Ann Munby; the next was the old house with land which Mr. Henry Cock had held, and behind which his brick kilns were situate, but which in 1768 belonged to Benjamin Blaydes, Junr. Miss Jane Wilkinson owned one of the farmsteads that lay opposite to the way leading down into the Carr. Then came the manor house of the Corporation of Hull (to the east of the present Elm Tree House), rented by Thomas Atkinson, yeoman. Where the Reading Room and the Railway Station now stand were four small enclosures, from which the cottage farms had wholly disappeared. The parish gravel pit was at the place where the road goes down into the Carr. This was called the Marr Lane, commemorating the ancient Sutton Marr.

The site of the ancient Rectory, or Mansion House of the College of St. James, with the more modern buildings and the old Tithe farmstead I have already indicated. Within living memory there was a large house on the old Tithe farmstead, the farmyard coming close up to the street, where a fine group of chestnut trees formed a prominent feature.* Next came the Hastings Manor House, that belonged to the family of Sedgwick. Eastward of this were the old enclosed lands of Mr. Thomas Mould and of Mr. T. G. Champney, extending as far as the tillage of the East field.

* I owe this description to the kindness of Mr. Francis Jackson, of Wawne, whose grandfather lived there, and who remembers the house.

TOWN OF SUTTON

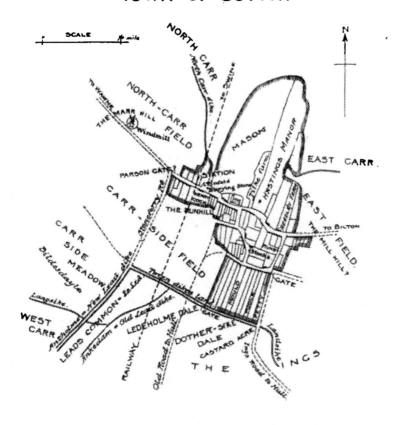

NOTE.—The dark edging surrounds the ancient enclosures as shewn on a map dated 1770. Everything outside was open tillage or grass land. I have supplied the names, some of which will be recognised as having been in use in the 13th century.

The street which runs from the Wawne Road to the Bilton Road is called in legal documents the Highgate, High Street, and Great Street. The short street nearest to it on the south, and parallel to it, is Fynkell Street. The street of irregular course which runs from the Highgate to the gate leading to the Ings is Lowgate. The narrow lane between Highgate and Lowgate towards the east is of the shape of a ploughed land, and before the town extended eastward was probably part of the East Field.

On the south side of the Highgate, near its eastern end, there were three or four farms, and the more important residence of the Munbys, a large house that stood facing the street. The front garden of the house of Mrs. Ross now occupies this site. In 1751 Mr. Broadley bought "a garth facing the Church." Leonard Chamberlaine's farmstead must also, I think, have been in the centre of the town. It probably consisted of separate portions abutting on the Highgate, and on Fynkell Street at the rear.

The Mansion House of Mr. Thomas Mould, a merchant, having also a handsome old mansion in Hull, stood in extensive grounds in the angle formed by the southern portion of Lowgate near the Stocks. I have been unable to connect this property with any of its former possessors. The small farmsteads in Lowgate and the back street have been already sufficiently distinguished. The last farmstead at the east end of Lowgate, at the corner of the road to Hull, was that of George Petty, yeoman. There was a gate across the end of Lowgate, and two houses were on the left-hand side, outside the gate.

The Windmill Hill by the side of the Wawne Road would then have one of the old wooden mills, specimens of which may still be seen. In 1715 William Munby bought of Ralph Peacock a "land end" in the North Carr Field, ten yards square, being part of the fifth land west of the first balk next to Sutton, on which to build this windmill.* The balks had evidently disappeared to a great extent by that time, so that there was no longer one balk to each land.

In 1783, the parish register records the burial of Jenny Farthing, spinster, killed by the "East Mill." If no mill existed at the east end of the town, this record must refer to the mill then lately erected near to

---

* I have already suggested that there must have been a windmill at the east end of the town ; perhaps the first hill in the East Field was called Mill Hill from this mill.

Salts House, on the Holderness Road, where a more modern mill is, I think, now being demolished.

The town was shut in by gates at the ends of all the streets. The old names of Parson's Gate and Parrock

TOWN OF STONEFERRY

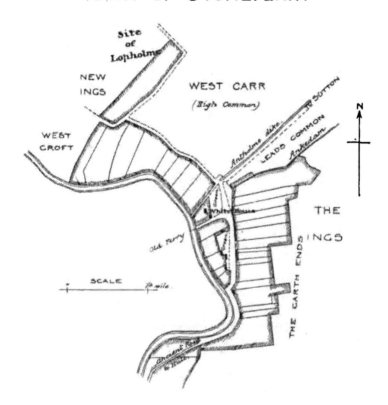

Gate seem to have been lost. Casterd Gate may have been the gate in 'Tween Dikes Lane, where the Casterd Dale represented the ancient "Catesterte." Highgate and Lowgate remained as names of the chief streets.* The gates kept the cattle from straying

---

* Neither name has been used in modern times, unless in a conveyance.

into the town. It is probable that all the footways
were protected by posts and rails, as shewn by the
engraving on page 94. A few years ago posts and
rails still protected the footway between Stoneferry
Road and the mill.

Beyond the Carr Side Field, the Ings and Leads
Common was the town of Stoneferry, with its farms
more scattered, and having liberal shares of enclosed
land.   There was six times as much enclosed land by
the river at Stoneferry as in Sutton.   The road went
through Leads Common as far as Antholme Bridge,
and then turned through waste ground past the White
House, where the lane branches off to the old ferry.
The town street beyond this lane seems to cross
the lands of an ancient tillage field.   The Poor-house
was in the northern part of Stoneferry.   There had
been an ancient road by the side of the river bank
to Hull; though long disused, it is not yet quite
obliterated.

The old Sugar House in Lime Street, close to
Witham, was built before the year 1752.   There would
be a few houses thinly scattered in that neighbourhood,
but the district called " The Groves " was then chiefly
an open field.

There are still several old houses in Sutton which
preserve the appearance of the houses of the last
century.   Some of these may be as old as the reign of
George the Second.   They consisted of a ground
floor of two rooms, the front room being the common
entrance and living room, the back room forming the
kitchen.   There was a low garret with dormer windows in the roof.   There would be no ceiling to the
lower rooms, and everything could be heard, if not
seen, through the chinks in the boarded floor.   As
times improved, it became the practice to improve
these houses by raising the roofs so as to convert the
garrets into good square bedrooms, and sometimes
they were enlarged at the front or rear.   One example,

the easternmost house on the north side of the High-gate, will illustrate both these processes. The precise shape of the original house can be traced at the junction of the old work with the new. Many of these houses must originally have been thatched. It is not very long since the last specimens of thatching disappeared from the streets. A town like this, with farmsteads closely packed together, was always in danger of total destruction by fire, and care in the use of lights was a matter of public concern. By the regulations of some manors there were penalties for laying straw or sticks near to the hearth in any house, and for carrying fire from one house to another, except in a covered vessel.

AN OLD HOUSE ENLARGED.

Outside the town gates there were only four public thorough-fares for carts—the ancient road that extended from Wawne to Bilton ; the Leads Road, which ran by the side of the *leda* to Stoneferry ; a portion of the Holderness Road ; and the Ings Road, then called the Hull Road, originally granted to the nuns of Swine as a way from Catesterte to the sheep-fold of Martin de Ottringham. When this came into public use as a road to Hull, the old road leading straight across the Ings to the Groves became a foot-road, as it is at present. Besides these, there were of necessity foot-ways and cart tracks all over the fields to enable the occupiers of the small patches of land to reach them from the public highways. None of the cart roads could be more than barely passable. There was no public cart road from Stoneferry to Hull, and, except as to foot traffic, Hull could be reached only by way of Sutton or by boat on the river.

There were then very few roads in England that

could have been traversed by a light cart. Rich people might ride in heavy carriages, drawn by horses or oxen, at a snail's pace. Even on turnpike roads there were sloughs in which vehicles stuck fast, ruts four feet deep, ruts in which a sheep might be lost, ruts unfathomable. Oxen at plough were often unyoked, to the profit of their owners, for dragging carriages out of the mire. Mason, writing from Aston, promised to go to York when he could muster courage to *wade* seven miles to a turnpike road. If the road were dry, it was intolerably rough. The farm wagon and the wain were used for getting in the harvest. Though these were only half laden, they were constantly being overturned. The Rev. Robert Banks, vicar of Hull, writing in 1707, says, " The ways in Holderness at this time of the year are next to impassable, and some have lost their lives who have ventured through them." In Burton's Monasticon, Swine is described as a secluded place where the land is so flat and the roads so deep that it is scarcely possible to get to it. Even after this period Arthur Young, the writer upon agriculture, travelled through the North of England, cursing the turnpike roads and counting the farmers' wagons that lay wrecked by the wayside.

There was then only one eligible mode of travelling. Mounted on a strong horse, and provided with a riding coat, high boots, and saddle-bags, a man might travel anywhere, and at a very good pace. A woman in cloak and hood would ride on a pillion behind a relation or a servant, and one man would ride behind another. Horsemen were tempted, by the absence of fences, to trespass on the adjoining lands, which would be cut up for fifty feet on each side, but the public sentiment was strongly against riding over wheat. It was not only unneighbourly, it tended to reduce the supply of food, which was a sin! In an old metrical form of examination for a penitent at confession, the priest asks such a question as this :—

"Art thou wont o'er wheat to ride
When thou mightest have gone by side?"

Nobody walked along such roads in bad weather, except those who were prepared to walk over ploughed land or marsh : of this we shall find some evidence amongst the parish records.   In the country every man above the position of a labourer went about booted and spurred, and looking as if he were ready to mount a horse.   The ordinary costume of such a person was a long coat over a long waistcoat, knee breeches, high boots, and a wide brimmed hat.   Such clothes, home-spun, descended from father to son.   The gentlemen whom I have named would have their best garments of rich brown, or green, or blue, which might be trimmed with silver or gold lace.   Their low shoes had silver buckles.   They would pin up the brims of their hats in some fashion ; the three cocked hat so commonly seen in pictures being the favourite mode. A wig was a necessity for anyone who pretended to be genteel or even smart.   Mason's portraits shew him as a clergyman in his periwig.

Old pictures represent country women in gowns cut low and with kerchiefs round the neck.   A large white cap was worn, and for greater protection, a home-made bonnet or a cloak with a hood.   The ordinary material was Duffel grey.   For church and for grand occasions there were hats, with garments of more elaborate design.

The parish registers for this period tell us something of the occupations of the men.   Husbandman, or farmer, and labourer are the most frequent entries. Weaver, webster, carpinter, blacksmith, tailler, fisher-man, pinder, milner, schoolmaster, and innholder occur. A sugar boiler in 1735 and a bandmaker indicate that these occupations had already been established near to Hull.   About 1734-6 Christopher Danby, yeoman, a papist, and children of Blythe, Temple, Gunby, Morton, and Chapman, yeomen, were buried.   Two "grassmen," whose occupations would be in the meadows and pastures are mentioned. Trowell, grassman, lived at the cottage farm at Castle Hill. Spinsters are common, and one man is distinguished as a " Batcoler."

The work of the farm changes slowly from generation to generation. This was the period immediately before the introduction of machinery. Corn was thrashed by the flail, and winnowed by being poured slowly in a thin stream from a wide-mouthed basket in the draught of the barn door. I have heard no tradition of Sutton women going out to plough or using the flail, but they would have to work in the harvest field, and to be handy among the cattle in the homestead. During a great part of the year they would go out milking in the open field. The poet Mason notices the winding path of the milkmaid as she walked through the fields from stile to stile ; and, indeed, we could ill spare that picturesque figure from the eighteenth century landscape. In the dairy, cheese was made of skim milk, and butter was produced by the slow process of working the plunger of a hand churn.

All the spare time of the women was occupied in spinning, wool being spun as well as flax. In those days wool would be spun on the great wheel. The spinster stood at her work, whirling the wheel round smartly with her hand, then stepping backwards and drawing out from the point of the spindle the lengthening thread. Returning towards the wheel, the thread was wound upon the spindle as it continued to revolve. This process required a good deal of movement, and has been said to have produced attitudes, which, for grace, might be compared with such as are caused by playing the harp. It is pleasant to think of this constant occupation of our great grandmothers in such an aspect.*

* I more often think of an old village farmer who showed me where his mother used to bring out her wheel in the moonlight, when everybody else was in bed, and the children lay awake long after midnight listening to the whirr of the spindle and to her footsteps going backwards and forwards across the village street.

Woollen yarn could be sold or woven by the webster into the homespun cloth in which ordinary people were clad. Linen was for nicer uses. There was no cotton. Of the small spinning wheel, with which flax was made into thread, I have some precise information relating to a more recent time.

The farmer took his corn to Hull on horseback—a sack at a time, as it was thrashed—and stood it up for sale. The wife might ride or carry her dairy produce along the foot-road. A Lincolnshire song says :—

> " The farmer doth to the market go
>   To sell his barley and wheat ;
>   His wife on a pilloring seat rides behind,
>   Dressed up so clean and neat—
>   With a basket of butter and eggs she rides."

The farmers used very little money, living principally on the produce of their farms. There were no weekly markets for cattle. The fortnightly market at Hedon was not established. The farmers looked forward to certain annual fairs—Maudling fair, near Hedon ;* Holy Rood fair, and Michaelmas fair. There was no winter feeding of cattle with turnips. They sent their corn to the mill, the "milner" paying himself by taking toll. They had their poultry and eggs. but during half the year fresh meat was scarce, and beef as well as bacon was salted down. With such a diet a good supply of vegetables was necessary, but they had very little space for gardens. Potatoes, very small and waxy, were being slowly introduced in certain places. In the farm inventory of 1748, already quoted, is an item of 15s. for a "fence round potatoes." Were it not for that entry, I should have felt quite certain that they were still unknown in this locality. We shall see that at good dinners in Sutton they were not actually used.

---

* Held on Magdalen Hill, but suppressed some years since on account of the cattle plague.

There were no ovens or ranges. Coal must have been used to a small extent, but turves burnt on the hearth with refuse wood were the ordinary fuel. Even after 1768 rights of turbary were still put in a Sutton conveyance of land. Nearly all the meat would be boiled, and the juices came to table as broth rather than as gravy. Plates and dishes of pewter were used by the few, flat wooden trenchers by the many. Bread was leavened by using in each batch a piece of old paste that had been saved long enough to turn sour. It was baked on the hot hearth under an iron cover. Such bread is substantial, with a slightly sour flavour that is not unpleasant. The men ordinarily used their own clasp-knives at dinner, and were unaccustomed to a fork. Tea would be known in the very few households that could afford to pay twelve shillings to a guinea a pound. Small beer or skim milk was generally drunk at meals, strong beer being for festive occasions. Spirits were beginning to be known as a convivial drink. In the reign of George the Second gin was coming in as a substitute for the safer but slower, and less effectual, ale.

The Plague was by this time almost forgotten, but they had two diseases which custom must have made familiar. The moist meadows, the wet pastures, and the Carrs, were a constant source of ague. One of its victims, sitting shivering by the fire, would be a common sight. Deaths were frequent, for no quick and effectual cure was then known. The small-pox came in periodical epidemics, but was never entirely absent. About four out of five children caught it, and one or two of these would be carried off. Those who escaped as children might catch it at any later period. Two-thirds of the population bore on their faces such marks of this frightful scourge as are now very rarely seen. The people were accustomed to this disorder, as their forefathers had been to the plague. In ordinary cases of sickness doctors were then thinking less of the treatment by salivation and more favourably of bleeding, which was practised to an incredible extent. They probably did best in most cases who did nothing, and let nature take its course.*

Skin diseases and insect pests were favoured by the wearing of grey woollen clothes, and were the terror of every housemother. Personal washing beyond the hands and face was little known. There was no place where men could bathe, and, though the sea was only a dozen miles away, sea bathing was hardly thought of, except as a remedy for the bite of a mad dog. There was one place in the parish where washing seems to have been practised as a curative measure. Down in the East Field, near to Spring Cottage Farm, was the Blindwell, to which the people had access. If they used its waters freely when suffering from sore eyes, their faith would probably be rewarded.

Neither Leonard Chamberlane nor Ann Watson had included writing among the things to be taught to their scholars. At a parish meeting in Sutton, five out of eight of the principal farmers were unable to sign their names. Sometimes they made their marks ; sometimes the clerk would write all the names down to save trouble. At weddings one or both of the parties would be unable to write. In the case of one marriage by license neither party could sign the register. Nobody wrote letters, or was very anxious to receive them. Even rich people hesitated to write to their friends, for the receiver paid the postage, which would be from eightpence to fifteenpence. Business was done, and news spread abroad, by word of mouth. About the middle of the century two attempts to establish newspapers in Hull failed for want of encouragement. The Bible and Prayer Book,

* Nothing can be stronger than that which has been written by medical men of their predecessors. Horace Walpole, however, managed to express with a kind of humour his indignation upon hearing that a Professor had refused to get up in the night to attend Gray in his last illness. He asks, " Is their absence to murder us as well as their presence ?"

with the Pilgrim's Progress, would be within the reach of most children. Gulliver's Travels and Robinson Crusoe would be lent from house to house. Novels, and books interesting to children, were just beginning to be written for the rich and the children of the rich.

Superstition and credulity flourished. Everybody who believed in anything, believed firmly in witchcraft and ghosts, in signs good and bad, and in seasons of good and evil luck. Horace Walpole, writing to Mason, asks for some good ghost stories out of the North. In addition to the badness of the roads, the possibility of meeting an unearthly wanderer tended to keep the townsfolk within the town gates after nightfall.

Within those gates they would be cheerful enough, though their seasons of merry-making might be few. I find no trace of May-day sports, but the Maypole would probably be reared where the feast is still held on St. James's Day. Such festivities then meant outdoor games, with dancing and feasting in public. The gentlefolk (when there were any), the farmers, and the labourers joined heartily in them, or showed their sympathy by their presence. These are amongst the most pleasant memories of the good old times.*

The Fishery Feast. There was one day of festivity of which we have some precise details in the Records of the Corporation of Hull. Annually on Midsummer Eve, which is the eve of the Feast of the Nativity of St. John the Baptist, the Corporation exercised their right of fishery as the owners of Salvain's sixth share of the Manor. That was usually the termination of the close time for fishing in such waters as these. Sutton Marr seems to have disappeared, but there remained the Filling and the "Old Williams" in the neighbourhood of Castle Hill. The drains seem, in respect of the fishery, to have

---

* In the last chapter will be found the local evidence on which most of these items are founded.

been apportioned amongst the several Lords of the Manor, and the Corporation fished only these two waters. But the fishery must have been of some importance, for in 1727 Richard Trowell, fisherman, is named in the register, and he had successors who fished with boats and nets down to the reign of George the Third.

The oldest record of the fishery feast, which the Corporation possesses, is the following. There is nothing to shew where it is held, but all the feasts mentioned in the later accounts were held at Sutton.

FOR THE FISH DINNER 22TH. JUNE 1695.

To: 30: Bottles of Blenkard *	-	-	-	£03 : oo : oo
To Ale Beare and tobacko	-	-	-	oo : 10 : 06
To: 3: Cool Tankerds	-	-	-	oo : 08 : oo
To: 1: Botle of Canary	-	-	-	oo : 02 : 04
To Victuals -	-	-	-	- .	02 : 08 : oo
To the servants by order	-	-	-	oo : 05 : oo

$$£06 : 13 : 10$$

Hull: 24th : June 1695.

Recd : of the R^t worpp^l Henry Maister p. the Hands of Ro : Raikes in money fower pounds eighteen shill : and Sixpence; and one pound fifteen shill : I allow for a mass fatt I bought of the Towne is in all Six Pounds Thirteen Shill : and Six pence in full of this noat : I say recd. - - - - } 6 : 13 : 6

by me Tho : Lambert.

The later accounts, dated from 1745 to 1766, give much information as to the proceedings of the annual fishing, and as to local habits in the middle of the eighteenth century. The Mayor and some members of the Corporation, with the principal officers, went to Sutton in procession, and, no doubt, in some state. The Mayor had a chaise and pair. The Town

* I can hear nothing about any liquor so called. It must have been a kind of wine.

Clerk, the mace-bearer, and three or four others, had horses hired for them at 1s. 6d. per day. The rest, to the number of seven or eight, found their own horses. They would be off in good time; on one occasion, at least, they had some refreshment with drink before starting. They must have made a brave show.

Toll was paid at the Summergangs turnpike gate; sixpence for a chaise and pair, threepence for a chaise and single horse, and a penny for a saddle horse, for all which the toll keeper had to make out a bill. Robert Tayler, who made all the arrangements, presented the bills, adding his own payments to them. When the party arrived in the Carr their horses were held by boys at the cost of sixpence. Once, when the horses broke away and got as far as Summergangs gate, a man was paid sixpence for fetching them back. In 1757 there is a charge for holding horses at Frierdike, a name used elsewhere for Foredike.

The Fillings had to be dressed or cleared of weeds in preparation for this expedition. James Trowel was ready with four or five boats and the same number of men, and they drew the nets so as to drive the fish to places where they could be taken out. The men had a shilling each for the day. When dinner was given them it cost sixpence each. The charge for boats was a shilling each, and Trowel charged about three shillings for the use of his nets and for his own trouble. In 1751 he charged a shilling "for dressing the old Williams." He was, perhaps, the last fisherman of that family, for Edward Butters was employed in the later years.

The fishery feast was held at the village inn, but there are charges for carrying liquor, and for a man to assist the carter. No doubt there would be ale and the lighter refreshments down at the Fillings. Once Robert Tayler had a bread and cheese lunch before going into Carr. But the more serious elements of the feast were beyond the resources of the inn, and had to be brought from Hull. Robert Tayler himself in the first instance, and afterwards John Nicholson, who supplied refreshments at the Town Hall, bought the necessary provisions. Nicholson charges for a horse to take them to Sutton, with the usual sum of half-a-guinea for cooking them there. Matthew Leng, the innholder, had his bill for ale and tobacco, with other light refreshments, and for his "trouble of house." One of the feast days must have been wet, for he makes a charge for coats for the gentlemen.

I will give the bills for eatables and drinkables consumed in the year first named. As it was then usual to sign with a mark, we will not too closely criticise the performances of the few who wrote : and it is only fair to say that he who wrote the best spelled the worst. But even this free spelling has its value. Such an item as "chease keaks," which occurs in one of the other bills, evidently reproduces the local name of that popular viand.

EXPENSES AT SUTTON JUNE 22ND, 1745.

	£	s	d
Six Gall^{ns} and halfe wine	1	15	9
Rum and Brandy	0	15	6
Lemmons	0	2	3
Beefe	0	7	0
12 Chickens	0	5	6
Suger	0	7	8
Ham	0	3	6
Two Geese	0	3	10
Two q^{rs} lamb	0	4	0
Bread	0	2	0
10lb Butter	0	8	4
Vinegar, Mustard, Salt, and Capers, &c.	0	3	8
Tobacco, &c.	0	3	0
Pees, Sallit, and Colly Flower	0	5	6
Glasses and bottles broak	0	3	0
Mrs. Loyd (the cook)	0	10	6
	£6	1	0

The large quantity of butter would be required chiefly for frying the fish, of which mention is once made. No doubt we ought to add this item to the other provisions consumed at the feast. The second bill is that of Matthew Leng, the innkeeper of Sutton.

June 22, 1745.

A note of charges at Sutton when fillings was driven. By the Honourable the maior and burgesis of hull to me, Mathow Long.

	£	s	d
For alle and bred and chees, and hay for the horses	2	6	8
for tartes and cheeskaks	0	10	0
for hous and tendance	0	12	6
4 glasses broken	0	0	8
paid for eges for salets	0	0	3
halfe grose pipes	0	0	8
halfe pound candels	0	0	3
	£3	11	0

Received the 28th day of June, 1745, of Mr. Robt. the contents of this note in full for the use of the corporation.

Recd. I say p Mathow M Leng.
his
mark.

The charge for vegetables varies considerably ; they were brought direct from the gardener in Hull. In 1753 John Nicholson paid Mrs. French, whose name and occupation are perpetuated in " French's Gardens," Mason Street, a three and tenpenny bill for vegetables which included 4 peckes peasse, torneps, carets, *Enens*, 4 cabages, 2 cowcombers, and a half-pennyworth each of sage and of parsley. With all this minuteness of detail, no mention is made of potatoes. It seems certain that if they had then been in general use in Hull, and its neighbourhood, they would have been provided at these feasts, and mentioned in the bills.

The cost of articles named in different bills is as follows :—Beef, 3s. 6d. a stone ; a ham, weighing thirteen pounds and a half, 4½d. a pound ; a side of lamb,

5s. to 6s. ; a leg of mutton, 2s. ; a quarter of a stone of salt, 3½d.; loaf sugar, 8d. to 1s. a pound ; wine, about 16s. a dozen ; three bottles of port, 2s. each ; best foreign brandy, 8s. 6d. to 10s. a gallon ; best Jamaica rum, 9s. ; lemons, 1d. and 2d. each ; cheese, 2½d to 4½d., and butter usually about 5d. a pound. Upon one occasion a bottle of cyder was supplied, at another time a pottle of mead ; they mixed the mustard with vinegar as French people still do. A quart of "aleker," a kind of home-made vinegar, being sour ale or beer, cost 4d. Anchovies are mentioned. A charge for "cherries for the gentlemen" is the only indication of dessert. Tea at Sutton is once charged at sixpence a head, at another time tea was supplied at the same cost in Hull, probably after the return of the party. Upon the whole there is less difference than might be expected between this feast and the roughly plentiful dinner to which a similar party might have sat down a century afterwards.

No doubt the whole village shared more or less in the Fishery Feast. It cost some ten or twelve pounds, and was intended to be remembered in case the rights of the Corporation should ever be questioned. Nobody who assisted, if only by looking on, would be altogether left out. There were not enough drinking vessels in the inn, and some appear to have been borrowed in the village ; in 1749 they were hired in Hull. The bill for hiring includes three dozen wine glasses, one dozen water glasses, six punch bowls with six ladles, two decanters weighing four pounds eight ounces, and one weighing one pound fourteen ounces, with two small porringers. There were usually breakages—"glasses and bottles broak," "four glasses broken," "two mugs," "five glasses broke of Thos. Atkinson," "one chaney basin," "a punch bowl broken," this last by a servant, whose name, after being entered, was very considerately obliterated. But glasses and crockery are fragile, and the break-

16

ages at such a feast might have been very much worse.

The accounts for these festivities end significantly with those for 1766. In the following year the common fields were being allotted, and such expeditions as this may then have been thought to involve more interference with private ownership than the occasion justified. Yet even in the next generation owners of other shares in the manor thought it worth while to maintain, by stipulations in deeds, their rights of fishery in the ancient water courses.

Two years before the last of these expeditions, there occurred another disastrous flood, which is recorded in the parish books of Patrington. In 1764, from the sixth of January to the first of April, the whole of the land between Bilton and Hull was under water, so deep that the turnpike houses were deserted, and there was no travelling, except by boat, between these places for months together. A man and horse were drowned in attempting to go through the water. This means that the whole of the meadows and pastures in Sutton lay under water for that length of time. The farmers with their cattle would be prisoners upon the ancient island of Sudtone, looking out, as its first inhabitants had looked out, over miles of inland sea.

There was, however, at that time, a project on foot for putting a stop to the frequent floodings of the Carrs. In 1763 an Act of Parliament was passed for cutting such a drain as had been projected by Sir Joseph Ashe ninety years before. In a paper containing elaborate calculations of levels, this drain, now called Sutton Drain, is described as extending through the Ings and Carr Side meadows to Foredike, at the place called "Double Dikes." At that time the "Sutton dyk" of Sayer the Second, running by the side of Foredike, must have still been conspicuous throughout its whole length, so that the place where the two dikes joined, once called Helpstone Grainings, was chosen as the termination of the new drain. Except on the pasture land, it has now been nearly obliterated by the plough.

There was a serious project of making the proposed Sutton drain into a canal, with locks and places for passing, and for landing goods. But the effectual drainage of the flood waters from the country beyond Benningholm was much more important, and the drain was adapted for that purpose, though the question of canal traffic was not forgotten.

We have some materials for judging of the condition of the Church in Sutton in those days. In 1740 the living of Sutton, which had been held with Marfleet by the Rev. Thomas Patrick, became vacant, and the elder William Mason presented his nephew, the Rev. Arthur Robinson. In the same year Henry Waterland, of Hedon, who, with Hugh Mason, had acquired from Brodrepp the patronage of Marfleet, presented Mr. Robinson to that benefice. Towards the end of the same year he was presented by the Chancellor of York to the vicarage of Wawne. The Chancellor was the Rev. Daniel Waterland, and this series of appointments no doubt bears the aspect of a comfortable family arrangement. It is, however, probable that the arrangement was also a desirable one for the parishes, for each living was extremely poor, and their combined income would scarcely be adequate to the maintenance of a minister.

The parish books shew that Mr. Robinson began by giving close personal attention to each parish, signing the registers and records of the parish meetings. After a few years the names of curates, Hebden, Dawson, Dowbiggin, Lewis, and Thompson appear in the Sutton registers, with that of Arthur Robinson, who calls himself " minister." About 1754 he had been presented to the vicarage of Holy Trinity, in Hull, where he must have always lived, and thenceforth he would be less able to pay personal attention to his country livings. He held the four livings together until 1783, when he resigned that of Holy Trinity, retaining the three small livings until 1789, when he resigned these also.

Whatever might be thought now of such pluralism, we must remember that the practice was then as common as it had been in the fourteenth century, and it does not indicate that the duties, such as they were, failed to be performed by some duly qualified clergyman. The Rev. Arthur Robinson was the nephew of the Vicar of Hull, and the cousin of a Canon and Precentor of York, whose writings are distinctly noted for their high moral tone. He was himself undoubtedly respected as the Vicar of Hull, and there is no reason to think that he fell short of the standard of Churchmanship prevailing in his day. Amongst the little that is known about his connection with Hull is the presentation to him by the Corporation, on his resignation of the living, of a testimonial in the form of a piece . of plate of the value of fifty pounds.*

The records of Queen Anne's Bounty throw a curious light on the conditions under which the living of Sutton was held by the Rev. Arthur Robinson. In 1743 the clear yearly value of the benefice is said to be about £24, arising in this way :—

> "Ten pounds per annum chargeable upon the estate of the Rev. William Mason, Impropriator, and has been paid time immemorial.
>
> Five pounds per annum left by Mrs. Ann Watson, of Stone-ferry, to be paid by ye trustees of her will out of ye rents of her estate for an anniversary sermon to be preached on St. James' Day, which has been paid nigh twenty years.
>
> The rent of a piece of pasture ground (communibus annis), five pounds per annum, which is a gratuity of the parishioners, and what they may at any time withdraw.
>
> Surplice Fees."

* Two of the aldermen having waited upon him, he selected a tea-vase. The old silver tea-vases that I have seen are covered jars, about ten inches in. height, richly ornamented. They were used to treasure the precious and costly leaf as a caddy is used now.

Another entry gives an answer to the question,
" Does the present certain income not exceed £10
per annum ? "

> " Yes, If ye bequest of Mrs. Watson is considered as a
> certain income, which indeed is somewhat precarious, for ye
> heir-at-law pretends to dispute Mrs. Watson's having a power to
> dispose of the estate (out of which ye five pounds per annum is
> paid) and threatens a suite."

From all this it appears that the sixteen pounds paid
a century before by Christopher Brodrepp had in some
way shrunk to ten pounds, and that fifteen pounds
was the full certain income, the five pounds continuing
to be paid by Mrs. Watson's trustees.   An entry in
1802 states that the duty was formerly performed once
every fortnight, and this throws light on Mrs.
Watson's directions that her school girls should go to
church every Sunday to hear divine service and
preaching *when there should be such service.*

The standard of Churchmanship, or indeed of
Christianity, in that day would not be thought much of
now.   It has been asserted that the country parson
differed little from the rough country squire, and that
the sermons of the more polished town clergy might
have been preached in a Unitarian chapel.   This
account is probably inexact, but the earlier sermons of
Precentor Mason, though admirable in their tone and
tendency, would teach his hearers more about Stoics
and Cynics, and Epicureans, about Aristotle and Seneca
and Locke than about any doctrines especially Christian.
But neither the sermons of the clergy nor their walk and
conversation seem to have had much influence on
those whose condition I have been most concerned to
investigate.

They were of the religion of the Tiller of the Soil,
whose eyes turn even more anxiously upward for sun-
shine and rain than earthward to the culture of his fields.
For husbandry they would hold themselves respon-

sible.   They did their duty to their neighbour, and
saw that he did his duty to them.   They told no lies.
They kept their word.   They rarely swore, were
sober as a rule, and went to church—when there was
service—as regularly as to fair and market.   They
could not question the existence of the Providence
whose energies they were daily called upon to direct,
and whose shortcomings they so often had to supply.
They might not be able to quote chapter and verse, but
they felt that between It and them there was an honourable understanding.   It would have shocked their sense
of fairness to be told that, hereafter, things might go
wrong with a Holderness farmer of this stamp.

On such a sturdy stem as this Wesley and the
Milners and the Venns, and many a grafter since,
have raised boughs of fairer blossom and richer
fruit, but, underneath that clustering verdure, there
might, even in later years than these, be observed the
hardy shoots of the original stock, uncultured and
root-grown.

The summer of 1766 was the last that saw the grass
wave over the great unbroken stretch of meadow
which we have so often mentioned as the Ings.   There
and in the Carr-side and Soffham meadows, and in
Risholm Carr, the last hay crop was then gathered
from the unenclosed land; the whole population, young
and old, going out together to the most delightful outdoor occupation of the year.   But the surveyors had
already been busy measuring and arranging and
mapping the new allotments and the roads.   The
stipulations of the award in respect of the off-going crop
shew that in 1767 the East Field was the last to
grow the accustomed crop of wheat, and the last in
which the harvest home could be held with the
boisterous gaiety of the olden time.   It was only when
the harvest was being gathered in common that the
race to get in the last load could cause any excitement.
We can picture the condition of the town when the

wagons came in by the Bilton road with their mixed teams of oxen and horses, and laden with harvesters and children, whose merriment was enhanced by the dangers they had encountered on the way. Only in the publicity of this merry contest, and not in the seclusion of a modern farmstead, could there be any real appropriateness in the harvest song beginning :

> " Wo-hever, wo-hever, at our town end,
>   A cup of good ale and a crown to spend,"

which has come down to us from older times than these.

NOTE.—In 1623 the Corporation let to John Lister, Esquire, their "royalties, Courte Leetes, Courte Barrons, liberties of Courtes, wardes, marriages, releifes, amerciamentes, weyfes, estrees, fisheinges, fowleinges, and profittes of courtes whatsoever," without any reservation of Midsummer even.

In 1677 the Mayor and Burgesses granted to Robert Barnes, of Sutton, Gentleman, for six years "their sixth part of the mannor of Sutton with the priviledges, liberties, and royalties of courts and of Fishing and fowling belonging to the same," except "the honour or royalty of fishing and drawing their nettes first through Sutton Fillings and other Fishing places within the said Lordship of Sutton upon every Midsummer even." The annual fishing expedition may therefore have been instituted between these dates.

THE ENCLOSURE OF THE COMMON FIELDS.

THE most important undertaking of modern times affecting English agriculture and the general appearance of the country was the enclosure of the common fields. This was carried out by a long series of Acts of Parliament, passed chiefly during the eighteenth century, which nearly completed the transformation of the old ploughlands, meadows, and pastures into their present state and aspect.

For generations the owners and occupiers of the best land in the country had been fettered by a system that had long outgrown its original purpose, and had been denounced by all the more intelligent of those concerned with it. In Queen Elizabeth's days, Tusser, the author of *Five Hundred points of Good Husbandry*, writing in prose, and in his quaint doggerel verse, told how one acre of land that was "several" or enclosed was worth three acres of "Champion" land, or that which lay in the open fields.* Arthur Young, writing in 1771, says that on land which has been enclosed, one sheep yields as much wool as three did before, and that the profit upon one sheep is as much as the profit had been upon five. No one seems to estimate the improved value of land when enclosed at less than double the original value. Upon every consideration it was high time that so serious a matter should be taken in hand.

* Champion—Champayne.

As early as the reign of Charles the Second, the parish of Brandesburton, a few miles distant from Sutton had been enclosed.* The reasons for this step are well set out in a decree of the Court of Chancery, dated 1667.   Every man's land lay intermixed in "several" places and by several quantities together. There were two fields, only one of which was sowed one year, and the other field the other year.   Thus "one field was lying fallow every year, and no profit made thereby."   There were 123 commons or gates in these fields after harvest, until the land was tilled and prepared for sowing again.   These commons were to be taken without intermission in certain grounds in the parish, which were good grounds, but they were "drowned" and of little or no profit.   Such language as this might have been used a century later to describe the condition and the value of the Carrs and of the common fields of Sutton in the early years of George III.

At that time Charles Poole, the grandson of Hugh Mason, and the cousin of the poet, owned the tithes together with the tithe farmstead, that adjoined the east side of the churchyard, as well as certain farms in Sutton which he had bought or inherited.   His interest in the improvement of the parish was then greater than that of any other person, for the tithe owner suffered even more than others from the existing agricultural arrangements.   When the crops and the stock had been produced under that antiquated system, the tithe owner had to collect his tenths as he best could.   It was one of the most important points with the farmer to keep the tithe down to the lowest possible amount.   Our grandfathers had their traditions of disputes over the tithe pig, and of the cottager who, having sent for the parson to see him gather apples, tricked him by gathering only nine.   There is a Lincolnshire ditty which may serve to shew the spirit

* Poulson's History of Holderness.

in which the struggle was sometimes carried on.   It
says :—

> " We've cheated the vicar, we'll cheat him again,
> For why should the vicar have one in ten ? "

At Patrington, if the parson refused the lamb that
was offered as tithe they put it into the quire of the
church to take its chance.

It did not usually suit the convenience ʾor the
dignity of the tithe owner to engage personally in
such struggles, and there grew up a class of tithe
farmers who paid annually an agreed amount for the
privilege of collecting the tithe, getting what they
could from the occupiers of the land.   No great
proportion of the money strictly due to the tithe
owner found its way into his pockets.   He had
therefore every inducement to assist in bringing the
system to an end, and this could be very effectually
done under an act for the enclosure of the common
fields.   Charles Poole's monument in Sutton Church
expresses the best opinion of his day on the subject of
these enclosures.   It tells of " his spirit and example
opposed to the prejudice of ages against improvements
in agriculture, by draining, enclosing and planting the
adjacent country."

The Act for the enclosure of the parish of Sutton
was passed in the third year of George III.   From it
we gather the names and the areas of the several parts
of the townships of Sutton and Stoneferry that then
lay open and, under different conditions, common to
the lords of the manor and their tenants.   They were
as follow :—

	Acres.
Tillage in the East Field, the West, or Carr-side, Field, the North Carr Field, and the Clough Field -	780
Pasturage in West Croft and New Ings of Stoneferry -	56
Meadow in Sutton Ings, Carr-side Meadow, and Riseholm Carr · · · · · · ·	1200

	Acres.
Pasturage in East Carr, the Salts, Bransholm, and North Lands, in which there were 640 cattle gates	700
Open Commons called Sutton Common, Stoneferry or West Carr Common, North Carr Common, with other commons and waste lands - - - -	1500
	Total area: 4236.*

There were "several large pieces of open or unenclosed meadow or pasture ground contiguous to the said several arable fields commonly called the Balks," which were the remnants of the ancient boundaries between the selions or groups of selions, and which appear to have been included in the measurement of the tillage fields.

The owners of messuages and cottages, tofts and toftsteads, and lands, had immemorially enjoyed a right of common for their commonable cattle over the 1,500 acres of open commons, a right of common at certain seasons over the East Carr, Salts, Bransholm and North Lands, Common of Average for all sorts of cattle over the Arable Fields with the Balks, and a right of common at a certain particular season for their commonable cattle over the Ings, Carr-side Meadow, and Riseholm Carr. The dispersing and intermixing of these lands in small parcels had been found to be attended with inconvenience and detriment to the parties, and it was considered that the dividing and allotment would be advantageous to all persons interested. In the allotment of the lands the shares of the respective owners were to be made tithe-free, and an allotment consisting of one-eighth of the whole, quantity and quality being considered, was to be made to the owner of the tithes.†

The rights of Mr. Charles Poole, the tithe owner, are described as :—

---

* The old enclosures in Sutton and Stoneferry amount to about 534 acres.
† The tithe on the ancient enclosures was not dealt with at this time.

"The tithes great and small and of what nature or kind soeve
and Ecclesiastical dues, except the accustomed fees for
Churchings, Marriages, and Burials, and all other surplice
fees yearly at two pence a head for every communicant
and also a certain annual payment called Smoke-money
which were to remain payable to Arthur Robinson, clerk,
the then present curate or minister of the church of Sutton."

For carrying out the enclosure, John Dickinson,
William Iveson, John Outram, John Lund, and
Edward Holgate, who were persons of position
much concerned in business relating to property in
the district, were appointed commissioners. Surveys
were made and particulars taken of every man's
interest in the lands, the area of his tillage and his
meadow, the number of cattle gates to which he was
entitled, and any pighills which he might possess upon
the meadow lands. The tofts and toftsteads in the
tillage fields were also taken into account. These and
the pighills alike were thrown into the new allotments
and have disappeared from fields and meadows.

Early in the year 1767 the new allotments had been
staked out. They are fully described in the award,
dated January 5th, 1768, deposited in the vestry
of the church, and are shewn upon certain copies of
a plan of the parish that was made at about the time
of the enclosure.* The award shews evidence of
great care and judgment in allotting to each owner the
land that lay most conveniently with respect to his
farmsteads and ancient enclosures, certain of the
owners making exchanges of small pieces of land to
facilitate the arrangements.

But while the new allotments were being made, the
corn crop belonging to the old proprietors was ripening,
and in the autumn of 1767 it was harvested by them.
The new proprietors had therefore to be compensated by
the owner of each land or selion that had been cleared

* One of these is in the possession of the Corporation of Hull, there are also
one or two copies in private hands. Printed copies of the award are in the
possession of the Corporation and of private persons.

of the off-going crops, and the commissioners settled in minute detail the sums, which, on a balance of all the separate accounts, were to be paid by certain of the proprietors, and the sums which were to be received by others. And thus the changes of ownership were effected by about the end of the year 1767.

The award also dealt with the public and private highways, and footways, and with the drains. The public highways were staked out practically upon the lines of the old highways, straightening the irregularities that had been produced by the traffic of centuries. Thus, though much of the old roadways was re-used, a good deal of the ploughed land was occupied by roadway, as may still be seen where the ends of the selions appear in the grass of the roadside.*

But whether the road ran over an old or a new track, it was thought best to provide by the side of every highway, except the Holderness turnpike road, a footway over the lands of the several owners, so that foot passengers were separated by hedge and ditch from the roads used by vehicles and cattle, and the landowners were ordered to provide stiles and plank bridges where the footways crossed the boundaries between their fields. I believe there are places where the hawthorn in the hedges has never yet grown so as to obliterate the marks of these footways.† Clearly it was not contemplated that the highways, now so smooth and clean, would be fit for the use of foot passengers.

Some of the allotments made under the award are interesting. Mr. Witham, the chief owner of the manor, received the lands adjoining the Castle Hill, and now forming Castle Hill farm.

* The old course of the Wawne Road may still be traced in the field to the right of the modern road from Castle Hill Road to West Carr Lane, and to the left of that road in the fields beyond West Carr Lane.

† The footway to Wawne ran on the right hand side of the highway, passing *behind* the windmill and crossing the highway at West Carr Lane, from which point it ran on the left hand side as far as Foredike. Indeed, it kept near to the ancient line of road.

To Charles Poole in respect of tithes, was awarded a large and valuable allotment in the eastern corner of the parish. It included the Salts and North Lands, the hill now called East Mount and Riseholm Carr, with large portions of the East Field, the Ings, and the East Carr. The area of this allotment was 438 a., 3 r., 3 p. He obtained also, by an exchange with Ann Munby, the Sydings, or Side Ings, at Bell Field, which has been mentioned as the site of an ancient sheepcot belonging to the lord of the manor. He also received in lieu of tithes an allotment of 52 a., 1 r., 29 p., beyond Soffham in that part of the West Carr which had been held by the monks of Meaux. In lieu of the lands that had been purchased by him of Miss Antonina Willoughby, he received an allotment running over Soffham Hill, adjoining the Wawne Road and Foredike, and a small allotment in the Ings, together containing 128 a., 2 r., 4 p. His other allotments included 8 a., 10 p., in lieu of lands inherited from his father, and 57 a., 39 p., in lieu of lands bought of the executors of Hugh Mason.

The Rev. Arthur Robinson owned the ancient enclosure called Oxlands farm, with tillage and meadow in the open fields, and three and a half land-commons, but no house-common. He received an allotment in the Ings adjoining the Oxlands, and another in the West Carr, amounting together to sixty-six acres.

Robert Quokes, Yeoman, received 3 a., 37 p., of good land close to the east side of Sutton town in lieu of a "house common," or the right to depasture thirty sheep and eight large animals, which he enjoyed in respect of his ancient cottage or toftstead." * Two more allotments of the same area to other persons shew that this was the proportion of land awarded in lieu of each house-common. It shews, I think, how small was the real value of the right to depasture sheep and

* This name is written Cwookes in the parish register.

cattle in the moist or drowned carrs and the bare commons of Sutton.

Another allotment has a special interest.   Mr. John Windham Bowyer, who then owned the parish of Wawne, was also the owner of a small piece of land in the Carrside Meadow, and the commissioners, according to their practice, allotted to him the equivalent of 1 rood, 37 perches, next to his own estate.   This could only be done close to the river bank, at the outlet of Foredike, where the mills of the Abbot of Meaux had stood.   The fact that this piece of land was in Sutton seems to have been forgotten, although it is so shown upon the old maps, and the ordnance surveyors have included it in Wawne.   The ordnance map which gives the area of Sutton as 4,739 a., 3 r., 15 p., is therefore deficient to this extent, unless this little allotment is to be considered as lost to the parish.

The ancient water-courses were also adopted by the commissioners, and formally described as public drains. But even while they were preparing their award the new drain was being cut to take the water that came down from a great district to the north-east, and which was to protect from floods all but the lowest portions of the North and East Carrs.   This is the old Sutton Drain before mentioned, which discharges into the river Hull, near the North Bridge.   Poulson notes that before the enclosure, the lands in Sutton were so subject to floods, that many hundreds of acres were valued at 2s. 6d. per acre, which, from the salutary effects of this drainage, were soon afterwards let at 28s. per acre.   The fisheries in Sutton are also said to have extended over "many thousand acres," an exaggeration which contains a large measure of truth.*

Under the Act of the fourth year of George III.,

* The Award does not treat the western end of the ancient Foredike, where the Raw ran between it and Sutton-dike as a public drain, but it names it as the boundary of the lands awarded in the north-western corner of the parish.   This seems to have been an error, for the Raw or Rawbank belonged to the lords of the manor.   The actual boundary of these lands was Sutton-dike.

which was passed chiefly for the making of Sutton Drain, the commissioners estimated the improvement in the annual value of the lands in the North and East Carrs at from 10s. to 20s. per acre. Out of the total expense of £24,000, the owners of land in Sutton had to pay £6,582 5s. od., which was a fraction over £8 for every £1 of increase in annual value.*

The smaller allotments continued to be attached to the old farmsteads in Sutton town—indeed this is still the case to some extent—but all the large allotments would require to be provided with new farmsteads of substantial construction conveniently placed upon the land. Such farmsteads were provided at once for Castle Hill and Soffham farms. The former had been purchased from Mr. Witham by Mr. Thomas Broadley, and the land on which Soffham farmstead now stands had been left by Miss Jane Wilkinson to Mr. Charles Poole. The farmsteads on the right of the road to Wawne, with the farm of Riseholm Hill, were also erected soon after the enclosure. Low Bransholm farm, which was allotted to Benjamin Blaydes, Junior, seems to have already had some kind of farm building. It is the only one that is shewn in that vicinity upon the map of Sutton, dated 1770. A very old building still exists at this farmstead.

The original position of High Bransholm farmstead is worthy of notice. It was built for the Corporation of Hull upon their chief allotment, in the position which must then have been thought the most suitable —close to the drain once called Thirty-acre-dike, the boundary of Swine, and far away from any public or private road. There could be only one reason for this. There seemed to be no hope of getting the produce away by road from such an out-of-the-way farm, so it was intended to convey it by boats along the dikes, just as the farmers of Holland and Flanders still carry

* Acts of Parliament for Holderness Drainage, with plan, by A. Bower, Surveyor, 1781.

their hay and vegetables, and their tubs of milk, in boats along ditches even smaller than these. The next generation found out that it was better to incur all the perils of the roads, and the existing farmstead was built near to Bransholm Lane, a deep and miry roadway, unendurably bad until it was made passable in our own day.

The immediate result of this award must have been such a demand for labourers as the parish had never before known. Every allotment had to be enclosed with hedge and ditch. Gates, stiles, and planked bridges had to be provided. The erection of so many farm houses was a considerable undertaking. In connection with such work in Sutton, and also in Wawne, the name of Munby has come down in tradition. In 1715, William Munby, who married Ann Cock, had built the new windmill. In 1743, a William Munby was carrying out fencing and the cleansing of drains at High Bransholm for the Corporation of Hull. He was, I think, the eldest son of William and Ann Munby, who, by will in 1754, left the Sutton and Keyingham property of his family to his four brothers, through one of whom, Benjamin, a considerable portion of the property descended to the family of Ross. A high house, built as if for their own residence, stood on the site of the Munby's old farmstead, opposite to the Reading Room, some twenty years ago.

As a result of the enclosure and the cutting of the Sutton drain, the value of the lands and the value of the tithe-owner's interest must have been at least doubled, but in some cases more than quadrupled. The owners had, however, to bear their proportion of the cost of these undertakings. The effect upon the tenant farmers would depend upon the arrangements they might make with their landlords in respect of rent, but in other respects, they would find the change entirely to their advantage. Their work lay close to

17

their homesteads. For the first time each one could
manage his land to his own liking. The more
enterprising among them could now improve the
accommodation for their cattle. Root crops and green
crops might now be introduced by the few farmers of
that day who dare venture out of the beaten track.
The thorough drainage of the land by ditches and by
pipes, and the introduction of modern inventions, then
undreamed of, were now made possible. The
balks and other grass divisions in the tillage fields
that still remained would be ploughed up, and
much of the driest of the meadow and pasture land
would be turned into tillage, in view of the rising
prices of wheat.

In such enclosures of parishes it must have happened
in many cases that the cottagers who were of the
labouring class, having no title to the land, lost the
chance, which they before had, of turning a cow, or a
few sheep, or a flock of geese on the commons and
wastes that were not held by the farmers under the
system of pasture-gates. There were, however, few of
such cottagers in Sutton, where the smaller houses
had been diminishing in number, and the demand for
labourers increased so greatly through the Enclosure,
that they must have been well compensated for the
loss of the very indifferent pasturage. Besides
this, the rising town of Hull offered high wages
and absorbed all the local surplus labour. The
labouring population of Sutton was largely com-
posed of new settlers from the "East End" of
Holderness, who occupied the old farm houses
which the farmers had left. For such families to be
without land was no doubt an evil, but it cannot be
charged against the improvements, which gave them a
footing in the parish. It is everywhere an evil for
labourers to be without a chance of bettering their
condition, and the provision of allotments, for working
men has not been undertaken too soon.

ANTIQUITIES OF MODERN SUTTON.

PART I.

THIS subject completes my story. Although it deals with a period extending backward one hundred and twenty-eight years, those years have seen no change sufficiently striking to suggest a dividing line. They form a period distinctly modern, and people whom we have known lived through the earlier years. This period has, nevertheless, its antiquities, for practices have existed in it, and things have happened, which are as utterly forgotten as if they belonged to the days of the ancient lords of Sutton. Many an item in this chapter is my authority for some statement on an earlier page that is not otherwise substantiated. If I have to draw rather freely on the experiences and the recollections of those with whom I have been best acquainted, it is because I have sought for outside help of this kind almost in vain. The events which seemed worth recording are arranged as in some former chapters, not chronologically, but in such groups as the nature of the materials seemed to suggest.

We have seen how the value of the manorial rights had dwindled. In the eighteenth century nothing of a practical nature was heard of copyholds or of "services" in the shape of hens. Even the fishery rights had been neglected, and, except in legal documents, these rights quietly vanished with the enclosure of the common fields. But, though the position of a lord of the manor has ceased to be of substantial value, those who have traced the line of the ancient lords of Sutton from Grinchil and Lanbert and Syward through Sayer the Second and his successors, will feel that, if only on sentimental grounds, their former power and dignity should not be clean forgotten.

A confused account given by Poulson * seems to imply that Charles Poole the elder had disposed of his sixth share of the manor, probably derived through Bromflete, to Hugh Mason, and states that the royalty of the fisheries was divided into 9 parts, of which 4½ parts had belonged to Mason, 3½ to Witham, and the remaining part to the Corporation of Hull. This was probably the proportion in which the owners of so much of the manor as could then be traced considered it to be held by them.† Immediately after the enclosure, Mr. Witham's share was acquired by Mr. Thomas Broadley, and from a conveyance referred to below, it appears that in 1799 Mr. Robert Carlisle Broadley then acquired Mason's share. Thus was again brought together after four hundred years, nearly the whole of the manor which had been dispersed on the death of Sir Thomas de Sutton.‡

There was, however, another portion which does not appear to be included in the above reckoning; that which had descended in the family of Blaydes. This was sold in 1828, by Mr. Hugh Blaydes, of London, together with Low Bransholm farm, to the Corporation of Hull. In the conveyance it is thus described :—

---

* History of Holderness, vol. ii., p. 329.

† Mason had acquired from the Daltons only eight-ninths of Bulmer's manor. Poulson says the Daltons "reserved" the remaining ninth, but Bulmer's share had fallen amongst heiresses, and it may be that the Daltons had never acquired this portion.

‡ I will give in the appendix some account of the descent of the three shares in the manor.

"All the lordship and manor of Sutton in Holderness with all the rights, royalties, members, and appurtenances to the same belonging or appertaining, wastes, fishing places, hunting, hawking, fowling, turbary, suit sole, mulcture, free warren, mines, quarries, escheats, heriots, courts leet and view of Frankpledge, perquisites and profits of courts and leets, and all that thereto appertaineth, goods and chattels of felons and fugitives, waifs and strays, deodands, villains with their sequels,* fairs, markets, pie-powder courts,† stallage, tolls and customs whatsoever to the said lordship and manor belonging or appertaining."

But although the Corporation had now made some addition to its sixth share of the manor, it does not appear to have kept up any practical assertion of its rights.

Nevertheless, courts were regularly held in Sutton down to the year 1847. Soon after Easter and Michaelmas in each year there was held, by Mr. Thomas Thompson‡ or his deputy, the "Court Leet, or Law day, and View of Frankpledge," the Court Leet being a King's Court, in which twelve of the principal farmers and tradesmen were sworn as "the jury of our Sovereign Lord the King and the Lord of this Leet." There was held at the same time, and with the same jury, the Court Baron of Henry Broadley, Esquire, the lord of the manor. The book containing the last Rolls of the Courts, beginning with the year 1834, is an interesting record, if only as shewing how these ancient institutions dwindled to their extinction.

It is prefaced with the statement that "from memorandums on all the lists of Freeholders and Occupants from the fifteenth century to this time," there is payable by every freeholder upon admittance 6d., by every occupier upon admittance 4d., by a freeholder who does not attend court, and is not fined

---

* Bondmen with their families. I was too hasty in saying upon page 136 that the grant from Henry VIII. there quoted contained the latest suggestion of the condition of serfdom among our townsfolk.

† Courts held at fairs, where disputes between parties were decided while the dust was on their feet.

‡ The Town Clerk of Hull.

but essoined (or excused)—for his essoin 2d., and by
an occupier for his essoin 1d.—but there is no trace of
any of such payments.   Once a member of the class of
freeholders attended the court and, as he departed
during the proceedings, and did not return, he was
fined two shillings.   He came no more.

The whole of the business done belonged to the
Court Leet, which dealt with public matters and with
persons who had neglected to cleanse their ditches "as
in duty bound," or who had encroached on the waste
of the manor "to the common nuisance of the King's
liege subjects," and who were therefore "put in
mercy."   The amercements, or penalties, were from
two shillings to thirty shillings, which, if not paid, were
levied by the bailiff, who would seize the offender's
cattle, impound, and, if necessary, sell them.   For
these and other purposes there were appointed at each
court two "Affeerers," experienced farmers, who
assessed the amercements   Constables, varying from
twenty-two to half-a-dozen, two Haywards or Pinders,*
and two Byelaw men.   There was also a bailiff.
You might then know when you were in the house of
a Constable, by the staff, which usually hung in his
sitting room, but the duties were as a rule performed by
one only in each township.   The Byelaw men had no
duties, as the common pastures over which they had
formerly exercised jurisdiction had been enclosed, and
the separate sittings of the Courts Baron, which
dealt with offences committed in them, had ceased.
It appears, from an early roll, that there had been
great laxity on the part of the suitors in their attend-
ance, and that penalties had not been duly exacted,
but that it was now intended to put the powers of the
Court Leet in force.   This resolve was kept to for
some years, but the business grew less, and the attend-

---

* The Sutton pinfold was on the site of the parish gravel pit, eastward of the
station-master's house.   The Stoneferry pinfold was close to the bridge over
Antholme.

ance grew more difficult to secure.   It was a custom
of the court for the lord of the manor to present at
Easter three guineas towards the expenses, out of which
money each of the jurymen and pinders received a
shilling to pay for his dinner.   The affeerers and byelaw men had each a shilling in addition.   The roll of
the Court Baron always records that the homage was
duly sworn, and that, no person appearing, the court
was adjourned.

Upon June 16th, 1847, the courts met as usual.*
The Court Leet proceeded to its duties with some
vigour, amercing the parson, for the second time,
in the sum of ten shillings, in respect of a nuisance and
obstruction in one of his ditches, and dealing with some
smaller offenders.   The courts were then adjourned
until further notice.   But they never assembled again,
and since that time there has been no manorial
business.   Thus unceremoniously, these ancient
courts, without which the old village community could
not have held together, came abruptly to their end.

The ancient Berewic or Manor of Hastings, which
had been bequeathed with his other property by
Thomas Dalton to his widow, did not descend through
Mr. Witham.   At the enclosure in 1768, Elizabeth
Sedgwick, and Richard her son, received 121a., 1r.,
20p., in lieu of their lands and pasture-gates in the
common fields, and of two house-commons and five
land-commons in the commonable places—

> "belonging to their said lands and their ancient messuages or
> cottages in the parish of Sutton, and also in lieu of a pighill or
> piece of ancient enclosed land in the said Carrside Meadow, and

* Jury :—John Cowl, foreman, Geo. Thompson, Junr., James Blenkin, Thomas
Hart, John Robinson, George March, Wm. Thompson, W. B. Hewson, Wm.
Rodmell, John Barker, James Carrick, Thomas Sissons.
  Affeerers :—George Thompson, Junr., Wm. Rodmell.
  Constables :—James Carrick, (sworn), Thos. Tindall, John Pearson, James
Blenkin, Henry Decker, Wm. Simpson.
  Byelaw men :—John Cowl, W. B. Hewson.
  Bailiff :—Thomas Richardson.

also in lieu of a road herein awarded over the old enclosed lands of the said Elizabeth Sedgwick."*

This description conceals the berewic.† In the time of Edward I., John de Meaux had claimed "wayf, the assize of bread, ale, etc.," in Sutton in respect of it. In 1774, when the Sedgwicks' property was sold, their claim to manorial rights was in respect of fishery only, shewing how the fishery had been divided amongst the several lords of the manor. The drains had been cut up into imaginary lengths or "setts," and these were supposed to be fished by the parties entitled to the respective setts. We have seen that the Corporation fished the Fillings and the Old Williams only. The Sedgwicks claimed to hold

"One fishery in the Middle Sett in Foredike, in the Middle Goat, and the Middle Sett in Lea Dike, and also one sett in the upper end of New Lea Dike."

The middle "Goat" may be the long narrow drain which runs through the middle of Sutton Carrs. Lea Dike is, no doubt, Lead dike, and this description refers to the two watercourses which enclosed between them Leads Common, viz. : the ancient Ankedam, now nearly forgotten, and the more modern *leda*, or Antholme dike. The old homestead of the owner of the berewic passed from the Sedgwicks through the Frosts, amongst other families, until the terraces of houses eastward of the churchyard were built upon it and upon the tithe homestead of the College of St. James which the Frosts‡ had acquired from the representatives of Charles Poole.

* This road was taken from the old enclosed field called Langcroft, to form the oot-road to Hull along the drain bank. Langcroft with Hedoncroft belonged, at this period, to the Sedgwicks.

† Headley farm left by Thomas Dalton to Champney (see p. 161,) adjoined this property on the east. I think it had formed part of the berewic, and also the other property lying eastward of it. Before the enclosure it was bought of the Champneys by Thomas Mould.

‡ Mr. Charles Frost, F.S.A., the author of the "Notices relative to the Early History of the Town and Port of Hull," was one of these.

The last record of the old rectory house of the
College is derived from documents relating to the sale
of the property of the Masons.   At the enclosure, Ann
Mason, the widow of the Rev. William Mason, Vicar
of Hull, received 139a., 1r., 26p., in lieu of lands and
pasture gates in the common fields and of one house
common and seven land commons belonging to her
lands and "Ancient Messuage House."   This house
was, I think, close to the west of the churchyard
(which has since that time been very much enlarged),
and upon ground behind the site of the old Workhouse.

Mrs. Mason died in 1776, and the Rev. William
Mason, her step-son, at length succeeded to his paternal
estate, which he enjoyed till his death in 1797.   His
"little sister" was married to the Rev. Henry Dixon
of Wadworth, and in 1799 Mr. R. C. Broadley acquired
from Mr. and Mrs. Dixon

> "All that the Rectory, Church, or Chapel of Sutton in Holder-
> ness in the County of York and the scite of the College of
> the said Rectory or Mansion House of the Collegiate Church of
> Sutton," also "all that capital Messuage or Dwelling-house,
> barns, stables, outhouses, orchards, and closes of ancient
> enclosed land in the back side thereof, and adjoining upon the
> same, and thereto belonging.   Also all that piece or parcel of
> arable meadow or pasture ground in Sutton called or known by
> the name of Rowbanks."

With this went the new enclosures and all that the
Masons had possessed in the parish.

Rowbanks is, I have no doubt, the share in the
Raw or Roe Bank by Foredike which the several
owners of the Manor appear to have divided amongst
them as a token of their manorial rights, and with this
Mr. Broadley obtained the four and a half parts of
those rights, which had been held by the Masons
He now held the Castle Hill, and the Raw. the two
pieces of property which in old times had been held
with the manor.   The ancient mound, called in old

deeds the Castle Ring, is well seen from the Bilton Road ; it is covered with a clump of high trees. The enclosing ditch is much shallower than formerly, having been partly filled up. The adjacent earthwork is called in old deeds the Castle Hill. In a lease of 1613, by

CASTLE HILL AND RING, WITH SWINE CHURCH.

the Corporation of Hull to Nicholas Cooke, of Stoneferry, labourer, their sixth part of the ring and the hill is said to contain about three acres.

Mr. Charles Poole had built for his occupation, in the best position on his large allotment, some kind of residence, but not the existing house. His farm of Soffham he had called "Weston Farm," but the ancient name prevailed. When in 1787 it was advertised for sale together with the tithes on the old enclosed lands of Sutton, with Drypool and South-coates, it was pointed out that the Sutton drain would enable farm produce to be taken to Hull, and manure to be brought to the farm.* Soffham together with the tithes was bought in 1798 by Mr. R. C. Broadley. Mr. Charles Poole, of East Mount, died in 1799.

In 1762, a new College was built at Stoneferry, and the ladies were transferred to it, Ann Watson's old residence, the White House, being afterwards occupied as a farm. Bearing in mind her careful provision for the widows and daughters of clergymen, the then condition of the college is interesting and instructive. She had desired that relations of her family, though not answering that description, should have the preference, and these had so multiplied, and had asserted their

---

* It is quite possible that the drain may have been so used. There were times when the best team on the farm could not without great risk draw a load of corn through the mire from the farmstead to the high road.

claims so successfully, that none of the widows or daughters of the ordinary clergy could gain admission to the college.   It was only through a suit in Chancery, decided in 1801, that this preference was brought to an end.   And it was not until 1817, or ninety-six years after Ann Watson's death, that any of the ladies who were the objects of her charity were admitted to its benefits.

The new Hospital or College built by Ann Watson's trustees, in 1762, was inhabited by her kindred for about sixty years.   The Rev. J. H. Bromby, who became Vicar of Hull in 1797, remembered seeing the ladies carried to Sutton Church on horseback, according to Ann Watson's directions, perched on pillions, behind the tenants of the College estate.   This procession would make a quaint picture, especially in the last century, when costume was picturesque.   A newer College was built about 1816, in a more convenient position at Sutton, but some of the older inmates declined to move into it, even though their incomes were to be increased. After their time the old Hospital was inhabited by labourers until the row of modern cottages took its place.

I have no doubt that while the White House was inhabited by the ladies on Ann Watson's foundation, it was called the College or the Hospital.   But no other name was given to it afterwards.   I will therefore continue to apply to this old building the name of White House, which connects it with the olden time.

I am indebted to a lady who remembers her visits to my mother's family, five generations of which occupied the house after the removal of the College, for a description of that old-fashioned establishment, as it appeared seventy-five years ago.   It consisted of several rooms in pairs of one large and one small room, just as they had been apportioned to the ladies of the College.   There was a carved oak staircase, a large kitchen with coppers, and a large "best room," with its oak dresser filled with pewter, brilliantly polished, but never used. Some of the rooms upstairs were used for storing apples or feathers, and for keeping the spinning-wheels. The children delighted in it. The description of Mrs. Poyser's household in Adam Bede brought to mind old recollections of this house, which, however charming it might be in Summer-time, was not in accordance with modern ideas of comfort. It was taken down some seventy years ago, except the portion described on page 214.

The enclosure of the common fields deprived the town of Sutton of the greater number of its resident families of the farmer class, and of all the life and activity of their village farmsteads. To these families the comparative solitude of the "odd" or isolated farms must have been a novel sensation. The farming arrangements of that period have to some extent come down in tradition, and much valuable information respecting the practices of a later period may be gained from the minutes of the Holderness Agricultural Society, established at Hedon in 1795.* It is interesting to note the condition of agriculture, the great industry of the parish, in the times immediately before our own.

In treating of oxen and their relation to the land, I have failed to give any idea of the ox of mediæval, or even of more recent, times. Down to the latter part of the last century, the cattle were small and lean. They ran in the open fields unsheltered in all kinds of weather, and there was a strong prejudice against pampering them by over-indulgence. No pains were taken to breed from the best animals ; indeed, all were

---

* See extracts from its minutes compiled by the late Mr. Wm. Bethell, of Rise. Leng & Co., Hull, 1883. It was founded and carried on by well-known squires, farmers and professional men interested in agriculture. Such names as Stovin, Stickney, Raynes, Iveson, Frost, Dr. Alderson, Sherwood, Champney, Strickland, Tatton Sykes, and Broadley, often occur in its annals.

alike bad. The calves were very ill kept. If a cow dropped her calf upon the snow, there was no hurry about getting the pair under cover. As the oxen would not fatten until they were about six years old, they were made to work in harness for three years, and were then fatted, so far as that was possible, by grazing, in preparation for one of the fairs. In hard weather they might have hay scattered over the grass fields, but there was no question of stall feeding with roots. Improvement in the breed was effected by irregular stages. In 1770, it was said that cattle and sheep had improved three-fold within living memory, but I think that improvement did not extend in this direction. It is said that the Holderness cattle were of a superior breed that had been imported from Holstein by Sir William St. Quintin, but from neglect had much degenerated. When, in 1805, the Holderness Agricultural Society discussed the question, it was said that great improvement had been caused recently by the introduction of new blood from the neighbourhood of Darlington. The idea of keeping an animal in good condition from the time it was weaned was dawning on the farmers. Previously they had been kept in "good holding order," which might mean just safely alive.

The sort of care that was taken of cows a century ago, and the work which women had then to undertake, are well illustrated by two incidents remembered by our grandmothers. One of them told of the girls, upon a large farm near Keyingham, having to borrow boots from the men when they walked through the snow to milk in the open field. The other, whose home had been near Beverley, spoke of milking being done while sitting upon a snow-drift.

Draught horses were used to a considerable extent, but draught oxen were generally preferred. In 1771, Arthur Young found that on large farms one ox was kept for every fifteen acres of tillage, the exact quantity which had been fixed as an oxgang in the most ancient times. A team of oxen would plough an acre in eight hours, which horses would plough in six hours. Speed, however, was of minor importance.

In 1798. the Holderness Agricultural Society, having discussed the question, seemed to conclude that a more general use of oxen, particularly by small farmers, would be advantageous. In 1822, Mr. Strickland, in his "Agricultural Survey of the East Riding," said that forty or fifty years previously oxen did all the heavy work. They had, however, gone out of use, but were then coming in again on account of the dearness of horses. Two or four oxen were used in a wagon, or one or two horses would be yoked before a pair of oxen. Oxen had worked with greater facility and freedom in a wain (a cart with a pole), but this vehicle was then forgotten. Upon light land in Holderness four oxen would be yoked to the plough, with a horse as leader. Oxen were used for drawing out manure, and for hauling lime over the indifferent roads, they being more suitable than horses over soft ground.*

While the original house at High Bransholme existed, that farm was cultivated by oxen, but they were then going out of use. It was not later than the year 1839 that I saw one or two oxen, assisted by a horse, drawing a load of corn from the fields in the Carr, behind the existing school. The use of oxen for draught was brought to an end by improvements in breeding and feeding. The modern ox is well fed and well sheltered from the first, and is ready for sale when only half or one-third of the age at which the unimproved breed could be sold. There is, therefore, no period during which he can be put to work on the farm.

Pigs were not improved until within living memory.

---

* I have to thank Mr. W. R. Park, of Catwick, for information as to old farming customs.

The old English pig was a long-legged, sharp-nosed animal, covered with long hair, variegated with tints of red, black, and yellow.   It had disappeared from this neighbourhood fifty years ago, though it might have been seen in some backward parts of the country long after that time.

The Holderness breed of sheep was so inferior at the beginning of this century, that, by crossing it with the Leicester, the offspring were heavier at one year and a half old than the Holderness sheep were at two years and a half.   In 1838, it was said that sheep were now ready for the butcher as "shearlings," which in the olden times would have had to be kept for two or three years more.   Such particulars enable us to form some idea of the kind of sheep which the monks of Meaux turned out by thousands in the moist pastures of Sutton; these were, however, valued for their wool rather than as mutton.

The work of a large farm two or three generations ago was laborious, while the hours were early and long.   The members of the Holderness Agricultural Society were, however, from the first endeavouring to introduce machinery which led to shorter working hours. One of those whose names I have quoted above would encourage his servants by telling of the time when he used to put off his clothes on going to bed, and have them on again before they were cold!   Corn was harvested by hand labour, and thrashed by the flail.   Swarms of Irishmen and their wives came over in the harvest time, and with their sickles reaped the heavy crops that were too roughly laid to be cut with the scythe.*   Their rough, tattered garments of blue homespun wool, and their eager unintelligible talk were curious to see and hear.   They brought smuggled whisky from their own illicit stills, but were them-

---

* About 1780 none of them were as yet to be seen in the neighbourhood.

selves generally temperate, and as reapers, untiring.
Beer was often home-brewed, and the duty of cooking
for a household where farm servants were kept fell to
the women.   Some of the kitchen fireplaces in the new
farmhouses, and perhaps all, were built for turf fires in
the hearth.   A century ago turves were so burnt in
Beverley Parks, and leavened bread was still baked.

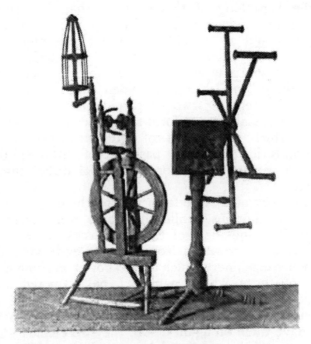

AN OLD UPRIGHT SPINNING WHEEL.

Hardly anything used in the household at that time
was bought ready made.   No table delicacies were
bought at a shop.   The tailor and mantuamaker came
and exercised their skill in the house.   They brought
news.

But the occupation most characteristic of the women
in farmhouse and cottage was spinning, and every
minute that could be spared from the other work of

the house was spent at the wheel.   Maid servants
were required to spin a given quantity of yarn during
their year of service.   When the weaver called for the
yarn he took his instructions and duly returned it in
the shape of household linen, which, if rather cold to
the touch, had nevertheless to be worn, for cotton was
not to be thought of in households such as these.
Fine linen was hoarded.   The jewelled spinning

LATEST PATTERN OF SPINNING-WHEEL.

wheels which were the toys of princesses, and those
used by fine ladies, which were inlaid with ivory and
pearl, cannot have given the solid enduring pleasure
that was afforded by the plain wooden wheels of our
grandmothers.*   When the girls on Ann Watson's
foundation ceased to be taught to spin in the White

* The illustrations represent spinning wheels and implements for measuring the
yarn, and making it up into hanks selected from those used in the household or
Samuel Hudson, of Stoneferry, from about 1800 to 1829.

house, the task was taken up naturally by the women folk of the family which afterwards occupied it.   There, in the leisure of the summer afternoons and in the long winter evenings, three wheels gave their steady accompaniment to the ebb and flow of talk.   But when, in those long evenings, sitting in the glow of the fire, the brothers of the household began to tire of that music, the wheels, after many hints, would have to be put aside so that the fiddle and flute might accompany the voices in song.

Spinning, which must have been practised by the first woman that stood dryfoot on ancient Sudtone, ceased suddenly about the end of the reign of George IV.   From old habit and from pure liking, it was kept up here at Stoneferry until the head of the household protested that it was sheer waste of time, as linen could be bought at the price of the unspun flax.   So the wheels, with the other machinery, were stowed away, and lay forgotten for fifty years.   The spinsters had, however, completed their task, for they took with them to homes of their own, linen that lasted to their old age.*   About 1835, an old woman was still spinning in one of the small houses in Sutton opposite to the mill.

Sixty years ago, Stoneferry still retained its old-world air, and much of the quietude of Sunday afternoon. There was amongst the Stoneferry folk something like a family relationship evidenced at times of sorrow and of rejoicing.   At a wedding the whole hamlet had outdoor sports and indoor feasting.   When a death occurred, every householder was asked to the funeral, and there was bread with cheese and ale before the procession set out for Sutton.   These were old customs—once more wide-spread—that lingered longest with this rather secluded community.   The

* One of them told me, as an excuse for leaving a portion untouched, that it was spun and woven in view of her marriage, and had been so prized that she had not the heart to use it.

existing cart-road to Hull, which was then almost impassably muddy, was made private by locked gates. The footway might be practicable, even in winter, for pattens. The shy moorhens ventured away from the reedy margin of old Antholme to feed in the courtyard with the ducks and hens. Occasional vessels stole silently up or down the river.* The ancient ferry which had once carried all the traffic between South Holderness and the country to the west, was by this time moved lower down the stream, and a vehicle would sometimes require to be boated across. There were, however, days when the farmers were fetching lime, and when clattering waggons and free voices would drive away the peace and quiet. Stoneferry is now a part of the town of Hull, with smooth roads, and gas and manufactures of its own. Every characteristic feature with every landmark of the olden time will no doubt be soon effaced. †

I know of no family, of the class of landowners or merchants, that, at the time of the enclosure, remained resident in the parish. The chief people were then the farmers and the old yeomen, some of whom rented more land than they owned. If there was an exception it was Mr. Thomas Mould, a wealthy merchant, resident in the High Street, Hull, who owned several

---

* There are occasional notices of this old ferry at the existing landing-place. It is mentioned in a fine of the third year of Richard III.—Ralf de Hastynges, plaintiff, and Thomas de Ughtred, deforciant—as "the ferry of the water of Hull," then held by William Burgyn, and Elizabeth, his wife for the term of her life. The Patent Roll, 4th and 5th, Philip and Mary contains a grant to Sir Henry Gate and Thomas Dalton of parts of the possessions of the Carthusian Priory at Hull, including small properties in Lopeholme, Sutton, Stoneferry, and Drypole, and a piece of land near the ferry held by "the farmer of the water of Stoneferry."

† The derivation of the name of the hamlet from Sutton Ferry, seems so probable that it has been easily assumed. But in the earliest documents dating from the fourteenth century, it is called Stanefery and Stanfery; names which in the seventeenth century become Stone Fery and Stoneferry. It lies at some distance from the Marr which anciently existed at or near to Summergangs and the dailes, but this seems to have been called Staynmarr, Stainmar, and Stannmar. Robert de Stanernia was a frequent witness, and perhaps the writer of thirteenth century charters. These latter names do not seem to have been derived from Sutton, which gave its name to the Marr in the North and East Carrs.

pieces of property in Sutton, including that in the angle formed by Lowgate, where two good residences have been built in recent times. It is probable that the large house, which previously stood there, was built and inhabited by him. It was, to some extent, inhabited by his legatee, Mr. John Graham, afterwards called Graham-Clarke, a wealthy merchant of Newcastle, whose daughter, Mary, was married to Mr. Barrett, and became the mother of the poetess, Elizabeth Barrett Browning.

The Sugar House, close to the town of Hull, was owned principally by the Thorntons, a family distinguished by their generous support of religious movements. With them were associated two or three generations of the family of Wilberforce, whose name heads the list of those who a century ago were pleading the cause of the poor and the oppressed.

Eight or ten houses were built early in this century upon the most favoured sites by persons of leading positions in Hull, who constituted a new and increasing class in the parish. Sutton House, long the residence of Mr. George Liddell and his descendants, was built upon the allotment of George Petty, chief among the old yeomen, whose farmhouse stood opposite, at the corner of Lowgate and the Hull road. East Mount was bought from the Pooles by Mr. Thomas Priestman, and the existing house was built by him about 1813. His cousin, Isabel Richardson, who kept house for him in Humber Street, used to walk there while the work was in progress, going on foot, and usually wearing pattens "to keep her feet out of the water, so abundant in that locality." *

The mill built by William Munby was represented fifty or sixty years ago by a four-sail mill of moderate height. It was afterwards raised and furnished with five sails, when it formed a very fine object, and was

* Records of a Quaker family.—*Mrs. Boyce.*

prominent in views of Sutton, from such heights as Beverley Minster and the Wolds.   Steam machinery was added in due course, but on a day in 1884,

SUTTON MILL, 1884.

people far away noticed a column of smoke rising from it—it had taken fire, and was practically destroyed.   The loss of it has greatly changed .

the appearance of the western end of the town.*

We cannot realize the condition of our townsfolk a century ago merely by considering them in full health, at home amongst friends and neighbours, or going about where they were known in broad day. All these conditions, of which we think so little now, were of grave importance to them, for, until recent years, there was very little security for a man outside his daily routine. A century ago, this country was engaged in a struggle for existence, as it had always been, for no such peace, as it has enjoyed since Waterloo was remembered, or could have been foreseen. † The authorities inflicted barbarous punishments upon the few criminals whom they caught, but took no reasonable steps to prevent outrage; indeed they added, by their own action, to the general sense of insecurity. People had to take care of themselves.

When the country was at war, the press-gang was especially " hot " in the neighbourhood of Hull, and it was unsafe for a lone man to be abroad near Humber side after nightfall. ‡ About 1780, my grandfather, Robert Blashill, then living near Patrington, was pursued by the press-gang, and had to take refuge with the village blacksmith, who defended his doorway with a red hot iron bar until the neighbourhood was aroused. His wife's brother, the only son of Edward Truslove, and the last male of that branch of the family, disappeared after a sea voyage, and there was reason to believe that whatever may have happened to

---

* A lease by the Hull Corporation, dated 1611, includes in the Carr-side field "three stengs beyond the Mylne." There must therefore have been a mill at that time nearly opposite to the Railway Station, and this is a likely position for the ancient mill of the lords of the manor. The Munbys had a house there, and it seems probable that the mill, built in 1715, was a substitute for the more ancient mill.

† The popular feeling against the French is shewn by the name of The Anti-gallican, applied to a house, which in 1769, had lately stood in Groves, near to the outfall of the Sutton drain.

‡ See Sheahan's " History of Hull," 2nd Edition, p. 192.

him happened at Hull. If one of the Sutton landowners wanted to go to London in safety and comfort,
he might advertise for one or two to join him in a post
chaise, and they would be sure to go armed with pistols
against the mounted highwaymen, who infested all the
great roads. The Royal Mail Coach, from Hull to
York, was then advertised to go with a guard well
armed. If a Sutton man thought of going to Hedon
on a quiet day he might ponder the fate of Mr. Lockwood of Beverley, attorney at law, who in 1788,
was robbed near the turnpike house in Preston
Fields. The footpad swore that if he did not
immediately deliver his valuables he would shoot
him ; so he had to part with his watch and his
guineas.

There is in the churchyard a gravestone to John
Taylor of Soffham, who was murdered on the footroad
to Hull on February 24th, 1814. He was returning
homeward about seven in the evening, and when he got
a little way past the place where the railway now crosses
the footroad, between tillage fields, a man sprang out
of the hedge, and without saying a word, fired
a pistol into his side. Taylor, who was a powerful
man of sixty-two, struggled with the robber,
but, through loss of blood, was overcome, and
lost thirty pounds in notes and gold, his assailant
expressing surprise that he was not Mr. Liddell, the
banker, who might have been supposed to be laden
with money. Taylor managed to reach his son's
house in Sutton, but died after lingering for a week.
James Forbes, an Irishman, was apprehended, and
when taken to his victim's bedside, was very positively
identified, but as there was no corroborating evidence
at the trial at York a month later, he was acquitted.
Farmers who might be supposed to have received
money at the market, were watched out of Hull by
these footpads. An attempt was made to stop Robert
Blashill—Taylor's successor at Soffham—somewhere

on the bank of Sutton drain, and his son had a similar
experience.

It may be said that such incidents might happen at
any time, but there were far too many of them within
a small compass, and we may be sure that very many
were unrecorded. The *Hull Advertizer* did not
inform its readers of the murder of John Taylor until
more than a month after it had been committed ; it
was in no hurry to report the robbing of Mr. Lockwood
on Preston field. But local newspapers did not much
concern themselves with local news, which everybody
might be supposed to learn from other sources. They
told of foreign wars and sieges, shipping matters, and
distant markets, brightening their columns with Court
gossip, stories of calves with two heads, and amusing
incidents such as would now find a place in a column
of jokes.

At a meeting of the Holderness Agricultural Society
a month after Taylor's murder, a member suggested
that travellers would be greatly benefitted by the
erection of labourer's cottages, at convenient distances
along the high roads. He urged that they would
afford shelter from a shower of rain, and would be useful in case of robbery or of accident, and proposed that
a bell should be attached to a conspicuous part of each
cottage, by ringing which. a person who had been
robbed might bring assistance, and a line of communication might be established far and near. He also
though that the hoisting of a lantern or other signal,
by way of telegraph, might be adopted with great
success. He was perhaps over timid, but the King's
highway was doubtless made for the timid as well as
for the bold.

It was not ,only on the King's highway that people
were anxious about their money. It was very
hazardous to put confidence in a bank. Gold was
hidden away in thatched roofs, and in chimney nooks.
Less than a century ago an old house near to

Antholme brook was owned by one of the yeomen, whose niece lived at the White House. One day she observed that the bricks in the floor had been disturbed, and it was whispered to her that they had been changing the hiding-place for their guineas.

The good old days when everybody was strictly looked after by the parish constable, and when the villagers would set their dogs at a stranger, were gone, I am not sure that, on his own authority, the constable could even have clapped a vagrant into the stocks. The stocks, however, still stood some fifty years ago in fair working order, by the roadside near the end of the narrow footway in Lowgate. They enabled the schoolboys to bring down upon each other in play the terrors of the ancient law. I think I once saw a tramp sitting in them in sad earnest.

The death roll in the parish register varied considerably in the period immediately after the enclosure so as to suggest the occurrence of epidemics, and a very large proportion of the names were evidently those of children and young persons. We must, however, look elsewhere for evidences of the diseases which were prevalent, and the ages of the victims. From 1778 to 1783 the Vicar of Keyingham, a few miles away, entered in the register of burials the causes of death. Out of 62 deaths so noted, 26 were those of children, 11 of whom died from fits. Of the whole number 26 died from fever, 6 from consumption or decline, 2 from dropsy, 1 only in that period from small-pox, and the remainder from various causes.[*] All the elderly people died from fever, including seven aged from 68 to 84. It seems indeed that they might die from anything except old age.[†] I know of

---

[*] Scientific accuracy is scarcely to be expected ; fits which carried off all the infants, must have been a symptom of one or more disorders, that now go by other names.

[†] Some idea may be formed of the population from the entries in the Parish Register. A friend tells me that there may have been some eight hundred inhabitants in Sutton at the time of the Enclosure.

no reason for thinking that our death roll differed materially from this.

It was not till towards the end of the last century that the ravages of small-pox were checked by the practice of inoculation, which, however, communicated small-pox itself, though usually in a mild form. It was not until the early years of this century that vaccination provided a safer protection against this dreadful malady. It lingered, however, for many years amongst the poor, and there were children in the schools whose faces were very badly scarred. Those who would form an idea of what small-pox was, may read Mr. Lipscomb's Newdigate prize poem of about 1780, upon inoculation, and the poet Bloomfield's prose and verse on vaccination. The delight expressed at the introduction of these remedies is a measure of the prevailing dread of the disease. The ague, or "shakings," was still common in Sutton, but by this time those who were stricken could find a remedy in quinine. In 1832 the first epidemic of cholera was severely felt in Hull and the neighbourhood. On April 1st, in that year, Robert Matthews, of Stoneferry, was buried at Sutton without service, "he having died of the Cholera Morbus," as certified by the clerk.

An excessive dread of skin diseases lingered a long while. Some ninety years ago a young gentleman was sent to the village school with strict injunctions as to his being kept from contact with the village boys. His mother thought it necessary to come during the first forenoon and satisfy herself as to the condition of the boy who sat nearest to him by turning down the collar of his shirt.*

The fear of ghosts lingered into the early part of this century, and perhaps lingers yet. The murdered wife of Drogo de Brevere still "walked" in white, and veiled, in Skipsea Lane. A monk of Meaux Abbey

---

* That boy was a bright old gentleman seventy years afterwards when he supplied me with this illustration of ancient manners.

might then be met in the most solitary part of Meaux
lanes.   Seventy years ago, upon account of a something
which was supposed to appear, nothing would have
induced the more timid of those at the White House to
venture alone after nightfall across the garth that had
once been part of the Village Green.   There was in
the Back Street of Sutton an old house with one
solitary inhabitant. . Even in broad day we used to
peer through the rusty gate whispering the name of
him who was said to walk in the melancholy shrub-
bery.   The place where John Taylor was shot was
manifestly shewn by a gap in the hedge where the
hawthorn had refused to grow.*   Children inherit and
servants cherish the cast-off superstitions of a family.
When the widowed mistress of the White House died,
both nurse and maid declared that they had heard some
supernatural noise, such as in their view was proper to
be heard at the moment when the head of a family passed
away.   There was a fearful pleasure in listening to
blood-curdling tales of this kind, told by servants over
the kitchen fire.   They could have amply satisfied
Horace Walpole's desire for ghost stories out of the
North.
    A witch is, I think, always depicted in a red cloak.
There used to be in Sutton, a poor old woman who
went about so clad.   Upon asking whether she was
really a witch as the boys supposed, I got a sharp
rebuke, but was consoled by the following story.   A
generation back there had lived in the parish an old
woman who really had that evil reputation.   Upon a
summer day, she was found by a waggoner gleaning
in a field before the corn had been cleared away, and,
upon being ordered off, went muttering as an old woman
would.   The waggoner's first load fell over, which was
not a very uncommon occurrence ; but when it fell over
a second time, he knew what was the matter.   There is
only one way with a witch—you must see the colour

* I am afraid the gap was fifty yards from the real place.

of her blood.   Straightway he marched off to her
house, where she sat spinning, and having entered
unheard in the whirr of the wheel, he pulled a nail out
of the wall, drew the point of it smartly along her
naked arm, and thus effectually broke the spell.

ANTIQUITIES OF MODERN SUTTON.

PART II.

THE old idea of school is, I suppose, obsolete, but, sixty years ago, knowledge was imparted by force, or by threats that had the effect of force. Parents might be very poor judges of the things that a boy ought to be taught, but they could form a liberal estimate of the extent to which he would need to be flogged.* There was then no profession of teachers for village schools. No pictures decorated the schoolroom, and interesting books were few. There was, however, usually in a village, some man and some woman of rather superior education, and with sufficient force of character, who set up school and, with poor materials, did their best. The parish clerk was usually the schoolmaster in Sutton. A prim old lady tended her meek-looking flock in a little room in Stoneferry. In Sutton, a single room, under a mistress of whom her pupils retained a kindly memory, held all the girls and infants. Threatenings, which at times passed even childish credulity, were her chief weapons.

Eighty years ago, the master of the Sutton school with its small endowments, though a good master, was noted for his vigorous use of the cane, and those who had suffered under him always expressed doubts as to the capabilities in that respect of his successors. They

---

* I have been assured by old pupils of an important public school, that in one class the swish of the cane was never out of their ears. They admitted, however, and their attainments proved, that the master could teach.

had, I think, small ground for anxiety on that score, but the two whom the town possessed at a later date were respected, all parties recognising that school was a place where war had to be waged, and going through their respective parts with firmness and fortitude. No boy was such a sneak as to carry tales home.*

Outside the few who felt a real pleasure in their tasks, and who themselves came off fairly well, school was liked as little as physic is liked, and the boys who left, not so badly prepared, for some academy in Hull, or for a more distant seminary of learning, found that they had changed the arena, but not the nature of the strife. Most of those who passed through this ordeal, might afterwards be seen upon high stools or behind counters in Hull ; the rest who stayed at home would be all the better for their discipline.

But the inducements to reading and writing were then few; the days of cheap books, and frequent newspapers, and letter writing had not come. Sixty years ago, an inhabitant of Sutton could get a letter only by inquiring at the post-office in Hull, and on payment of eightpence, or tenpence, or fifteenpence. Twice a week the carrier would call there, and bring the letters of those who he thought would repay him the postage. On the following days he would go to Stoneferry, and so in the course of time a letter would be delivered even there. Then there was a chance that somebody would see your letter stuck in the window of the post-office, and it is amazing how rumour will fly. People were so accustomed to this system, and had so little correspondence that there was no burning desire for change, and few believed that the penny post,

---

* When after my time, a new master came who was mild and kindly, and tried to rule without the cane, he was misunderstood. One afternoon, drawn by a sort of hankering towards the old school, I found him standing outside in deep embarrassment. I burned with shame—his boys had locked him out, and were stipulating through the keyhole for an extra holiday !

established in 1840, would succeed, or that letters would in time be delivered at every door.*

Our more recent forefathers were not over well off for amusements. A hundred years ago, football was the most popular amusement in all our villages and smaller towns. Hedon and Preston were old antagonists. On Sutton feast Sunday the ball would be thrown up on Foredike bridge for a contest between Sutton and Wawne, and, in the anxiety of each party to get it home, serious accidents were unavoidable. This, no doubt, helped to bring the game into disfavour, and in the next generation football was as obsolete as cock-fighting, traditions of which long survived. Wrestling went out probably about the same time as football, and before cricket in any serious form had taken the place of these rather rough pastimes.

I suppose fighting must be classed among amusements, at least by the spectators. Upon Sutton feast Sunday, young men who had quarrelled would, by arrangement, fight their quarrel out in the "First Close," —before it was walled off from the foot-path to Hull. They were sure of a good company to see fair play, and upon that greensward blood would flow pretty freely. This, however, need hardly be recorded, except as an example of the general roughness of the times.

The sports of hunting and fishing were kept up, though not by the lords of the manor. There were Hull hounds in 1794, for according to the *Hull Advertizer* of Nov. 15th, they were to throw off on Sutton Common on the Saturday following. † There is, I suppose, some gratification to be obtained by

---

* In that year I heard the new system discussed at a tea-table, where a set of people of considerable intelligence frequently assembled. There was quite as much diversity of opinion upon the question of its utility as usually shewed itself when the ordinary subjects of religion or politics were under discussion.

† The West Carr was called the High Common. The North Carr was called the Low Common. Sutton Common, mentioned in the Enclosure Award, was not one of the Carrs. It may have been a name for Leads Common, but there was not at that date a yard of common or waste land in the parish.

standing on the bank of Sutton drain watching a float, but there is nothing now to remind us of the times when the parish was half drowned, and when rights of fishing in all its ditches were jealously preserved.

Dancing and card playing were popular until about seventy years ago. Not only the country dance but reels and hornpipes used to be spoken of by our old people, and there were traditions of merry parties guided by a lantern to a dance at a neighbour's house. They never got so far as the quadrille, and dancing became discredited about the same time as cards; which came to be spoken of with nothing less than horror. If only a few of the stories we used to hear of ruin brought about by cock-fighting and card-playing were true, it was time they disappeared on that ground alone. There was, however, very little indoor amusement left, except parlour games more suitable for children than adults, and if a young fellow sought companionship at the public-house there was small cause for surprise.*

It would have rejoiced the heart of Arthur Harpur, whose endowment made in 1631 was by this time lost, if he could have foreseen that two hundred years after his time, the fifth of November would still be celebrated. After parading the Guy with appropriate ceremonial, the bonfire was made in the 'Tween dikes lane, and the boys, when they had sufficiently thrashed each other with "babbles," threw them into the flames. These weapons were made of leather, wetted, rolled, hammered, and tied up with whipcord, They were much more efficient scourges than any used in schools. I am assured that these old customs

---

* Hull was, towards the end of the last century, one of the gayest places out of London. Theatre, balls, suppers, and card parties were the delight of the principal merchants and their families. They dined at two, and met at each others' houses at six for sumptuous suppers, with cards to follow.—*Life in the Provinces —18th century.*

of flame and flagellation were survivals from times more remote than any herein noticed.*

The fifth Sunday in Lent was always observed by the eating of Carlins, which are peas soaked and fried in butter with seasoning of salt and pepper.   Frumety,

A BABBLE.

which is wheat creed and boiled, milk with spices being added, was always eaten on Christmas Eve.   On the 21st December, the feast of St. Thomas, the old custom

* I have to thank Mr. H. Syer Cuming, F.S.A.Scot., fo his drawing of a babble that was made for me in 1869 by old J. Saunderson of Sutton, to shew me how the weapon was made when he was a boy.   The dimensions are reduced to a third. I am told that the babble has gone out of use.

of "gooding" was kept up, the labourers' wives and children coming to the farm-houses for a small measure of wheat.   Gleaning and gooding have come to an end, mainly through the cheapness of corn.   Early in January the plough-boys came round—farm-servants, who had failed to get suited at Martinmas, or who preferred to have a frolic.   They were picturesque with ribbons, "Bladder-Dick" and "Besom-Bet" being the leading characters, and their antics were amusing.   "Buy-a-broom" girls, with the quaint, tight head dresses one sees in some parts of Germany, brought amusement to the children, particularly those at the farms.

Sutton feast was observed as now on St. James' day, with many stalls in the Highgate, with swings, round-abouts, cheap Jacks, and perhaps a canvas theatre.   One heard and saw more of these things than of the annual sermon about which Leonard Chamberlaine and Ann Watson were so anxious.   I have suggested that this feast was a survival of one of the two ancient fairs, but there is actually a tradition of stalls having been set up under the Chestnut Trees on Sunday mornings, for the sale of meat by butchers from Beverley to people who came from Hull.   If that be true, it was probably a result of the restrictions upon trade, which, until the passing of the Municipal Reform Act, kept business in the hands of the freemen of corporate towns.

The dress and general appearance of our townsfolk have changed a good deal during the present reign. Let us try to realise them as they were.   In the earlier days the three-cocked hat worn by some old-fashioned gentlemen, was just remembered. while the enormous neckcloths of the days of the Prince Regent actually survived.   The smock-frock of the labourer was going out.   Knee-breeches were commonly worn, with gaiters for Sunday.   For riding the farmers wore boots with white tops—a sign of the condition of the roads even then.   But anyone

connected with Hull would wear a swallow-tail or
"dress" coat, probably of a dark blue colour with gilt
buttons. A buff waistcoat, below which hung a bunch
of seals, grey trousers, and a white hat, with long nap,
made up a handsome summer costume for a staid middle
aged gentleman. Such costumes are put in pictures
now. Some of the younger men wore in summer
white duck trousers, tightly strapped under the boots.
Neither beard nor moustache was ever seen. Even in
Hull, where foreigners were common, such a sight,
except in the case of a working sailor, would excite
comment and some dislike.

A straw bonnet long treasured as a curiosity,
having been worn early in the reign of George IV.,
was twenty inches long, and was trimmed with a
broad green ribbon, with a deep curtain to protect
the neck. Early portraits of the Queen shew the
enormously wide bonnets hung with lace, which we
saw after her Majesty's accession. A Bird of Paradise
made a handsome decoration for that head-dress
when its size was somewhat reduced. Families
connected with Hull brought new and startling
fashions which were first looked at disdainfully and
then quietly adopted.*

The general effect of dress was exceedingly bright
and gay. Dress, however, could not have been what
it was, but for the protection afforded by an invention
which was then modern, and which early in the
century was new. It is difficult to realize that down
to that period the people, with whose affairs we have
been concerned, managed to get on without umbrellas.
About 1810, the mistress of the White House, then
forty years of age, ventured to buy one as a protection
for her new silk gown. It was the first in Stoneferry.

---

* It must have been a visitor who first displayed at church a bonnet which
permitted a small atom of the wearer's face to be seen in the side view,
suggesting the enquiry "what next?" If, now, the handsomely dressed group
that on Sundays used to exchange greetings after church should be reproduced in
any public place they could hardly escape being mobbed.

She had, however, not realized that she would have to carry it when it did not rain, and on the first Sunday on which the sky looked threatening, she directed her boys to carry it for her.　Both refused ; so she carried it close by her side, concealed in a fold of her dress.　But when the service ended, and a heavy shower was falling, she made her way boldly through the crowd in the porch, and unfurled her umbrella, determined not to be ashamed of it again.

We have seen that in 1743 the regular stipend of the minister was ten pounds, and that his full income was no more than twenty-four pounds ; including the five pounds which the parish then allowed him to receive, but of which no more is heard ; and including Ann Watson's endowment.　The income was, however, slightly increased about that time, the Governors of Queen Anne's Bounty having made a free grant of two hundred pounds, which was drawn by lot and invested by them.　The living was augumented by two hundred pounds, drawn in the same way in 1772, and again in 1802.

The Rev. Arthur Robinson resigned his livings of Sutton, Wawne, and Marfleet, in 1789, having held them for forty-nine years.　He died in 1793.　He had lived in his own house in Postern Gate, Hull, his friends being amongst the most prominent and most respected people in the neighbourhood.　Upon his resignation, the Rev. William Mason, the patron, presented his curate, the Rev. Michael Brunskill, who, however, continued to act as the curate at Aston until 1801. In a legal document he is frankly described as of Aston, and I cannot find that he performed any regular duty in Sutton, nor is it probable that he did.　He appointed as his curate, the Rev. George Thompson, who had assisted Mr. Robinson and who had succeeded him in the livings of Wawne and Marfleet.　Mr. Thompson doubled the ordinary duty by performing Divine Service every Sunday—

morning and evening alternately. He and everybody must have forgotten the existence of Mr. Brunskill, for when in 1795 a new peal of three bells was provided they bore the name of the Rev. George Thompson, Minister.* The Rev. John Foster was presented to the benefice in 1815, and the Rev. G. J. Davies succeeded in 1819. In his day there was morning and afternoon service every Sunday. The Rev. Nicholas Walton was the incumbent from 1839 till his resignation in 1847. He lived on his own property in the parish, being probably the first resident minister in modern times.

The whole aspect of the Church, with the mode of conducting the services, has changed so much during the half-century that has since elapsed, that we may treat the former arrangements as a matter of antiquarian interest. The church had been fitted with pews long before that time, and there had been a western gallery with pews under it, quite close to the cross passage. The easternmost pews originally extended no further into the quire or chancel than the ancient screen shewn on the plan on page 96. In 1763, Mr. Charles Poole and Mrs. Mary Mason who, as impropriators of the Church, were charged with the repairs of the chancel, applied for a faculty to remove the old roof which was much out of repair, to sell the lead, and not only to make a good roof, covered with slate, but also to beautify the inside of the chancel. Upon the report of a Commission the faculty was granted and the work carried out, the beautifying consisting apparently in whitewashing the walls.

In, 1785 a faculty was obtained, and a loft or gallery erected over the south aisle, between the first and second pillars from the east end of the nave.

In 1824, the old western singing-loft or gallery, and

---

* Mr. Brunskill can hardly have gained anything by his living, beyond some improvement in his status as a beneficed clergyman. At Aston, he signed the register first as curate, but afterwards he signed as minister.

THE CHURCH, 1895.

the seats under it, were removed, and a new western gallery was constructed. This was set back under the tower, new pews being made in the space between the tower and the cross passage, where the old gallery had been. The font was then placed on the north side of these new pews. An organ, that in the first instance was worked by a handle, was soon afterwards provided. In 1841, a new loft or gallery was erected over the north aisle, occupying the three bays of the nave arcade nearest the east.

PIERS UNDER TOWER.
(Seen from the South Entrance.)

All the best pews were square, having seats on all sides with a flap-seat that fell across the doorway. The family sat round such a pew, no one kneeling. The graver men stood up on entering these high pews and said a prayer, covering the face with the hat. Two or three of the best pews were surrounded by brass rods and green curtains, so as to entirely hide the occupants except from the pulpit and galleries. The

Stoneferry folk sat principally on the north side of the church, where there was a large pew belonging to the White House. The pew belonging to the old tithe-farmstead and to Soffham was on the south side of the quire, the dwarfed remains of the old screen forming its eastern side. New pews had been added in the quire, and the monument to Sir John de Sutton still stood in its original position in the centre. The effigy was called "Old Morell," which

EAST END OF SOUTH AISLE.

was the name given to the effigy of Sir John de Meaux in Aldbrough Church.*

The handsome old pulpit stood across the middle passage elevated upon four columns to the level of the galleries, so that one could pass under it; the reading-desk and the clerk's desk were on the north side where the pulpit now stands. There was a painting of St. James the Great in the front panel of the pulpit. A sounding-board supported on two columns was over it, and a dove with gilded rays was carved under the sounding-board. The chancel arch was blocked by a plaster partition on which were fixed the Royal Arms with the Commandments, the Lord's Prayer, and the Apostles' Creed. In the clerestory wall above the south gallery was the hatchment or coat of arms of some parishioner recently deceased.

I have never seen public worship conducted with

* Morell probably means model, or likeness, or image.

more perfect decorum.   Morning service commenced
with the Morning Hymn.   All the responses were made
by the clerk, and he gave out the Psalms from the Prayer
Book version.   As soon as the first lesson began, the
churchwardens took their hats and gravely left the
church.   They went to search the two public-houses,
each of them visiting one.   This was a senseless
survival from the old time when the churchwardens
perambulated the town to drive stragglers into church.

THE CHANCEL OR CHAPEL OF ST. JAMES.

I feel bound to accept the assurance of some of those
who were most frequently hiding in the houses at such
times to the effect that none of them were ever
discovered.*

Before the sermon the clergyman walked down
the church to the vestry which was on the south

* A few weeks ago I was told by the old clerk of a church in the West Riding,
that in his recollection, the same ceremony took place there, the churchwardens
invariably refreshing themselves at the village inn.

side of the tower, followed by the clerk. When
they returned, the clergyman, vested in a black
gown and black gloves, ascended to the pulpit,
the clerk securing the door after him. When the
black gown ceased to be worn, I was told that it
had been introduced within living memory, the

THE CHURCH, 1848.

surplice having been worn formerly throughout the
service.

Sutton church, although its internal arrangements
were incongruous, was kept as clean as an ordinary
house ; yet no one then thought of removing his hat,
except in service time, as he would do on entering a
house. Much of the old spirit, not altogether

irreligious, to which I have before alluded, is traceable
in the modes of treating certain of the services.
The influence of successive incumbents was, however,
in the direction of greater reverence, and their
sermons were appreciated and discussed more than
was then usual.   .

Baptism, except perhaps in the poorer families, was
always performed in private houses, being made an
incident in a family feast.   The marriage service might
be an affair of a few minutes, the parties always desiring
that it should be as short as possible.*   I am sure that
there was no conscious idea of irreverence, but on the
other hand it may be said that there was not much conscious reverence.   These were occasions of great rejoicing, when friends were entertained with feasting
and games.   The idea of solemnity, however, seemed
to be reserved for burials.

Until the construction of the railway, the old parish
gravel pit which formed an approach to the path
anciently called the Marr Lane, was unfenced from
the town street.   In front of the space was a large stone
known as the " burying-stone."   It is highly probable
that it was all that remained of the ancient cross which
would be set up in such a position.   Funeral carriages
were little used, and indeed could hardly have travelled
over some of the farm roads.   There was a sentiment in
carrying a farmer to his grave in his best waggon
drawn by his favourite horses.   By old custom the
funeral parties from Stoneferry and the west end of
the town, rested their burden on the burying-stone,
and a procession was formed to the church, accompanied with singing.   There was a " burying-tune,"
and everything was done to mark the solemnity of the

---

* At the wedding—about 1837—of one of the spinsters, to whom I have
alluded, the scarlet postilions had leave to go their own pace. Their pace was a
gallop, and, though the distance from Stoneferry to the church is over a mile and
a third, the wedding-party was absent from the hamlet only twenty minutes. The
last to marry was detained at the altar-rail of Hull High Church five minutes by
my watch.

occasion. The stone, or what remains of it, is now under the stile that leads to the Carr.

In 1868 the Church was reseated, and the roofs were reconstructed. At the same time the massive brick pillars were replaced by stone of more slender proportions, and the chancel arch was reconstructed at a higher level.

In 1852, the commutation of the tithes of the old enclosed lands was effected.* The amount then payable to Mr. Henry Broadley, was £33 8s. 7d., and some small landowners had acquired the tithes on their land to the amount of £3 4s. 6d.

These figures, however, give no idea of the value of the property anciently set apart for the service of the Church, and once belonging to the Rectory and College of St. James. We must look for the substantial portions of this endowment in the broad acres allotted to Mr. Charles Poole in and around East Mount, and in the West Carr, and in the lands near to the Church and elsewhere, formerly belonging to the Rectory and College. In respect of part of these lands the Patron still pays to the Vicar ten pounds annually, which represents the salary enjoyed at the Reformation by Thomas Whyt, parochial curate. Together with the offerings of the inhabitants, this would make up a sufficient income for him, but we have seen how inadequate it must have become, owing to the altered value of money, and how it was augmented from time to time. Further grants from Queen Anne's Bounty of £400 and £200 were drawn in 1812, and £200 in 1820. At present the total income from every source

---

* Their total area was 547a. 3r. 20p., but of this area Southowscroft and Hirncroft, now forming part of Frog Hall farm, were, by prescription, tithe-free. These were the old possessions of the Cistercian monks of Meaux, who paid no tithe. The Oxlands and the Hills adjoining the churchyard were also tithe-free, having belonged to former tithe-owners who had, no doubt, so arranged. The tithes on 98a. or. 15p. of other lands, had been merged by their owners. The prices per bushel on which the commutation was calculated, were, for wheat, 7s. 0½d. ; barley, 3s. 11½d. ; and Oats, 2s. 9d.

is about £115 with the vicarage-house—surely a very inadequate endowment !

The earliest trace I can find of the great religious movement of the eighteenth century, outside the Church, is in 1775, when the Archbishop gave his license for a meeting-house for Protestant Dissenters in the house inhabited by Robert Robinson, wheelwright, at the east end of the town.* Sixty years ago meetings were held in a sanded kitchen in Stoneferry.   Small chapels, and then larger, were the outcome of these beginnings.   There was, no doubt, in the people a · strong root of religious sentiment which only needed to be cultivated into life.   The fruit of it was evidenced by the conversation of those who hoed in the field, and who thrashed in the barn.   They who dissented from the Church were not the spiritual successors of the Quaker Ellikers, but of the Churchman Wesley and his associates ; they agreed very well with the clergyman, and might often be seen at church until they had morning service in their own chapels. Camp meetings were occasionally held in the " First Close," and hymns with tunes in which everybody eagerly joined, made such gatherings cheerful and attractive.

Notwithstanding all that had been done to protect the low lands in the parish from floods, the North and East Carrs were, within living memory, still liable to be flooded, and in one case at least a voyage was performed from Fairholm to Sutton village in a boat. About the year 1835, a new drain was cut, under an Act of the 2nd William IV., through the Carrs to take the low-land waters to a new outlet at Marfleet, and if this has not entirely remedied the mischief, it has left an occasional reminder of the far-off time when the Carrs were marshes, and the

---

* Hull was made the head of a circuit, and the first Wesleyan Chapel was built there in 1771.

lowest portion of them was occcupied by Sutton
Marr.

When on Easter Monday, 1864, the Hull and
Hornsea Railway was opened, access to the Sea
Coast and to Central Holderness was for the first
time easily practicable, and the parish then possessed
the freedom of communication with the whole country,
which is one of the great characteristics of our age.

———

They who have followed the course of this story
have learned something of the life and ways of the
generations that trod the streets, worshipped in the
Church, and tilled the land with which we are so
familiar. They have become acquainted with the
lords of the manor, vassals themselves of over-lords,
the free-tenants fettered to the soil, and the bondmen
struggling to be free. They have watched the
fortunes of the non-resident landowners, with the
farmers and labourers whose life routine, pursued
in happy ignorance of better things, seems to
us bondage under another form. Forerunners
were all these, but not many of them forefathers,
of ourselves. Since Commerce struck root by the
deepened channel at the river's mouth, our native
population has drifted easily away towards fields of
richer promise, making room for fresh immigrants out
of the Holderness East End. Such may be the
course of future events; for the qualities which urged
our forefathers hitherward seem to be serviceable for
many and varied uses. At home or abroad they will
find their market. And when the young inheritors
of those endowments remember the conditions under
which former generations have lived and worked
they may look forward with confident hope to
a brighter and a happier life.

Appendix.

THE SUDTONE OF DOMESDAY.

Page 7. In eighteenth century documents the mound with its encircling moat is called the Castle Ring, the mound on higher ground on which the farmstead now stands being called the Castle Hill.

MEDIÆVAL SUTTON.

Page 20. John de Sutton, junior, succeeded his father in 1338. Thomas de Sutton succeeded his brother in 1356.

SAYER THE SECOND.

Page 29, line twelve from bottom, omit "the second."

Page 42. In 1246, the Archbishop quit-claimed the advowson to Sayer for one "sore" Sparrow-hawk—a young bird in the reddish plumage of its first year.—Feet of Fines, 30 Henry III. The more noble kinds of falcons and hawks could be used only by persons of high rank, the sparrow-hawk being assigned to priests.

Page 44. The relations between Sayer and the nuns of Swine are well illustrated by a Fine (York, 20 Henry III.), in which Sayer is plaintiff and Sibil, Prioress of Swine, is deforciant. The date is Easter-day, 1236. Sayer had complained that the Prioress had deforced him from the advowson of the church of Dripol, contrary to a Fine made in the King's Court before the Justices in Eyre at York between himself "petens" and Helewyse, late Prioress of Swine, "tenens." But Sayer quit-claims to the Prioress his right to the advowson. He also grants to the church of Swine and the Prioress 80 acres of marsh, measured by a perch of 20 feet, in the south part of the marsh of Braneceholm, next to the 30 acres of marsh in Braneceholm, which she before had of his gift, with the right of hedging and ditching both these pieces at will, he and his heirs having no right in the dykes so made. He grants also his right in the watercourse which extends from Feirholm to the marr of Swine, and the fishing thereof, together with land six feet in breadth on the west side of the watercourse.

The Prioress grants that she and her successors shall find daily a chaplain and clerk, books, vestments, light, and all necessaries to celebrate divine service in the chapel of St. George at Gaghenstede (Ganstead) for the souls of Sayer, his ancestors and successors; also that he and his heirs shall have a free chapel in his manor of Soutecotes and a free chantry as he had before in the said chapel, at his own charges saving harmless the mother church of Dripol. She also quit-claims to him and his heirs her right to common of pasture, of turbary, and of faggots in Braneceholm, and Sayer grants the tithes of Braneceholm, so far as is in his power, to her and her successors.

Thus was permanently severed from Sutton the land lying northward of the map on page 14, now called Thirty Acre Farm, but not, I think, the 80 acres herein mentioned.

SAYER DE SUTTON THE THIRD.

Page 53. The preceding note shews that in the time of Sayer's father the perch had measured twenty feet.

SIR JOHN DE SUTTON, SENIOR.

Page 82. The date of the fine mentioned in the note is 1432, seventy-six years after the death of Sir John de Sutton, junior. Joan's father must have been descended from another member of the family, probably from Nicholas, who was a resident in Sutton.

Page 83. The year in which Sir John de Sutton, senior, died was 1338.

Page 84. An entry on the Patent Roll, 1 Edward II., part 2. m., 4d., 1308, throws light on the condition of the neighbourhood in the time of Sir John de Sutton, senior. It is a Commission to John de Creppinge and Roger de Scoter on the complaint of John de Sutton, that certain persons had at Sutton, without authority, distrained and impounded his cattle and killed several of them. They were Hugh de Hilton, Thomas de Vielle, John the son of Reginald atte Howe, William the son of Alice, John the son of Thomas, John the son of Helewysie, Hugh the son of Matilda, Stephen Buffel, and Peter Huesknave de Hilton, who were to be called to account and dealt with according to law.

Entries on the Patent Roll, 1 Edward III., part 3. m., 24d., tell of similar outrages which happened in 1327. A Commission was then issued to Thomas Wake of Lidel, Alexander de Cave, Robert de Scorburgh, and John de Thwayt, on the complaint of John, the son of John de Sutton, that certain persons had beaten and wounded him at Drypole to the peril of his life. They were Geoffrey the son of Hugh, Conan de Birton, and Robert the son of Hugh; all of Kyngeston-upon-Hull; Thomas son of William Scayle, Richard del Ker Servatus Tunnok, Richard de Swyne, Woll-portour, William de Watton, Edward Quarel, William del Weende, Alexander Mattesone, John de la Trinite, Trumpour, Simon del Wyk, John de la Chambre, Thomas de Yafford, Stephen son of Alan le Ken, William le Botiller, William de Feryby, John Busie, William Harow, Richard Jonesman, Rotynberyng, Geoffrey Ernerysone, Richard Coke, Geoffrey Portour, Hugh Portour, Robert Maldesman of the Ker, Richard Wyne-Portour, John Cokeswayne, Richard de Barton, Michael Stut, William Godkynsman of the Ry, and Robert Yole.

This mixed mob, as it seems, of porters, sailors, and runaway serfs, who, with other malefactors, had committed the outrage were to be dealt with according to their deserts. The formation of their surnames is interesting.

At the same time these Commissioners were to investigate a charge made by John de Sutton the elder that the same crew had entered into his free-warren at Sotcotes, Sutton, and Drypol, and had hunted hares and rabbits, and carried them away, beating and wounding his servants.

SIR JOHN DE SUTTON, JUNIOR.

Page 85. The year in which Sir John de Sutton, junior, succeeded was 1338.

Page 86. Barrow was held *in capite* by Sir John de Sutton, senior, as early as 1324. The Fine Roll, 18th Edward II., records a fine upon his entrance into the manor of Barrow without licence of the King. In 17th Edward III., Sir John de Sutton, junior, had a grant of Free Warren in Atwick and the Lincolnshire manors of Barrow and Maltby. There seems to have been some connexion between these manors and Holderness, for Poulson quotes a document, vol. 1, p. 193, which shews that early in the fourteenth century lands in Barrow were held of the King as of the Honour of Burstwick by knight service.

Page 96. This drawing was made thirty years ago from two pieces of screens that remained. The upper panels are from a large piece that stood as a reredos behind the altar, but is now under the tower, as shewn on page 295. There are five panels, the one on the right differing from the others by having tracery of a perpendicular character. The lower panels of this piece are plain. The lower panels in the illustration are taken from a piece of the chancel screen, consisting of four panels that still stood in its original position on the south side of the central passage, but had been cut down so as to form the back of the seat assigned to Soffham. With its upper beam or cresting, it must have formed a very handsome division between the parochial chancel and the chapel of St. James.

Page 97. The date of consecration was fixed by entries in divers calendars of old books belonging to the church. Under the 12th September was written in an old hand as follows:—"Consecracio Cimiterij Capelle Sancti Jacobi de Sutton A° Domini Millimo CCC^mo XLIX."

Page 97. As this grant to William, son of Henry le Clerc, is the only clear documentary proof of the existence of a son to Sir John de Sutton, junior, I will here give the original text.

Grant in tail by John de Sutton in Holderness, Knt., to William son of Henry le Clerc of Sutton, of a bovate of land in Sutton (which the grantor inherited of Nicholas de Sutton) for a yearly rent of a pair of London gloves, with specified remainders.

Dated, Tuesd. Nativ^y of the Blessed Mary, 8 Sept^r, A.D. 1349.

Sciant presentes et futuri quod ego Johannes de Sutton in Holderness miles dedi, concessi, et hac presenti carta mea indentata confirmavi Willelmo filio Henrici le Clerc de Sutton unam bovatam terre cum pratis, pasturis, turbariis, et omnibus alijs suis pertinentijs que michi post mortem Nicholai de Sutton, jure hereditario descendebat in Sutton. Habendum et tenendum dicto Willelmo et heredibus de corpore suo legittime procreatis, de me et heredibus meis, Reddendo inde annuatim michi et heredibus meis unum par cerotecarum Londoniensium ad festum Pentecostes, et faciendo duos adventus ad curiam meam de Sutton videlicet ad proximam curiam post festum sancti Michaelis et ad proximam curiam post festum Pasche pro omnibus alijs servicijs, et demandis. Et si contingat dictum Willelmum sine herede de corpore suo legittime procreato obire, tunc predicta bovata terre cum suis pertinentijs remaneat Johanni de Eboraco filio meo et heredibus de corpore suo legittime procreatis. Tenendum de me et heredibus meis, Reddendo inde annuatim michi et heredibus meis unum par cerotecarum Londoniensium ad festum Pentecostes pro omnibus servicijs. Et si contingat predictum Johannem sine herede de corpore suo legittime procreato obire, tunc dicta bovata terre cum pertinentijs remaneat Johanni de Sutton fratri Nicholai de Sutton et heredibus de corpore suo legittime procreatis, tenendum de me et heredibus meis, Reddendo inde annuatim michi et heredibus meis unum par cerotecarum Londoniensium ad festum Pentecostes pro omnibus servicijs. Et si contingat predictum Johannem de Sutton fratrem Nicholai de Sutton sine heredo de corpore suo legittime procreato obire, tunc dicta bovata terre cum suis pertinentijs michi et heredibus meis revertet. Et ego predictus Johannes de Sutton miles et heredes mei predictam bovatam terre cum suis pertinentijs predictis Willelmo, Johanni, et Johanni in forma predicta contra omnes homines warantizabimus. In cujus rei testimonium uni parti hujus carte indentate penes predictos Willelmum, Johannem, et Johannem remanenti, sigillum meum apposui, et alteri parti penes me remanenti, predictus Willelmus sigillum suum apposuit.

Hijs testibus, Domino Roberto de Hilton et domino Johanne de Monceux militibus, Johanne de ffaucomberg de Bilton, Willelmo de Bilton, Johanne filio Walteri de Bilton et alijs.

Datum apud Sutton die Martis in festo Nativitatis beate Marie Anno gracie Millesimo Trescentesimo quadragesimo Nono.

Endorsed :—Scriptum domini Johannis de Sutton factum Willelmo filio Henrici le Clerc de Sutton de j. bovata terre.

The name of Nicholas, like that of John, occurs in different documents in ways that leave identification of the individuals doubtful. There is a Fine (York, 31 Edward III.) made on the quinzaine of Michaelmas, 1357, in which a Nicholas, son of Henry de Sutton, is plaintiff.

Page 99. "Johannes de Sutton de Holdernesse dat viginti solidos solutos in hanaperio pro pardonacione transgressionis quam fecit construendo quoddam Castrum carnellatum et batellatum apud Braunseholme. Teste Rege apud Westmonasterium quarto die Februarii."—Fine Roll, 26 Edward III., A.D. 1352.

On 5th April, 1356, the Warden of the Chantry of the Chapel of Sutton gave one mark, paid into the Hanaper, for licence to John de Sutton in Holderness, Chivaler, to assign one toft with the appurtenances in Sutton to the said Warden and the Chaplains "ad manum mortuam."

The year in which Sir John de Sutton, junior, died was 1356.

SIR THOMAS DE SUTTON.

Page 102. The year in which Sir Thomas de Sutton succeeded was 1356.

Page 110. The following details shew the descent of the three shares in the manor from the three daughters of Sir Thomas de Sutton, so far as I can trace the several items :—

The share of CONSTANCE descended in the families of Goddard and Stapylton, and, in 1527, was acquired from Sir Robert Ughtred by Cardinal Wolsey.

In 1529, Henry VIII. took possession of this property, and, in 1535, he granted it to Sir Marmaduke Constable. In 1629, Sir Philip Constable was "a third lord in Sutton."

In 1664, Thomas Watson, of Stoneferry, was settling lands which evidently belonged to this share of the manor. In 1665, he left to his nephew, George Bromflete, such manorial rights as he possessed, and Bromflete exercised his rights. His son Henry succeeded, and, dying childless, his property went to his uncle, Samuel Bromflete. The co-heirs of Samuel Bromflete were Jane, the wife of Noah Ellerthorpe, and her sister, Consolation Lythe, spinster, who sold her share to Thomas Eyres. From Ellerthorpe and Eyres the property was bought, in 1717, by Charles Poole. Poulson says that Charles Poole conveyed a sixth of the manor to Hugh Mason. This may have been all that Thomas Watson had possessed, or the third share may have been divided after the death of Samuel Brom-flete. In 1718, Hugh Mason, in a mortgage deed, mentions the Rowbanks, with the lord's rights of fishing and fowling, as possessed by George Bromflete and Thomas Eyres.

In 1799, Hugh Mason's grand-daughter, Mrs. Dixon, sold to Mr. R. C. Broadley all that she had inherited.

The share of MARGERY passed to her son Peter de Mauley the eighth, who had no children, and to his sisters and co-heirs, Constance, the wife of Sir John Bigod, and Elizabeth, the wife of George Salvain, each of whom inherited a sixth part of the manor.

In 1564, Thomas Dalton was buying of Fairfax and Boynton, St. Quinton and Curdeux, their interests which must have descended through Constance, the daughter of Margery de Mauley. This property was left by Thomas, the last of the elder branch of the Daltons, to his widow, whose great-nephew, M. H. Witham, sold it, in 1767, to Mr. Thomas Broadley.

The sixth share, which had descended in the family of Salvain, was bought, in 1536, from George Salvain by Sir William Sydney. It was acquired from him by Henry VIII., who desired to grant it to the Corporation of Hull. It was granted to them by Edward VI.

The share of AGNES descended in the family of Bulmer. Eight-ninths of the "manor called Boomers or Bulmers" was held by the younger branch of the Daltons, from whom it was bought by Hugh Mason, whose grand-daughter sold it, in 1799, to Mr. R. C. Broadley.

These particulars do not account for the possession of a share in the manor by the family of Blaydes. If this was part of the ancient manor acquired by them before the time of Sir Philip Constable, it must have been a portion of the sixth share which descended through the Bigods. If acquired after that time, it may have belonged to the Bigods or the Constables, or it may have been the missing ninth of Bulmer's manor. But I can trace no ownership by the Blaydes family of property in Sutton earlier than 1742, when Hugh Blaydes bought the principal farm and lands that had belonged to Henry Cock, and also some small pieces of his land in the centre of the town. I have suggested that the Blaydes manor had been assumed from the grant of Free Warren to the monks of Meaux, a part of whose lands appear to have come to Henry Cock. The Hull Corporation took a separate conveyance of the manor when they acquired the principal farm in 1826.

Upon the whole, it seems that the Corporation now holds a sixth, and perhaps something more, of the ancient manor, while the family of Broadley holds something less than five-sixths.

THE FIFTEENTH CENTURY.

Page 123, line two from bottom, for John read Joan.

Page 131. For Ravernspurn read Ravenspurn.

———

THE REFORMATION PERIOD.

Page 136. The condition of serfdom was actually assumed in the conveyance from Hugh Blaydes to the Corporation as recently as 1828; see page 261.

Page 143. Poulson gives lists of the Masters and Chaplains or Fellows of the College of St. James, taken from Torre's Peculiars, p. 503. The names of the Masters are interesting in relation to the disputes with the vicars of Wawne as to burials.

1347	Thos. Sampson.
1349	Wm. de Denford.
	Thos. de Lowthorp.
1373	Peter de Elyngton.
	Wm. de Barneby.
1402	Thos. de Poynton.
1410	John Poynton.
1413	Robt. Marfleet.
1432	Symon Seller.
1443	Wm. Simandson.
1458	Peter Ouste.
1470	Wm. Walsh.
1471	Robt. Tomlinson.
1472	Wm. Warde.
1487	John Curven.
1489	Robt. Ferys.
1499	Thos. Alderson.
1515	Chris. Crasse.
1517	Ralph Bulmer.
1522	Thos. Tenyson.
1528	John Brandesby.

———

QUEEN ELIZABETH TO QUEEN ANNE.

PART I.

Page 151. Sir Lancelot Alford did not succeed to the property of his brother John; see page 215.

Page 157. The oblations to the Vicar of Wawne were 10s.

Page 158. Two documents in the Corporation records throw

light on the interest of the St. Quintins in Sutton, and on the sizes of separate holdings. A lease from John St. Quintin, of Ganstead, to William Maughan, of Hull, cordwainer, relates to a half-oxgang farm, with its appurtenances, of which the homestead had the Queen's highway on the south, with tenants of Sir Marmaduke Constable's on the east, of the heirs of Sir Ralf Bowmer on the west, and of Christopher Stockdaill on the north. It measured 86 feet 6 inches towards the highway, and 67 feet along the rear. The eastern side was 171 feet long, and the western side was 168 feet long. Each piece of tillage and meadow is mentioned with the names of the owners of the adjoining pieces. Amongst these were some pieces called "the Quene's ground"— lands which had been taken from one or other of the religious communities. One piece of meadow in the Ings lay next to the "lead dicke," and a piece of tillage in the East Field had the "demaine medowe" on the south. This meadow seems to have come between the tillage of the East Field and the ancient stream called Landsyk, which forms the boundary of the Ings. There was in the Carr-side meadow, at the edge of the West Carr, a pighill, the lengths of the four sides of which were 179 feet 6 inches, 132 feet 6 inches, 163 feet 6 inches, and 183 feet, and upon it was a sheep-cote 18 feet long by 10 feet broad. There were fifteen leaseholders of this sort under John St. Quintin, and on the 18th February, 1566-7, he leased the reversion of the whole of their lands to Matthew St. Quintin, of Kilnesay for the life of Matthew, the consideration being £80, and an annual rent of £27 10s. His lease included all his manor of Sutton and Sutcotes, except fowling and fishing. This is described as a "fouert part of a thirde," and although this description is erased, it probably gives the proportion of Constance Bygod's share, which St. Quintin actually held.

Page 159, line 5, for 1547 read 1574.

Robert Dalton, Sheriff of Hull in 1584, and Mayor in 1588, is said by Gent to have been detected, while alderman, in sharp practice in the management of his mills. He had got possession of numerous mills, and had taken corn as mulcture instead of charging money for grinding; besides which he had adulterated his flour with "plaister." He got off with a humble apology. There were, however, many of this family, and probably others called Robert. I have seen "A Notte of my Debtes Owing and Dawngers I am in," which is a long account, drawn up in 1603 under twenty-one heads, of the debts and dangers of a Robert Dalton who owned mills. He had already endured imprisonment, and his properties seem to have been encumbered beyond redemption. He had borrowed £148 "upon pawne of Skytter Mylnes and Skytter Ferrye." He laments his farm insufficiently stocked, and pawned for debts, his commons void for want of sheep, and himself and children in want of apparel. He ends his pitiful moan with these words: "I may trewlye say wth

Jobbe Naked Came I forthe of my mother's womb and Naked shall I returne agayne. Blessed be the name of the Lorde."

Page 160. The Hall Coat Walls was "a parcel of ground" near to the Salts—probably the same as Hall-garth. It was always held with the Castle Hill and Ring. The sixth part of it contained about a steng or rood. See lease from Corporation to Nicholas Cooke, 1613.

Page 163. I think the statement as to the acquisition of part of the manor by William de Bursblaydes is erroneous, and the notices of the earlier generations of the family seem to be untrustworthy. In this appendix I have dealt with the probability of their having been lords of the manor in the account of the descent of the shares of the daughters of Sir Thomas de Sutton.

Page 165, also 211. A Fine, dated on the morrow of the Purification, 15 Charles II., Robert Berryer and Charles Vaux plaintiffs, Thomas Watson, gent., and Elizabeth his wife deforciants, relates to 4 messuages, 7 cottages, 45 acres of Tillage, 39 acres of meadow, 17 acres of pasture, and common of pasture for 35 beasts, 14 horses, and 280 sheep, with common of pasture for all cattle in Sutton, Stoneferry, Dripoole, and Sutcoates. This appears to be the property which Thomas Watson, in his will, says that he had settled on his wife, and which, after her death, was divided as "shift-lands." The land amounted to three oxgangs, with their appurtenances, besides which he left to his wife, for her life, one oxgang or five acres of his "best arable land" in each of the three fields. Other bequests of his "best" lands help to shew that on the whole he must have had a considerable estate.

Page 165. Note.—This John Truslove seems to have been a son, probably by a former wife. He is not named in any of the family wills. In 1679, the Mayor and Burgesses let to John Truslove, of Stoneferry, gentleman, land and beast-gates lately occupied by his father, John Truslove.

QUEEN ELIZABETH TO QUEEN ANNE.

PART II.

Page 173, line 13, for Mausdell read Mansdell.

Page 180. Christopher Broadrip, here said to be of Somerset-shire, was of Mapperton, in Dorset, where the family of Brodrepp was of considerable importance. The Rectory, with the property of the College of St. James, was so long held by them, together with the Alfords, that some account of the family connexions of the parties will be of interest.

The Alfords claimed to hold the Rectory and lands, which had been forfeited by Sir Michael Stanhope, on lease from Queen Elizabeth, and were in actual possession; see page 156. The reversion was granted by James I., as stated on page 157, to Morrice and Philips, and from them was bought by Dame Katherine Moore. She was one of the daughters of Sir Thomas Pakington, of Aylesbury, and married, first, John Davis or Davye, of Wiltshire, secondly, Sir Jasper Moore, and, thirdly, Sir Richard Mompesson, who held property at Fawley, in Buckinghamshire, where John Alford and Henry Alford lived. Her son and heir, Thomas Davye, was the father of the three heiresses mentioned on page 216 as plaintiffs in the cause against Henry Alford. Richard Brodrepp, of Mapperton, is said by Hutchins (Hist. of Dorset) to have married Catherine, daughter and co-heiress of John Davy, of Sutton-in-Holderness, and it was his grandson, Richard Brodrepp, who sold the Rectory and lands to Hugh Mason. There were leases from the Corporation of pasturage, in 1583, to John Alford, of Fawley Court; in 1604, to Richard Mompesson; and, in 1625, to Henry Alford; and of meadow or pasture in the Great Oxlands, in 1685, to Richard Brodrepp, of Mapperton; and, in 1706, to Richard Brodrepp, of Sutton. Brodrepp, who sold to Mason, is in one document said to be of Hull. Davye, and after him Brodrepp, may to some extent have occupied the mansion of the Rectory after the Alford lease fell in.

Page 181. The way in which a marriage was managed at that time is illustrated by the registrar's entries, and the magistrate's certificate in the register for 1657.

"James Morten came to me the 23th of May to desire me to publish him and Elizabeth Freman in the P'rish Church of Sutton afore said being bothe of the same P'rish.

The first time of thire publishing was the 24th of May and no exception made.

The second time of thire publishing was the 31th of May and no exception made.

The Last time of thire publishing was the 7th of June and no exception made.

James Morten and Ellzabeth Freman was married the 22th of June 1657 in the P'sence of us.   By me

 George Noell   Arthur Noell."
 Edw. Freeman.

The year in which John Dickinson became Registrar was 1663.

OLD-FASHIONED FARMS.

Page 189. I have to thank Mr. C. F. Hayward, F.S.A., for shewing me over some manors in Hertfordshire that are still unenclosed, the grass balk here illustrated being in one of them.

Page 194. On the 4th April, 1589, the Manor Court was held on behalf of the Mayor and Burgesses of Hull, Philip Constable, Thomas Dalton, John Rande, in right of his wife, Hugh Armyn, John Harrison, and Henry Watson. Among the suitors and jurors appear the familiar names of St. Quintin, Noddell, Hogge, Alford, Snaith, Lopham, and Shackells. The court dealt chiefly with those who had let their cattle stray in the corn-fields.

Page 195. Stainhood balk is probably the same as Standward balk, or the Standherd, in the East Field, mentioned in a Corporation lease of 1611. The same lease includes tillage in Foorde at Pyke-Cloote and Chopping-well.

Page 197. To the meadow in the Ings add Ledeholmdale.

Page 198. On the 16th February, 1555-6, the Corporation leased to Edward Thompson, husbandman, their messuage in Sutton, wherein he then lived with a barn " now beying in ruyne and decay," with half an oxgang and the appurtenances now or late in the occupation of Launcelott Alford. This seems to have been the cottage farm that had been leased to the Master and Fellows of the College (see page 135), whose property fell into the hands of Alford.
A lease to Gilbert Cowper, 31st October, 1611, describes lands belonging to his farm. There was—

In the East Field :—

Half an acre near the East Carr Gate.
Half an acre near the Blindwell.
One acre called Esopp-acre.
Half an acre near the Salts Gates.
Three roods and a half near Sykewell.

In the Carr Side Field :—

Half an acre at the Garth Ends, Sutton.
One acre at Grenebatt.
Three roods beyond the Mylne.
Three roods and a half at the Crooked Mare.

In the North Carr Field :—

One acre at the Marstall.
One acre at Nordale.
Half an acre at the Pyke Cloote.
One rood near Nordall Cross.

The Meadow comprised.

In the Ings :—

Half an acre at the New Ings—Sutton ?
One acre three roods and a half at Furram Coate.
One rood at Low Pighill.

In the Carr Side Meadow :—
> One acre wherein standeth a Sheepcoate.
> Three roods near Thomas Harryson's Coate.
> Three roods at Crossegate.
> One rood at the same gate.

In Rysome Carr :—
> One acre and a half.

Page 200. A four-acre patch of meadow called Rustgarth, belonging to the Corporation, appears to have been in the South Ings beyond Summergangs Gate. Another piece of meadow called the Bottome lay in Stoneferry West-croft.

Page 207. The conveyance from Martha Lacy, the heiress of Henry Cock, to Hugh Blaydes, now in the Corporation Archives, gives a clearer description of this property. There was the farmhouse which, some fifty years ago, stood opposite to the place where the Station-master's house has been built—an old house with a porch and a room called the Priest's Study, reached by a winding stair. There was also behind the house four acres and three-quarters, being nine ploughed lands, lying together at "Clay Pit Head," and running down to 'Tween-dikes Lane; one acre somewhat west thereof; one rood near the Kiln-nook, and a rood at the back of the barn. John Cock's kilns and his clay-pit were near to the old house. This large quantity of tillage lying near together almost proves that it had at some former time belonged to the demesne or home-farm of the lord of the manor. The Shifting Acre mentioned on page 208, was at Bessy Bell Bridge in the Ings, and there was in Rysom Carr another acre "called, or being, a Shift-acre."

There was payable in respect of this farm £13 7s. annually to Cyrill Wyche, Esq., "And formerly to the Common Wealth of England." I see some reason to suspect that this property is the major part of that described on page 138, then leased to Peter Snaith and others, which the Monks of Meaux had acquired through young Amandus de Sutton, and which they surrendered to Henry VIII. It had been called a manor, and I have found no other title that the Blaydes family had to call themselves lords of the manor of Sutton.

Page 212. Mrs. Ann Watson died in 1721.

OUR GREAT-GRANDFATHERS' DAYS.

Page 224. Opposite to the farmstead at the corner of the Stoneferry Road, on the west side of that road, was a pond which extended into the adjoining garden. It had probably been made for the use of the farmers when their farmsteads were in the village. The deep ditch in the Ings Road, opposite to 'Tween-dikes Lane, was called "Wash-dike" from the use to which it was put.

There was a pond just west of the old workhouse. By the margin of it and about the street sat or wandered the inmates until they were removed to the new union at Sculcoates.

An entry of the burial, in 1736, of "Milcah Cock, Widow, Gentlewoman," gives the idea that her husband, Henry Cock, had been a principal inhabitant of the parish. His kilns had probably furnished the bricks for the oldest houses now remaining.

Page 228. In the frontispiece to Gents' History of Hull, published in 1735, the Sugar House is shewn amongst the conspicuous buildings of the town.

Page 237. There is in France, in the Department of Gers, a commune called St. Blancart. Though it is a wine-producing district through which flows an affluent of the Garonne, it is so far from Bordeaux that its produce could hardly become well known in England; but the name may have been attached to some kind of claret then exported. Blancard is a French surname.

Page 240. In 1788, Red-nose Kidney Potatoes, which "for several years" had been much approved for planting, were advertised in a Hull paper, but they were still a luxury. In a small bill for vegetables, dated 1782, two pounds of potatoes are put down at a shilling.

Page 247. The best description of the Raw that lay between Foredike and Suttondike is given in the Corporation lease of 1677 to Robert Barnes. It included "the sixth part of one piece of pasture ground called the West-Raw, or the Raw, within the Lordship of Sutton, lying nere unto Fish House Clow."

THE ENCLOSURE OF THE COMMON FIELDS.

Page 248. Edward Anderson, the Yorkshire poet, put into rhyme many of the characteristic features of the old agricultural system. The following lines illustrate the inconvenience in time of harvest of the strips of tillage that lay side by side in the open fields :—

> " In harvest time, when it came a rainy day,
> The sheaves and pea-reaps oft were blown away ;
> Mixed, and against some balk or hill were blown ;
> The farmers then they could not know their own.
> Some then would take advantage of the rest,
> At such a time the strongest man fared best."
> —*The Sailor.*

This naturally led to quarrels and broken heads.

Page 253. One of the private roads awarded at the enclosure ran along the drain bank where the public footway to Hull now runs. It was called "Cockfolly Road," leading to Cockfolly Pighill. In 1712, Henry Cock had conveyed to Hodgson a steng of meadow in Sutton Ings, in a place called Little Folly.

ANTIQUITIES OF MODERN SUTTON.

PART I.

Page 268. About 1780, clover and similar green crops were still unknown, beans were never hoed, turnips had began to be grown upon enclosed land, but they were never hoed, and the land was so foul that it required to be fallowed after them.

Page 271. The minutes of the Holderness Agricultural Society shew that, in 1814, farm servants were allowed from a pound to a pound and a half of meat per day, with a quart of milk and two quarts of beer. Labourers then earned from fifteen to eighteen shillings a week, and paid twelve shillings a bushel for their wheat, unless the farmers agreed to let them have it at a fixed price of six shillings. At their own tables they had meat only once a week.

Page 283. It is difficult to realise the pilfering by gleaners when the cornfield was unenclosed, and wheat was at famine price. I have a brief that was delivered to Mr. Daniel Sykes for the prosecution of a woman who had persisted in gleaning amongst the stooks before the enclosure of Swanland Field. After dodging the farmer by moving on and off his narrow strip of land, she set him at defiance, and threw a stone that wounded him in the head. Counsel was to shew that "the common open fields are so robbed under the pretence of gleaning by a number of depredators, that the farmers must either seek redress, or submit to the greatest injuries and inconveniences." Things were worse in France in the famine times before the Revolution. At the town of Etampes, I found a record of the punishment of three women who, in 1731, had stolen wheat "sous prétexte de glaner." They were beaten naked with rods on a platform in the public square, placards describing their offence being hung upon them in front and in rear. The cause must have been starvation, and the farmers would not be much better off.

It was provided in the manor of Hibbaldstow, Lincolnshire, that "none shall glean within six lands of the standing corn or mown corn on paine of 5s.," and "none shall go and gather wool before the swineherd doth blow on paine of 12d."

ANTIQUITIES OF MODERN SUTTON.

PART II.

Page 285, line 9, for " was " read " were."

Page 290. The gipsies ought not to be forgotten. Until the County Police came into activity, it was not uncommon to see a couple of their tents by the roadside on the top of Nordale or Soffham Hill, the savoury smell from a spitted hedge-hog mingling with the smoke of their fire. Heathens as they were, if not robbers of henroosts, it was a pity that their picturesque encampments had to be prohibited. They continued, however, in more evident poverty and squalour to make flying visits to the old neighbourhood, getting harbour for a night in the corner of a field.

Page 300. The following is a list of the more recent incumbents :—

1839　The Rev. Nicholas Walton.
1847　　,,　　　,,　　J. A. Eldridge.
1858　　,,　　　,,　　H. T. Cattley.
1865　　,,　　　,,　　John Carter.
1878　　,,　　　,,　　H. A. Holme.
1894　　,,　　　,,　　G. A. Coleman.

In Mr. Carter's incumbency the parsonage house was built, and the church restored.

The total annual value of the benefice is made up of £48 from the Ecclesiastical Commission; £6 from Queen Anne's Bounty; £26 rent of lands (which used to produce £55); £5 from the North-Eastern Railway Company; £10 from the Patron; £5 from Watson's Charity, and about £15 from fees. In 1877, before the cemeteries affected the fees, they amounted to about £80.